Lynnette Porter's interest in Tolkien's works spans more than 30 years. She brings a decade of research to this book. She is a member of the Tolkien Society and the US Popular Culture Association. Her Tolkien-related articles and reviews have been published widely. Her books include *Unsung Heroes of* The Lord of the Rings*: From Page to Screen* (2005).

Purchased from
Multnomah County Library
Title Wave Used Bookstore
216 NE Knott St, Portland, OR
503-988-5021

The Hobbits

The Many Lives of Bilbo, Frodo, Sam, Merry and Pippin

Lynnette Porter

I.B. TAURIS

LONDON · NEW YORK

Published in 2012 by I.B.Tauris & Co Ltd
6 Salem Road, London W2 4BU
175 Fifth Avenue, New York NY 10010
www.ibtauris.com

Distributed in the United States and Canada Exclusively by Palgrave Macmillan
175 Fifth Avenue, New York NY 10010

Copyright © 2012 Lynnette Porter

The right of Lynnette Porter to be identified as the author of this work has been asserted
by her in accordance with the Copyright, Designs and Patents Act 1988.

All rights reserved. Except for brief quotations in a review, this book, or any part thereof,
may not be reproduced, stored in or introduced into a retrieval system, or transmitted, in
any form or by any means, electronic, mechanical, photocopying, recording or otherwise,
without the prior written permission of the publisher.

ISBN: 978 1 84511 856 3

A full CIP record for this book is available from the British Library
A full CIP record is available from the Library of Congress

Library of Congress Catalog Card Number: available

Printed and bound in Sweden by ScandBook AB

CONTENTS

ACKNOWLEDGEMENTS

I thank the many people with whom I have shared a love of hobbits at fan conventions or academic conferences, online or in print, via email or in person. In the past decade I have been welcomed by members of the Tolkien Society throughout the UK, US, Canada and New Zealand; your fellowship and hospitality, as well as your insights into Tolkien's many works, have been a highlight of my travels. I am indebted to everyone interviewed for this book.

Special thanks to Matt Blessing, Head of Special Collections, and the many kind staff members at Raynor Memorial Libraries, Marquette University.

As always, thank you to Bart, Nancy, Heather and Elvis, who understand and support my journeys 'there' but lovingly welcome me 'back again'.

INTRODUCTION

THERE AND BACK AGAIN

J.R.R. Tolkien's hobbits have indeed travelled far, from their home on the pages of a British book published in 1937 to the vast 'there' of cineplexes worldwide. Over the years they have brought generations of visitors 'back' to Middle-earth. Along the journey, hobbits have become an integral part of global culture, and just as they have influenced or perhaps personally changed us as we follow their adventures, so we have altered them over time. Hobbit fans (including myself) have a tendency to 'adapt' these beloved characters to fit into our specific time, place or culture – and our twenty-first-century globalised world is vastly different from finely detailed, lovingly described Middle-earth or Tolkien's England. If hobbits are to continue to survive, they must adapt to the expectations of new readers or, more recently, audiences for radio, television, theatre, film or electronic platforms ranging from CDs or DVDs to streaming or downloadable media. Popular culture is often Darwinian – only the most deeply ingrained stories or perennially relevant characters survive the onslaught of entertainment options and images available in the twenty-first century. Resilient hobbits, thus far, have been among the 'fittest' to survive.

Even those who are not hobbit fans are unlikely to escape hearing about Tolkien's most famous characters. Hobbits have become a popular-culture touchstone, as evidenced by one week in July 2011, during which such diverse sources as the entertainment mega-event San Diego Comic-Con (SDCC) and US politicians kept hobbits in the news.

On the first day of Comic-Con, representatives from the premier fan website for Tolkien enthusiasts, TheOneRing.Net (TORN), once again hosted a packed house. Over the years, TORN's SDCC panel has presented news and acknowledged rumours about director Peter Jackson's *The Lord of the Rings* (*LotR*) film trilogy (2001–3) and the development of *The Hobbit* – including its many setbacks – on its journey to becoming a trio of films to be released in 2012–14. TORN updates fans about the projects and professional lives of the artists, authors, actors and other creative, talented individuals who keep J. R.R. Tolkien's words alive in the twenty-first century.

Thursday 21 July 2011 could unofficially be dubbed the SDCC's 'hobbit day'. Although the first of three Jackson-directed *Hobbit* films was more than a year from release, fans crowding the ballroom where the TORN panel was held could barely contain their excitement. Unlike sessions in the previous few years – when the films had been stalled and no one, including Jackson, was certain when they could be made – the 2011 convention session was filled with hopeful hobbit lovers. Cliff Broadway, one of TORN's founding writers, proudly announced the official (no longer speculated) cast of the *Hobbit* films and showed the latest images released from the set.

The audience cheered loudly when photos of the lead hobbit – Bilbo Baggins (played by Martin Freeman) – appeared on screen. The fans approved of Freeman in hobbit costume, including wig, pointed ears and large, hairy feet. The photograph showed him standing in Bag End, Bilbo's home, which looked just as fans remembered it from the *LotR* films. The crowd collectively sighed, not only in anticipation that next year's Comic-Con might showcase film trailers and possibly feature appearances by Jackson or cast members. The sigh also signalled fans' relief that about 20 percent of the filming had already been completed.[1] Although Freeman was back in the UK to film his other iconic role as John Watson in the BBC's latest Sherlock Holmes adaptation, *Sherlock*, fans knew that he would be back on the New Zealand set after he finished filming the television series. At last the first *Hobbit* film could be pencilled in fans' day planners for December 2012. Hobbit mania had officially returned.

Because SDCC is the largest and possibly most influential fan convention, featuring nearly every imaginable aspect of popular culture, TORN's presence has become mandatory for legions of hobbit fans, whether they see the annual panel in person, live online, or via links to videos and blogs. The very fact that a fan-based organisation, born from news, expectations and rumours surrounding the filming of the *LotR* trilogy, has become so popular, both as a website and an annual SDCC panel, is testament to the continuing power of hobbits in the century since Tolkien first introduced them to the literary world. It also indicates the power of the most recent cinematic adaptations of *LotR* and *The Hobbit* and their continuing popularity, whether years after their release or in the years in which fans could only anticipate what the films might be like.

The sense that hobbits have been seldom out of the news and never far from Tolkien readers' thoughts was exacerbated by SDCC's fan costumes and further scheduling on 21 July. Arriving early in order to ensure seats at the TORN panel, three hobbit-costumed women stood in line and occasionally posed for photographs. Although the TORN panel was not scheduled to begin until ten o'clock that morning, the line to get in stretched around the convention centre's hallways hours earlier. While the hobbit trio waited, they held a rather serious discussion about how to carry their tankards. Whether those tankards contained coffee or something stronger was left to the crowd's imagination.

These three were only some of the many costumed fans from a wide range of fandoms attending the convention, but Tolkien fans were well represented. Throughout the day I saw numerous hobbits visiting San Diego from Middle-earth. Hobbits are still very much part of fantasy fandom, and those in costume seemed to have designed their hobbit wardrobe based on images from Jackson's films as much as Tolkien's books. Fan-created costumes themselves are an adaptation of the way Tolkien envisioned hobbits and provide a way for fans to re-imagine themselves as characters from the Shire.

Once a hobbit, always a hobbit (at least in fans' minds) – as Elijah Wood (who played Frodo Baggins) and Dominic Monaghan (Meriadoc Brandybuck) are continually reminded. Actors who had played hobbits in Jackson's *LotR* trilogy but were attending the 2011 SDCC to promote other projects were nonetheless persistently connected to the Shire. Wood attended Comic-Con to promote *Wilfred*, a US adaptation of the Australian television series broadcast on US cable network FX. Wood's character, Ryan, is about as far removed from Frodo as could possibly be conceived. The premise of the series is that Ryan sees the neighbours' dog, Wilfred, as a man in a dog suit. Randy, ribald Wilfred (Jason Gann) leads Ryan into all sorts of very adult-themed trouble.

During the panel Wood had to remind fans that 'This is a *Wilfred* panel, guys'[2] after the majority of early questions were about *LotR*. The reminder was said softly and politely, but it underscored Wood's continuing popularity as Frodo Baggins, Bilbo's nephew and the Ringbearer in *LotR*. Frodo's (Wood's) photograph had also been on screen at the TORN panel; according to TORN, Wood was scheduled to reprise his role from the *LotR* films in at least one scene between Frodo and his Uncle Bilbo. (Ian Holm, who played the much older Bilbo in *LotR*, also was reported to be making an appearance with Wood in the *Hobbit* films.)

Wood is as likely to be asked about Frodo, years after media frenzy over the *LotR* films has calmed, as to be interviewed about his more recent projects. Although Wood graced the cover of *American Way* magazine in August 2011 and the article was ostensibly about *Wilfred*, the feature also discussed his best-known role as Frodo and provided a photo of the actor-as-hobbit. The article added that

> Wood can't think of a single downside to the entire *Rings* experience. He feels the trilogy's enormous success (earning 17 Oscars and nearly $3 billion at the box office) afforded him many more acting opportunities, allowing him to consciously avoid the casting curse that inflicted [other actors] who played iconic fantasy characters.[3]

The same might be said of Monaghan. He too was asked about his role as Merry, and he referenced it himself during two sessions in San Diego. On 21 July, he was introduced to the SDCC crowd as a hobbit (as well as Charlie from the television series *Lost*) before his more recent role in a new web film was mentioned.[4] During the next day's 'Conversation with Dominic Monaghan', a fan Q&A held in conjunction with Comic-Con, *LotR* was a popular topic, and Monaghan acknowledged that Merry has become a part of him.[5] For the actors as well as their fans, hobbits are an enduring influence on their lives.

Although Peter Jackson appeared at SDCC in conjunction with Steven Spielberg's *Tintin* session, he managed to mention that he could attend the convention only because filming *The Hobbit* was delayed while Freeman played his other high-profile role in *Sherlock* back in the UK.[6] Jackson, as scriptwriter and director of the *LotR* and *Hobbit* movies, is now as inextricably linked to hobbits as the actors in his films. Even during a session about another long-anticipated project, Jackson namedropped *The Hobbit*.

Just as hobbits have seemingly become a permanent part of the world's largest and most publicised fan-and-industry convention that reflects the best of popular culture, so have they become a cultural reference outside Tolkien or fantasy fandoms. Only a few days after the 2011 SDCC, hobbits became linked to US politics during a particularly thorny discussion about the national debt. *The Wall Street Journal* described the policy proposed by the Republican party's Tea Party faction as something that the hobbits of the Shire might undertake, leading US Senator John McCain to decry those 'Tea Party Hobbits' in his party. The Tea Party movement within the Republican party was seen by Democrats and other opponents as overly conservative and obstructionist; Tea Party 'hobbits' were viewed as those who wanted to overthrow Democratic 'rule' and return to conservative values.[7]

Certainly, the hobbits of the Shire share some family values associated with this American political group, but, more important to a study of hobbits, the fact that the term 'hobbit' was used at all indicates the cultural permanence of Tolkien's characters. Everyone who used the reference in the initial *Wall Street Journal* article, picked up on it for rebuttal speeches or covered it in the news media (on internationally followed networks like CNN) assumed that the audience would understand the hobbit reference. No definition or description was provided.

Even in this political usage, hobbits were 'adapted' – or only specific characteristics emphasised – to make a point. Although Tolkien's hobbits certainly were not affiliated with an American political party, and the Shire's society, even with its conservative values, never debated a debt ceiling for communal spending, the political analogy briefly captured the public imagination and brought hobbits once more into the spotlight.

Whether using hobbits as literary, film or even political references, a global audience knows about hobbits. What they think of them and how they interpret them, however, may not reflect what Tolkien actually wrote. People adapt hobbits to fit situations that have meaning for them (and possibly for a wider audience). Peter Jackson envisioned hobbits acting in a certain way, and his vision became a series of films that influence the way audiences understand who and what hobbits are, where they live, how they act, and what they wear. John McCain's political analogy to hobbits (and his command that those 'hobbits' in politics should return to Middle-earth, far away from US government) created a different interpretation of hobbit values and hobbits' proper place in current political, and possibly social, culture in America. These and many other 'adaptations' of hobbits – whether complete stories modified from but based on Tolkien's works (for example, the *LotR* film trilogy) or cultural references (for example, the hobbit political analogy, fans' co-optation of hobbit fashion) – continue to change the way successive generations learn about hobbits and adapt them to fit contexts that Tolkien could never have imagined. The previously mentioned examples observed during two weeks in 2011, decades after Tolkien's *The Hobbit* was published, are just a few of the many current reminders of the continuing influence of Tolkien's most-loved characters in mainstream Western popular culture.

J.R.R. Tolkien's *The Hobbit* and *The Lord of the Rings* have become cultural touchstones, not only in literature, but in all aspects of popular culture and, as the political reference reveals, to the larger global sociopolitical culture as well. A large part of the resurgence in Tolkien's popularity undoubtedly lies with Peter Jackson's monumentally successful adaptation that took cinema by storm from 2001 to 2003. The continuing level of interest in *The Hobbit* and *LotR* pervades even unexpected corners of the world; a teenaged Guantanamo Bay detainee found the *LotR* story so mesmerising that his dearest wish was to see Jackson's films.[8] The power of these stories has touched the lives of millions.

Jackson's films may be the most popular recent adaptation, but Tolkien's hobbits have been adapted in other media in the past few years. The Toronto/London musical also kept *LotR* in the press as well as on stage in the mid-2000s. Online gaming and videogames encourage role playing, and the Internet helps keep Tolkienalia alive. Media outlets fuel fan interest by publishing more information about Tolkien's books and the latest news about forthcoming films.

In August 2011, a Google search for 'Tolkien' referenced more than 27 million general sites and several hundred recent news articles; a search for 'hobbit' retrieved 37.5 million entries. The number of websites and hits is yet another indication that hobbits are a perennially favoured topic of research and discussion, and a large part of the interest is a result of the many adaptations of Tolkien's original stories.

The original books and their many adaptations in multiple media encourage us fans to express our own creativity, too. Peter Jackson's official *Hobbit* blog best summarises movie fans' intense, abiding cultural interest in hobbits: 'We never cease to be amazed by all the energy, talent and creativity of fans of *The Lord of the Rings* Trilogy and *The Hobbit*.'[9] The popularity of this adaptation perhaps reflects the fact that filmmaker Jackson also is a hobbit fan, to the extent that he built a replica of Bag End as his guest house.[10]

Perhaps even more telling about the influence of hobbits, in particular, on popular culture are the many offhand references to *LotR* or *The Hobbit* that are assumed to be commonly understood by anyone watching TV, reading comics, or going to the movies. These ongoing cultural references are more subtle than something like McCain's political comments that make international news, less persistent than official blogs or studio publicity for hobbit-themed films, but more internationally influential than fan-created costumes or online fiction, which reaches a narrower audience.

US television series, in particular, frequently make general *LotR* or *Hobbit* references, or more specifically mention hobbits. Although these series originate in the US, American television shows are often exported around the world and reach millions living outside the US. Animated comedy series like *Family Guy* occasionally reference *LotR*,[11] as does *The Simpsons*.[12] A 2003 *Gilmore Girls* episode is entitled 'The Hobbit, the Sofa, and Digger Stiles'.[13] In a 2008 episode of the US version of *The Office*, one character baits a science fiction/fantasy geek by confusing characters from *LotR* with those on *Battlestar Galactica*.[14] On spy series *Chuck*, a gorgeous enemy overhears the title character compare her to an elvish woman; when she captures him, he gamely explains that his comment was a compliment based on his love of *The Hobbit*.[15] Popular US TV series *The Big Bang Theory*, which celebrates its characters' pop-culture geekiness, devoted an entire 2010 episode to a story in which the characters find at a garage sale one of the rings used in the *LotR* films. Of course, the Ring turns the friends into Gollums as each attempts to take and keep the Ring for himself.[16] The number of television series in which one of Tolkien's characters is mentioned far surpasses this brief list of examples, but they emphasise the point that hobbits are well referenced in US television series of the past decade.

Hobbit references also frequently pop up in films that are not directly adapted from Tolkien's works and, like the references in television series, are based on the assumption that audiences will be familiar with recent adaptations, if not the original text. For example, Ewan McGregor's character compares himself with a hobbit of the Shire in a passing pop-culture reference embedded in *The Men Who Stare at Goats* (2009).[17]

Frodo even plays a pivotal role in *Run, Fatboy, Run* (2007), starring Simon Pegg as a father who desperately tries to impress his Frodo-obsessed son.[18] Tickets to London's *LotR* musical become the battleground between the boy's biological father and soon-to-be-stepfather. The film humorously illustrates how obsessive *LotR* fans can become and indicates just how audiences expect Frodo Baggins to behave.

In Tolkien's story and the Jackson *LotR* adaptation, Frodo naturally is social, friendly and polite, even if he is also often quiet and bookish. Only when he is under the Ring's influence is he snappish, angry or otherwise antisocial. Jake, the young boy whose understanding of

Frodo is based on the Jackson films, pretends he is Frodo, as does a minor character later in the film.

Waiting for dad Dennis (played by Pegg) to arrive, Jake becomes so engrossed watching a DVD playing Gandalf's first scene with Frodo that he forgets to dress. Once he is ready to go out with his father, he wears pointed hobbit ears and proudly carries Sting, Frodo's sword; the youngster's mop of dark hair and wide eyes indeed make him look like a young Frodo (as played by Elijah Wood) from Jackson's films. Jake even plays hobbits and Orcs with his eager-to-please future stepdad Whit. To ensure Jake's love, Dennis promises to take his son to the *LotR* musical. Unfortunately, he fails to get tickets to the sold-out show and ends up going to jail for trying to buy tickets from a tout. Whit wins Jake's favour by procuring front-row seats a few nights later.

Hobbits become the standard of determining just how much Jake likes someone or something. The boy compares girlfriend Emily to tree frogs, leaving his bemused father to wonder whether that is good or bad. Jake explains he likes tree frogs even more than hobbits – a strong statement, given Jake's previous behaviour.

Even a casual encounter on a bus is hobbit-themed. After the theatre–jail debacle, Dennis catches the bus home and thinks of his son. He looks up to see a sleepy lad cradled against his father's shoulder. This boy, just like Jake, wears hobbit ears and looks remarkably like a miniature Frodo. In response, Dennis smiles hello and wiggles his fingers in a friendly wave. The frowning boy responds with an aggressive finger gesture, certainly not the response Tolkien might have wanted of young Frodo followers. What makes this scene amusing, other than the child giving Dennis the finger, is the 'hobbit' so rudely introduced within a modern setting. The child's unexpected 'anti-Frodo' behaviour is the basis for the scene's joke.

The film, as much as events like SDCC, further illustrates that fans often dress like or try to imitate behaviour of their favourite hobbits. Conventions and special gatherings often bring together fans of all ages who role play as hobbits of the Shire. At 'A Long-Expected Party' in September 2008, adults donned their finest Middle-earth wardrobe to celebrate Bilbo's and Frodo's birthday. Although elves, rangers and a wizard also came to the party, the Kentucky 'Shire' was filled with hobbits.[19] Even during events when hobbitwear was not required, almost everyone dressed appropriately for a day in the Shire. The event was so successful that plans began for a second Long-Expected Party, held in September 2011.[20]

Around the world, Tolkien fans annually celebrate Bilbo's and Frodo's joint birthday in September and, on 3 January, raise a toast to the Professor. In the UK, Tolkien Society events and conferences unite scholars and fans to discuss and celebrate the Professor's many works. Tolkien Society message boards and TORN regularly post announcements of gatherings like these worldwide. Adapting hobbits to fit specific contexts has become a popular, and often profitable, creative endeavour.

Adaptations fundamentally change the way individuals and the public in general perceive an original work. Tolkien's stories may explore a place outside recognisable time, but adaptations of Tolkien's stories often arise from a specific culture or time, as the previous examples indicate. Also, we fans likely remember the time when we first read the book or saw a TV special or film; we associate *The Hobbit* or *LotR* with a fond memory of that time. The increasing number of adaptations and ways in which the stories become personally important to fans or critics makes it progressively more difficult to think of or analyse the original work in isolation. *The Hobbit* or *LotR* as published books may be increasingly difficult to separate from the conglomerate *Hobbit* or *LotR* 'experience' based on fans' participation in conventions or enjoyment of multimedia adaptations.

Hobbits as a group are fascinating characters, but the ones who stand out are those Tolkien selected for incredible quests outside the Shire. In *The Hobbit*, Bilbo Baggins is the title character who best represents to readers just who or what a hobbit is. In *LotR*, Bilbo is still a character, although not featured in as many chapters, but his legacy of outworldly adventure and peril is passed to another generation of hobbits: nephew Frodo Baggins, Frodo's gardener and companion Samwise Gamgee, and Frodo's two close friends and kin, Meriadoc Brandybuck and Peregrin Took. Although these hobbits may be far from typical in their homeland, they represent the Shire to the outer world during the War of the Ring and, just as important, have won the hearts of readers for generations.

The Hobbits: The Many Lives of Bilbo, Frodo, Sam, Merry and Pippin highlights their individual and collective stories, as told first by Tolkien and later adapted for other media, including radio, television, film, theatre, music, art and fanfiction. What the many adaptations reveal about our understanding and cultural 'use' of hobbits, how hobbits have been changed by these adaptations to meet the cultural expectations of their time, and what the future might hold for hobbits – and Tolkien's stories – are topics discussed in the following chapters.

I

A KALEIDOSCOPE
OF HOBBITS

Tolkien provides the first images and descriptions of hobbits and their homeland, but once *The Hobbit* or *The Lord of the Rings* became adapted by others, a variety of sometimes conflicting portrayals emerged. Just as a kaleidoscope fractures the image a viewer first sees and recombines multicolour pieces into a new shape, so too can adaptations fracture Tolkien's complete picture of hobbits and focus on fragments of their appearance or personality, recombining them into pleasing, if very different, images for the viewer's entertainment.

In the 1960s, American readers, influenced by social and political upheavals occurring at home, may have viewed hobbits through a specialised lens – one that pitted Frodo against a backdrop of the Vietnam War or the hippie movement, for example. In the 1970s, audiences who watched Rankin–Bass television specials may have focused their attention on animated, family-friendly hobbits who reflected current fashions and values. In the decades since the first publication of Tolkien's books, the number of adaptations competing for hobbit fans' attention has increased. Audiences are presented with a currently in-vogue adaptation, one hyped by media marketing and entertainment news, but those who do not enjoy the current depiction can 'turn the kaleidoscope' – or go to another adaptation or back to the original text – to bring a different style of hobbit into focus. Kaleidoscopes, however, seldom keep one image in focus for very long, and by the time a viewer has seen the shifting play of colours and shapes several times, the original image is often lost from memory.

When audiences first see Peter Jackson's three-film *The Lord of the Rings*, they probably know, from media publicity or DVD covers, if nothing else, that the films are based on J.R.R. Tolkien's book of the same name – but they may never have read (and may never read) the original work. Even if they go to the original text, they may find their later reading of the book is overlaid with images and sounds from Jackson's films.

On the other hand, long-time book lovers who have read *LotR* dozens of times may avoid the films, or watch them very critically, because the cinematic trilogy cannot re-create each page in the beloved book. They may not want their understanding of hobbits, as set forth by Tolkien, 'tainted' by perceived lesser works that change aspects of the original story. These readers, however, lose out on a shared popular interpretation of hobbits, which becomes increasingly layered with meaning with each adaptation presented to the public. Book fans may not choose to look through the kaleidoscope, but plenty of other people will. Multiple resulting interpretations of who and what hobbits are will continue to influence succeeding generations of creative fans inspired by Tolkien's characters and the adaptations popular at the time.

Some musicians and artists who, in later chapters in this book, discuss how Tolkien inspired their own creativity often refer to the Rankin–Bass TV specials of their childhood. For many now-adult artists, the animated *Hobbit* was a first introduction to Middle-earth, one that they love, even though they may have gone on to read Tolkien's books. Even Peter Jackson admitted to his biographer, Brian Sibley, that he turned to Tolkien's when he couldn't understand the story as told by filmmaker Ralph Bakshi.[1] Although good or not-so-good adaptations may eventually lead audiences to Tolkien's original stories, these audiences often base their understanding of, or initial love for, Middle-earth on an adaptation, not the original.

Tolkien's detailed storytelling (as evidenced in the two hobbit-centric stories, *The Hobbit* and *LotR*) is often difficult to adapt, however. *The Hobbit* seems by far the easier of the two stories to tell in a non-print medium, but it also poses challenges, as directors of a *Hobbit* series of films in the 2010s discovered. Guillermo del Toro initially agreed to direct the films, as well as assist with the script, but, after a series of long studio delays, he left the project before his vision of the story could be realised. Peter Jackson, director of the *LotR* trilogy and another scriptwriter for the *Hobbit* films, became the director by the time filming began in 2011. During the project's long development, the directors and scriptwriters anticipated making more than one film, a seemingly impossible task, given the length of the book. The simpler story of *The Hobbit*, which is more of a children's story than the longer, more complex *LotR*, was reportedly expanded using information from *LotR*'s appendices as well as *The Silmarillion*. The resulting films were adapted from *The Hobbit* and other sources, creating *The Hobbit: An Unexpected Journey*, *The Hobbit: There and Back Again* and a later-planned third film.

From the beginning, the more complex *LotR* posed innumerable challenges for many would-be adaptors, who had a difficult time compressing the many subplots and characters into a coherent film or television programme short enough for audiences to sit through and still understand. The stories' continuing popularity makes the challenges attractive to innovative adaptors, and undoubtedly in the years ahead many other scriptwriters will want to tell Tolkien's stories in different ways, leading to even more adaptations.

Not only adaptations, but the original stories, went through many changes on their way to becoming the basic tales in print today. J.R.R. Tolkien's *The Hobbit* was first published in 1937; *LotR*, between 1954 and 1955. The stories, however, go back much longer than that, because Tolkien wrote and revised them during the course of many years, often stopping for a while and later returning when more time was available from his scholarship, teaching and family duties. Even when the books appeared in print, Tolkien worked to eliminate inconsistencies and errors, a revision and correction process that continued for the rest of his life.

In the decades since Tolkien's death in 1973, his son Christopher and other scholars, including John D. Rateliff and Douglas A. Anderson, have analysed the Professor's many handwritten or typed manuscripts to study these revisions and understand just how and why the changes were made. Although most readers of the books may never want or need to know about all transmutations that took place to bring their favourite characters into public view, fan-scholars have a wealth of information about how, when, and often why Tolkien changed names, dialogue and events. Those who want to know more about Tolkien's writing process as he described such a layered, complex Middle-earth are fortunate to have so many drafts and analyses of them; I doubt if any other author's long-term writing/revision/ publication/correction process has been, or will be, documented in quite so much detail.

Even J.K. Rowling's Internet-based commentaries, media interviews, public appearances, and planned *Harry Potter* encyclopedia may not yet come close, although in the future Rowling's work and number of materials surrounding the development of the Harry Potter novels may surpass the volume of information documenting Tolkien's written works. The accessibility of electronic information and the relative ease of revising text or documenting drafts have changed tremendously since Tolkien's day. Tolkien's handwritten or marked drafts required copious copying and typing, plus typographic revisions that could as easily introduce new errors as correcting previously published ones. In contrast, Rowling's word-processed text can be reproduced and changed many times easily and quickly, and the number of transfers from handwritten to typed (or simply word-processed) to typeset text is significantly fewer when a single file can be created, manipulated and ultimately printed (or presented as an e-book) by a publisher.

Since the publication of Tolkien's books, many artists have adapted *The Hobbit* or *LotR* professionally (for example, musicals, stage plays, animated or live-action films) as well as purely for personal enjoyment (for example, fanfiction, scene re-enactments at fan 'moots'). Although the plots of adaptations more or less follow the key points laid out in the original works, all adaptors make some alterations to characters, settings, timeline of events, and dialogue to fit their own creative views and the needs of the medium they use to tell the story. Adaptors usually modernise the tale for a specific audience.

Adaptations may come close to many aspects of the original works, but they more frequently differ in important ways. Different media may force a reinterpretation of information from Tolkien, such as an artist taking a prose description of a character or scene and rendering it as a painting. Although the artist follows Tolkien's description, the image in Tolkien's mind at the time he wrote (or revised) that passage is different from the artist's mental image. Sometimes an adaptation occurs because the person writing fanfiction, or developing a movie script, chooses to emphasise characteristics that are present but not given as much weight in the original work.

A look at the many live-action productions (on film or stage) and animated television specials reveals many different depictions of hobbits, although they all have some truth based on Tolkien's text. For example, hobbits may enjoy several meals a day, as supported by Tolkien's descriptions or dialogue. However, if Pippin is a writer's favourite character, emphasising Pippin's particular love of food and making him the focus of a song all about hobbits' eating habits (as in *Fellowship!*, a musical parody) might be a natural outgrowth of the canon. Meriadoc Brandybuck, literally described as a well-rounded hobbit, looked very rounded indeed in the *LotR* play premiering in Toronto in 2006, but the Jackson films slimmed Merry, especially the longer he journeyed from the Shire. Both depictions took aspects of Tolkien's description, but the elements, such as weight and costuming, varied greatly. In these and other ways described in later chapters about specific adaptations, audiences first learning about Pippin or Merry might think the adapted version is the 'true' or only correct one, because that is the one from which they first learned about hobbits.

The introduction to a collection of artist Ruth Lacon's art, aptly entitled *Illustrations Inspired by the Works of J.R.R. Tolkien*, summarises what motivates adaptors. Although *LotR* is specifically mentioned, the analysis also could be applied to *The Hobbit* and other stories delineating the complexities of Middle-earth:

The Lord of the Rings is a singular, contradictory work. Written in an almost archaic form, packed with strange words and historical details, and lacking the modern emphasis on the 'inner life', it is unabashedly antimodern. But at the same time its melancholy environmentalism and fully realised alternative world are very modern ... The enduring appeal, however, lies not in its literary oddness or straightforward action, but in its beautifully realised world and themes of loss, self-sacrifice, and friendship. In its wake, Tolkien's work left not only a host of sword-and-sorcery imitators and devoted fans, but a lasting legacy in the hundreds of virtual worlds that have come to life in books and films since. Tolkien's work has inspired (as he intended) many others in word, art, music, and drama.[2]

Imitation may indeed be the greatest form of flattery, and fans are often inspired by *The Hobbit, LotR* or other Tolkien stories to create their own works of art based on these stories or to re-create/adapt the stories for new audiences and different media. To get a better understanding of the different ways that people 'imitate' and, ultimately, change *The Hobbit* or *LotR* for their own or others' enjoyment, some terms first need to be defined: reproduction, revision, interpretation and adaptation. They illustrate the many ways in which Tolkien's work has been 're-imagined' in the decades since the books were first published.

'Copies' of the author's text were based on print. For example, when Tolkien handwrote a chapter, it then had to be typed. The typed manuscript, once it had been edited to the author's satisfaction, went to the publisher's editor, who might have negotiated further changes. When a manuscript was accepted, it had to be typeset and the page proofs read by the author or others, who then made changes that had to be implemented. That process could be time-consuming and relied on the production of several print versions even before the paper book was printed. After that point, a book could be reproduced, which could entail the addition of new materials or corrections that had not been caught in the production of the previous edition. If the reproduction required new typesetting, changes might be made inadvertently, such as a line being left out or a word accidentally changed.

In the following sections, several print as well as other media 'adaptations' are discussed that refer to changes made not through creative interpretation but largely as the result of the publication process being used in the years when Tolkien's books were first published. Print reproduction and revision are authorial and publication processes, whereas true adaptation may take the original print stories and turn them into something new – a film, play, song, painting or original fanfiction short story.

Print Reproduction

Reproduction refers to the supposedly faithful copying of the author's text. For example, Tolkien often wrote early drafts in pencil and later wrote over these drafts in ink. Often he simply rewrote the original words – that is reproduction. When Christopher Tolkien read his father's manuscripts and put them in order for publication in his many volumes of *The History of Middle-earth*, he strove to 'reproduce' his father's writing process to make it understandable for scholars and more general readers. Sometimes even the son could not read his father's handwriting and had to guess at the words; even Christopher Tolkien's attempt faithfully to document the words his father used and the many changes in his father's text might require him to act more as a 'translator' to infer meaning from the rest of the sentence, to make meaning from context rather than the actual words. The words Christopher Tolkien finally selected may be exactly what his father wrote, but then again, they may not. Even when the author, or someone other than the author, intends to reproduce a text, some original words may be lost or changed.

In 1988, Douglas A. Anderson published an annotated version of *The Hobbit*, complete with commentary about Tolkien's writing process; in 2007, John D. Rateliff published another analysis of Tolkien's writing process by documenting the many changes to *The Hobbit*. In *Mr. Baggins*, Rateliff, like Christopher Tolkien (and with his assistance), discussed the author's changes not only in word but meaning as the story eventually took shape for publication. Christopher Tolkien returned one more time to his father's unfinished manuscripts and, in a sense, co-authored *The Children of Hurin*, published in 2007; he reproduced his father's work to a certain point but then filled in the rest of the words so that the completed story could be published.

Reproduction also involves typesetters and publishing companies, especially during early publications of Tolkien's books, long before computerised typesetting or word processing. Even the most diligent typesetters who physically set lines of type based on the author's manuscript might skip a word or lose a line. This loss occurred not only when Tolkien's writings were first typeset in the UK for official publication, but during the famous battle between the Ace (unauthorised) and Ballantine (authorised) versions of *LotR* in the US.

In 1965, taking advantage of a loophole in copyright law, Ace published 150,000 copies of *LotR*, using text that they had reset, instead of using the official typeset text used for the UK edition. As a result of this reproduction, new errors were introduced into the text. Tolkien received no royalties from these texts, and US Tolkien fans who knew how the Ace copies had been created started a campaign against the publisher. For his part, Tolkien revised *LotR* to correct errors and make final changes to the official version of the text, which was published by Ballantine in the US later in 1965.[3]

The Ace and Ballantine versions published in the US are still in circulation today, and they illustrate the problems with the state of typesetting and publication available in the 1960s. (They also indicate problems with copyright, especially across national borders.) Depending on which version of *LotR* Tolkien's readers first encounter, they can have very different understandings of some passages and shifts of meanings created by the misprint or omission of a word here or there.

Revision of a Text

Revision also comes into play in the development of a printed book, especially in *The Hobbit* and *LotR*. Tolkien's many revisions to the text before it was submitted for publication attest to the small and large changes to character, setting, timeline and action. Not only does an author revise a text until it seems right – as Tolkien did particularly with the early chapters of *LotR* – but editors and publishers also have a hand in changing the text. The author usually retains the right to approve editorial changes, but the story, by default, is going to be different from the first-submitted words when critical readers look at the text with an eye to revising it. Even after publication, the text may be further revised, as Tolkien, or one of his representatives (such as son Christopher, who completed or revised his father's unfinished texts), did many times.

Interpretation of a Printed Text

Interpretation comes almost immediately when a reader opens a book. One of the joys of reading, and one of the problems of literary criticism, is interpreting a work. Readers may not interpret the book the way the author intended his or her meaning to be taken; critics, in particular, may attempt to derive meaning by looking at elements that the author may not even have been aware were in the text. Tolkien most likely did not plan to write a sexist or racist work, yet some critics over the years have seen *LotR* or *The Hobbit* this way because of their lack of women or people of colour.

Also, not all readers may interpret the text the same way. Some readers who become fanfiction writers find all kinds of sexual innuendo in the text – particularly between male characters – yet it is highly doubtful if Tolkien thought of the Frodo–Sam, Merry–Pippin, Aragorn–Legolas, or Legolas–Gimli relationships in the same way as modern writers who create slash (same-sex relationship) fanfiction.

Interpretation occurs when the work leaves the author's hands and makes its own way in the world. Different generations interpret a text differently; people who prefer to make meaning from a text using postmodernist criticism, symbolism or personal analogy, for example, will create for themselves a very different text than the author may have had in mind.

When Jackson's adaptation of *LotR* was released in the early 2000s, political interpretations of Tolkien's work regained popularity, and the events and characters portrayed in the book and films became perceived as metaphors for a post-9/11 world. In the past few years, that interpretation has begun to fade, as have previous political interpretations equating *LotR* with World Wars I or II, the threat of nuclear holocaust in the 1950s, or Vietnam.

Interpretation may be purely personal or based on academic literary theories; it may be revelatory for millions or something that affects a single reader. Interpretation goes beyond critical literary analysis; a text can also be interpreted by musicians, composers, filmmakers, artists, actors, and so on. Interpretation often leads to adaptation of a prose work into another medium, such as art, music, theatre or film. In this way, interpretation becomes closely tied to inspiration, a term used frequently in this book to describe original artworks that translate Tolkien's themes into different, sometimes abstract, media. Artists are often inspired by the original stories, which lead them to interpret Tolkien's themes in their illustrations or musical compositions. Fanfiction writers interpret theme, setting and character in short stories or serialised novels based on their perceptions of Middle-earth. Inspiration can also lead to formal adaptation of a specific character, setting or event, or even an entire work.

Adaptation of a Text

When artists (for example, scriptwriters, composers, illustrators) interpret a prose work and turn it into another form (for example, film, animation, painting, opera), that is adaptation. A prose work, such as a novel, may be adapted into another style of prose, too, such as a parody.

Renowned artists such as Alan Lee and John Howe interpret Tolkien's works when they look at themes and events portrayed in a specific story and then turn them into visual images. These inspired adaptations evoke emotional responses to the drawings and paintings, not only because of their beauty and inherent meaning as works of art, but because they harken to specific sections of Tolkien's prose.

When Peter Jackson, Fran Walsh and Philippa Boyens were granted permission (by Saul Zaentz, copyright owner of the *LotR* book) to develop a script for *LotR*, they based three films on key aspects of Tolkien's book, but they also added elements to the story, deleted others, and changed the order of events to make them better suited to dramatic high points on screen.

When Dean Burry (with permission) composed original music involving story and character elements of *The Hobbit*, he adapted the story as an opera, including original music to help tell Tolkien's story on stage. The medium helps shape the structure of the adaptation, but the story is still recognisable as Tolkien's.

Of course, there are good adaptations and bad, and critics (as well as audiences) may not agree on which are which. Perhaps the only effective measure of a 'true' adaptation is the way that it follows the basic structure and language of the original text, but when a text is transferred to another medium, a true, faithful adaptation may not be possible. For this reason Tolkien doubted whether *LotR* could ever be turned into a film. Even publishers were initially concerned that the book would be too long to be read – certainly such a lengthy story could not be successfully adapted for film. Nevertheless, over the years, *LotR*, in part or whole, has been adapted for stage, film, canvas, orchestra or band.

Some adaptations take on a specific genre, such as parody. In prose, Harvard Lampoon's *Bored of the Rings* became a successful parody first in 1969, with reprints available once again in the 1990s and after the Jackson trilogy arrived in the 2000s.[4] The characters' names were changed (Frito, Spam, Moxie and Pepsi) and the plot severely streamlined but mined for jokes (for example, 'Three's Company, Four's a Bore' instead of the 'Three is Company' chapter). The fun comes from knowing the 'in joke' of such a parody, from being familiar with the original and able to see the connections between it and the abridged comic form.

In the early 2000s, a Los Angeles theatre troupe created a musical parody, *Fellowship!*, and brought it back by popular demand in 2010 (New York) and 2012 (Los Angeles). They loosely adapted the words and events in *The Fellowship of the Ring (FotR)*. However, the characters' names and some semblance of their portrayal in Tolkien's tale have been retained. *Fellowship!* also modernises the story – for example, by implying that the hobbits' 'pipeweed' might just be 'weed'. Merry, in particular, seems concerned about having enough weed for the long journey. His song lyrics are modernised through lines like 'Maybe I'll find new things to smoke and get myself invited to a dwarven rave', which is sung as the hobbits think about the journey before them;[5] Merry later promises Pippin, 'I'm with you 'til the end; just don't bogart my last bag of weed', sung after the two have been captured by Orcs.[6] In this musical parody, even the Balrog gets a song ('The Balrog blues'),[7] and each member of the Fellowship is amusingly skewered through song and dance as the basic story of Frodo receiving and then agreeing to take the Ring to Mount Doom plays out on stage.

At the other end of the adaptation spectrum, dramatic readings interspersed between a narrator's summaries of the rest of the plot have also been popular over the years, particularly for university or community theatre. Actors, usually in costume, read the characters' words as Tolkien wrote them. Stage blocking and rudimentary scene changes, as well as assistance by a narrator reading verbatim or summarising the story, help audiences understand the rest of the plot not revealed through characters' lines.

One such reading took place at Southern Illinois University during the 1967–68 play cycle; *LotR* was presented twice over three successive nights in November 1967. The event was described as readings with costuming and dramatic lighting. Although billed as a dramatic reading of the book, Bilbo's birthday party was eliminated, and the story truly started with Gandalf's later visit to Frodo. When Gandalf explains the peril of the Ring to Middle-earth and the need to destroy it, Frodo is already reluctant to harm the Ring, showing how powerful it truly is. In part, Frodo responds by saying 'I do really wish to destroy it – or well, to have it destroyed. I'm not made for perilous quests. I wish I had never seen the Ring! Why was I chosen?' This 'adaptation' of Frodo, even within basically a shortened reading of the book, creates for audiences a depiction of Frodo they may not have picked up from reading the book. Other lines, such as the narrator's introduction that 'Bilbo and Frodo lived at Bagend [sic], the most luxurious Hobbit-hole in the [S]hire,' summarise background information while providing the adaptor's understanding of character and setting.[8]

Popular books like *The Hobbit* and *LotR* have intrigued other creative personalities who want to adapt the stories into forms suitable for specific audiences and situations. Like myths, which must be reinvented if they are to retain their power in a culture from generation to generation, some popular books attain mythic status. Although all Tolkien's stories remain popular with his readers and fans, *The Hobbit* and *LotR* hold a special place in popular literature and modern culture. They are likely to remain source material to be adapted by future artists. The hobbits – specifically Bilbo, Frodo, Sam, Merry and Pippin – are also adapted, sometimes in ways unfamiliar to readers of the original text. Therein lies both the beauty and the bane for the original work: prose stories adapted for other media help the stories survive to be told again to new generations, but the characters in these stories may be radically changed over the years as the number of adaptations increases.

In 1978, Ralph Bakshi, whose *LotR* film probably is the most often debated adaptation in terms of quality of storytelling and audience reception, summarised that issue:

> *The LotR* was not my story. And it no longer even was Tolkien's story. It already was a part of the public's consciousness, like an historical event or a myth or a folktale. And like any of those, everyone has his own interpretation of the meaning of the books, and beyond that, even what all the characters of the books looked like.[9]

Such is the problem of popular books being adapted into other media.

A Case in Point: Adaptation and 'The Road Goes Ever On'

A good example of adaptation involves a now almost-clichéd song from both *The Hobbit* and *LotR*, 'The road goes ever on'. Bilbo first sings the song in *The Hobbit*'s last chapter, indicating his relief at the end of his journey as well as his acknowledgment of how much he has been changed by what he has recently experienced. The pull of the Shire, not only for this now-worldly hobbit but for the Travellers who will one day follow him, also lures readers back to this comforting vision in the last stanza of the song/poem:

> Eyes that fire and sword have seen
> And horror in the halls of stone
> Look at last on meadows green
> And trees and hills they long have known.[10]

Tolkien revises the hobbit walking song into different versions suitable for either Bilbo or Frodo at different stages of their journey through life and on quests. The Professor inserts this song/poem and changing perspective on travels and home three times in *LotR*. Bilbo first sings this song as he departs Bag End after finally surrendering the Ring to Gandalf and leaving it to his heir, Frodo. The travelling song takes on a lighthearted air as newly 'freed' Bilbo leaves on what he plans to be a final journey:

> The Road goes ever on and on
> Down from the door where it began.
> Now far ahead the Road has gone,
> And I must follow, if I can ...[11]

This version is probably the best known, and it is the one used by Peter Jackson in *FotR*.

A few chapters later, in 'Three is Company', Frodo recalls Bilbo's song. His rendition, however, is more sombre, as he contemplates the quest before him. Bilbo once more murmurs the travelling song when the other hobbits have returned from the quest and are visiting Rivendell ('Many Partings'); the old hobbit falls asleep after 'singing' the song a final time. This time he changes the words so that they become an ending song. His life's work is completed, and he plans only one final journey, to Valinor.

Tolkien incorporates 'The road goes ever on' as a hobbit travelling song, but he links it metaphorically with the life journeys of two Ringbearers. Bilbo and Frodo ultimately hold very different views of 'adventure', based on their respective experiences outside the Shire, and changes in the situations and lyrics as the song is repeated throughout *LotR* illustrate Bilbo's and Frodo's personal quests.

This theme has been taken to heart by numerous writers and composers who later adapted either *The Hobbit* or *LotR*. Jackson first introduces the Shire by having Gandalf arrive singing the song. He sings under his breath as he drives a cart along the rutted road. Frodo becomes aware of the wizard's presence when he hears the song.

After the birthday party, Bilbo leaves Bag End and, as in Tolkien's book, sings the song. Jackson, however, never lets his characters complete the many verses Tolkien includes in prose; they only sing/hum the same tune and repeat the four lines from Bilbo's travelling song in *LotR*. It is telling that Gandalf knows the hobbit song well, and, musically, it provides a comfortable sense of tradition and warmth first as Gandalf travels *into* the Shire and, a few scenes later, Bilbo travels *from* the Shire.

Using Tolkien's song/poem to bookend audiences' first visit to the Shire both illustrates the hobbits' cosy homeland and Gandalf's long association with hobbits. At the end of Bilbo's song as he walks away from Bag End, the reflective music takes on first a note of melancholy as he leaves home for what he thinks will be the last time.[12] The music grows darker, with more ominous tones as Bilbo's words fade away. The change in key and lower range foreshadow Frodo's own travels that will not begin or end on a happy note.

The *LotR* theatrical musical turns this theme into a rollicking travel song for four hobbits, plus rangers and elves. Sam, Frodo, Merry and Pippin take turns singing their expectations for their journey. The lyrics, 'The road goes ever, ever on',[13] are decidedly upbeat and faster paced; this song provides a sharp contrast to the dangers the hobbits will soon face.

Dean Burry's *Hobbit* opera offers a very different sound for the song, one appropriate to Tolkien's lyrics and tone near the end of the book. Burry's slow, serious tune matches the returning Bilbo's understanding of the rewards – but also the perils – of travelling far from home. The composer understands how this song must change to reflect the situation being presented in Tolkien's books:

> Look at the moment in *The Hobbit* when Bilbo sings this song, practically at the end when he sees his home again. He realises the journey he has gone on and how much he has changed. In *LotR*, 'The Road Goes Ever On' happens at the beginning, which could very well be portrayed with vim and vigour, a chorus to get things going. However, in *The Hobbit*, it is a song of relief, reflection and

perhaps reluctance. Can the new Bilbo really live in the same old Shire?...This song is the most powerful and poignant part of the whole opera for me.[14]

Whether on film or stage, the 'song' presented as a poem in print must be turned into real music, and each person adapting 'The road goes ever on' has retained the song's purpose and thematic meaning while setting the song to different tunes, as appropriate for their adaptation. In several adaptations, including Jackson's and Burry's, the character who sings in the book is still the character (Bilbo) who sings on screen or stage. However, Jackson also gave the tune first to Gandalf, and all four hobbits, along with a large chorus, harmonise during the stage musical. While trying to keep the spirit of the song, those who adapt Tolkien's stories nevertheless manipulate the song's placement, musicality and lyrics to advance their own versions of the stories.

Adaptation by Genre

All adaptations discussed in this book owe their life to Tolkien's *Hobbit* and *LotR*, and each creative work portrays hobbits in slightly different ways. Each medium also presents its own challenges for adapting Tolkien's works. Jackson, for example, had to decide how much of the story to tell; he succeeded in presenting so much of *LotR* because he could develop three separate films for a combined running time of more than ten hours. When it came time to adapt *The Hobbit*, Jackson and a writing team of Fran Walsh, Philippa Boyen, and, as previously mentioned, Guillermo del Toro combined story elements from *The Hobbit* and other sources in order to develop the next three films. Although the projects had different amounts of source materials, they both faced similar cinematic limitations.

Some initial script limitations involved the time it would take to tell the story: how long would audiences sit still to watch a single instalment? How could each film end at a logical, emotionally satisfying plot point that would still entice the audience to return in a year to see the next film? How could a story which often requires parallel timeframes for characters in very different settings be told linearly to keep the action moving, but also not lose audiences unfamiliar with Tolkien's stories? Although Jackson ultimately ended up with multiple films, just as Tolkien ended up with three separately published 'books' within the one *LotR* master book, the writer/director broke the story in different places and rearranged scenes to fit the demands of film.

Composers must often give different musical voices to different characters or races. 'Elf music', for example, whether performed by an orchestra or sung by a soloist, must sound different from 'hobbit music'. The choice of instruments and the style of music help audiences identify characters and understand their current mood or situation.

These are only a few considerations for two types of presentational media. A successful adaptation requires many more creative decisions. Although adaptation may superficially seem like an easy task, given that the story already exists, the making of a successful adaptation that honours the source material while bringing the original text to audiences in a new way is a daunting job.

The Power of the Adaptation

With so many versions of *The Hobbit* and *LotR* available, which story, Tolkien's or an adaptor's, will people remember and think of as the 'true' *Hobbit* or *LotR*? For many fans, it will be the one by which they were first introduced to Middle-earth. Their ideas about what hobbits are, look like, sound like, and do will be largely formed by their first impressions, whether in the pages of a book, on stage, or in a cinema. The number of adaptations thus raises some important questions about the future of *The Hobbit* and *LotR*.

Is an adapted story, with cumulative changes over time, still Tolkien's story – or is it something new or someone else's invention? The basics of Tolkien's story will probably survive. Character names, the key plot points, and locations of big events, such as a kingdom or a battlefield, will undoubtedly be integrated or summarised into future adaptations, just as they have been in the past. However, new creations – such as characters a scriptwriter adds to a film – belong to the adaptors and may confuse future generations of audiences who then turn to the books for additional information. Fans of an adaptation may fault the original text or find it less enjoyable because of its 'missing' character or details, even though the adaptation is a much later work. More likely, audiences who watch a film or see a play, for example, will probably enjoy the entertainment but refrain from checking the original source.

This is the primary problem I find with adaptations, no matter how good they are. They may become the *only* version of a story with which a vast number of people will be familiar. The depth and breadth of Tolkien's world may some day be lost to the majority of the public who know of his work only through adaptations; fan-scholars or academics who study the Professor's words and care to read books may be among the minority who know the original stories on which popular adaptations are based.

Although e-books are easy to download, and reading is hardly an obsolete skill, Tolkien's style and language may prove challenging for readers who prefer modern terminology or quick reads. My traditional-age undergraduate students who prefer the action-oriented Jackson films to reading the more than 1100 pages of the one-volume, fiftieth anniversary edition of *LotR* are likely not in the minority. Although young readers of the Harry Potter series, for example, prove that reading is not dead and long books are still a lucrative business, Rowling's style is nonetheless far more modern and consistently worded than Tolkien's. The Professor developed different looks and languages for the different races of Middle-earth, and his literary style involves long sentences, descriptive passages with little dialogue, and turns of phrase not as familiar to modern readers. As Tolkien's style, as well as the habit of reading long books, moves farther from the norm for a mass readership, popular adaptations of his works may become increasingly important if the Professor's stories are going to remain a part of mainstream literature and popular culture.

Will audiences of films or stage productions know how much of the story is Tolkien's or someone else's – or does that even matter in the long run? For a story to survive, generation after generation, it must remain relevant to modern life. The number of adaptations of

The Hobbit and *LotR* help ensure that Tolkien's stories will survive into yet another century. However, I anticipate that many details will be lost or the stories irrevocably changed in public consciousness because of, in particular, cinematic adaptations.

In early 2011, when filming began on the *Hobbit* movies, the *Guardian* published an intriguing commentary on likely changes to Tolkien's story in Jackson's cinematic prequel to the *LotR* trilogy. The article's writer, Ben Child, concluded with the following, noting that the film scripts reportedly included

> Saruman, Galadriel, Ian Holm's elder Bilbo, Legolas and even Elijah Wood's Frodo (goodness only knows how they are going to shoehorn him in)…Part of me says more power to Jackson … The other part bristles at all this tinkering with Tolkien. I can already see myself being jolted out of my reverie in the cinema in six months' time when [Orlando] Bloom [reprising his role as Legolas] pops up out of nowhere, his shiny elf hair flailing out behind him in the wind, to take out some poor Orc who's been threatening mischief.[15]

Audiences who have never read *The Hobbit* may think that Frodo Baggins, like his Uncle Bilbo, is a character in that story or that handsome elf Legolas has a pivotal role in *The Hobbit* as much as in *LotR*. Just as action-elf Legolas was featured in battle scenes in Jackson's *LotR*, creating a different version of the character on screen to the one in Tolkien's book, so might the inclusion of characters not found – or described differently – in *The Hobbit* forever change the public's understanding of Tolkien's original story.

Another question revolves around the issue of mythology. Are Tolkien's works a mythology for England? Texts like *The Silmarillion* or *LotR* include extensive timelines, genealogies and maps written like historic documents, albeit of a time and place outside the world we know. Are Tolkien's stories thus rooted in a specific place and time, or are its themes universal? In part because of Tolkien's proclivity as an author to write in such detail, in part because of his vast scholarly research and knowledge of linguistic history, his fiction seems 'real'.

Although Tolkien's stories are not exclusively about a historic time in English history, many elements of the story resonate with official British historical documents or make the descriptions of the

Shire and great leaders like Aragorn sound familiar to British readers. Making hobbits seem like specifically English historical figures may endear them more completely to readers in the UK, but it also creates a cultural barrier between the hobbits and the rest of the world. In particular, because of Jackson's cinematic adaptations, New Zealand also feels a strong affinity for hobbits. Thinking of Tolkien's works as a type of fictional history may somewhat limit their appeal to readers who identify with hobbits but live outside the UK.

The idea that Tolkien created a mythology for England is well rooted in current websites with which recent *Hobbit* or *LotR* fans are likely to be familiar.[16] If Tolkien's story is considered more mythic than historical, its appeal is broadened across cultures, because a myth can have universal application. For example, the abiding friendship between Sam and Frodo or Merry and Pippin resonates with modern fans because of the timelessness of this friendship. The willingness to die for another, the hope to sustain a broken friend and heal him, the joy of being reunited after desperate separations – these elements of the hobbits' friendships are not specific only to one time or place.

Does the difference between a story's being specifically connected to one geographic location or having universal appeal make a difference to the way Tolkien's works may survive? Perhaps. When a story is deemed mythic, adaptors generally take more license in adapting plot or characters to make them relevant to modern audiences. Adding a new female elf to Jackson's *Hobbit* films, just as the director/writer expanded Arwen's role in the *LotR* trilogy, helps make Tolkien's stories appeal more to female filmgoers and improves the gender balance in Middle-earth. Also, a universal theme like love can be emphasised in an adapted film to make the resulting product more appealing, as well as relevant, to modern audiences.

The adaptations discussed in this book sometimes reflect modern (for the time in which the adaptation was set) concerns and trends more than the issues important in Tolkien's day or those crucial in the lives of hobbits living in a fantasy world set long ago. Some adaptations are more 'epic' or 'historical' in the way that characters and events are depicted. Some reflect universal themes – greed, corruption, love, hope – and illustrate these themes through the lives of specific characters. That Tolkien's work still provokes new interpretations and debate bodes well for its literary survival separate from the longevity of any of its adaptations.

The tale changes in the telling, but whether this is good or bad for the story itself as well as its author and audience can likely be determined only retrospectively many years in the future. No doubt *The Hobbit* and *LotR* will be around decades from now. They will still be inspirational and entertaining, whether in original text or new adaptations. Whether they will be recalled as *Tolkien's Hobbit* and *LotR* may be another matter.

The following chapters illustrate the many 'lives' of the hobbits: Bilbo, Frodo, Sam, Merry and Pippin from the many retellings of *The Hobbit* or *The Lord of the Rings*. Because *LotR* has been adapted more often, the chapters more heavily feature the hobbits of the Fellowship. Although this book summarises more than a dozen adaptations from print, radio, television and film (and the DVD versions of network and theatrical releases), theatre and the Internet, the *LotR* (or *Hobbit*) saga is far from over. Undoubtedly new generations of fans will enjoy new generations of adaptations. J.R.R. Tolkien could not have known just what he started when he wrote that fateful line, 'In a hole in the ground there lived a hobbit.'[17]

2

TOLKIEN'S REVISED HOBBITS

Christopher Tolkien's *History of Middle-earth* and John D. Rateliff's *Mr. Baggins* detail J.R.R. Tolkien's writing process and character revisions. A few changes that Tolkien made to hobbits, however, may help illustrate the point that even the author had different ideas about Bilbo, Frodo, Sam, Merry and Pippin; the final print version was the result of an ongoing creative process. After the publication of *The Hobbit*, Tolkien revised the riddle-game story and wrote a different version of it for *LotR*. The revision changes the way that Bilbo receives the Ring and the degree of his suspicion of Gollum. A note in *LotR* explains the shift in story, and *The Hobbit*'s first version of the riddle game was deleted from later editions.[1] As noted in Chapter 1, even within the published, or what most readers would assume is the final, text Tolkien continued to adjust the words to create the story he wanted to present to the public.

Whereas a revision to the riddle game involves some plot changes so that the game would be consistently portrayed throughout the entire hobbit saga, word substitutions may help create a more precise setting. The switch from 'tomatoes' to 'pickles' in Bilbo's larder from the first to second edition[2] is one such attempt to make even hobbits' everyday lives consistent with the precise geography and culture

Tolkien was establishing within Middle-earth. As Tolkien continued to develop his increasingly interrelated stories of Middle-earth, some revisions became necessary to avoid what would appear to be inconsistencies in the published works.

Revisions to *The Hobbit*

Tolkien's revisions to *The Hobbit* often took place in light of the expansion of hobbit lore and the cosmology of Middle-earth as told in later books. Nevertheless, some contradictions remain. Later hobbit folklore derived by *LotR* readers includes the ideas that hobbits fear water and those who enjoy boating or swimming are considered strange. The Brandybucks, for example, live close to the Brandywine River and might be expected to know how to swim, purely for safety reasons, as well as how to travel on the river; their comfort level around rivers or lakes helps mark them as eccentric or odd to hobbits living outside Buckland. Land-bound hobbits like the Gamgees, in contrast, normally would not live near enough to a large body of water to become comfortable with it, much less to learn to boat or swim.

Sam's reluctance around boats in *LotR* thus represents an understandable fear, one played up to dramatic advantage in adaptations like Jackson's *FotR*. Sam acts ill at ease when the Fellowship leaves Lothlórien by boat; he holds on to the sides as if he alone can steady the boat to avert its capsizing. He also would be well aware that Frodo's parents drowned, an unnecessary detail for the Jackson adaptation. Nevertheless, when Frodo paddles away on his own after the Fellowship breaks, Sam resolutely stomps into the river and refuses to go back, even though his attempt to follow Frodo nearly drowns him.[3]

Readers of *The Hobbit*, who follow Bilbo's plan to help the dwarves escape Mirkwood by bobbing down the river towards Lake Town in wine barrels,[4] may be confused if they assume Bilbo should be more afraid of water than of vengeful elves, something not indicated in the book. After all, Bilbo would seem to be one of those hobbits not brought up with knowledge of large bodies of water or experience on them; Bag End is a long way from a river. Even Frodo, because of his Brandybuck as well as Baggins lineage, would be expected to know more about boats and rivers than Bilbo would have learned.

Rateliff explained that this motif

> is another late accretion totally absent from [*The Hobbit*]; a hydrophobe would hardly propose barrelling down an underground river, and Bilbo shows no qualms about riding by boat from Lake Town across Long Lake and up the River Running (or indeed to staying in Lake Town, a city suspended above deep water).[5]

Tolkien did revise a section about Bladorthin's (later Gandalf's) propensity for sending youngsters off on 'mad adventures, everything from climbing trees to stowing away aboard the ships that sail to the Other side' (or Valinor). Although in the published *Hobbit* Bilbo does have to climb trees (for example, to escape wargs), he never is a stowaway on a ship; his later journey to Valinor is quite respectable. Rateliff noted that a change in this latter section was not made until the third edition of 1966, with the deleted stowaway reference and the insertion of 'sailing in ships, sailing to other shores!'[6] Bilbo seems to be comfortable with this concept, and both *The Hobbit* and *LotR* give examples of Bilbo's exploits in ships or lesser sailing craft, without the connotation of 'stowaway'.

Rateliff labelled as 'Plot Notes B' an early draft of the manuscript and several of Tolkien's notes about where the story was headed, most likely so that the author would not forget some ideas when he had to take a break from writing because of his university responsibilities. Rateliff noted more contradictions in hobbit nature found in this version of the story; although Tolkien always meant for Bilbo to return safely to Bag End, just how his adventures would ultimately affect him seemed uncertain. Tolkien wrote that Bilbo 'just becomes a hobbit again' but also indicated that Bilbo would be '"very different", a writer of poetry, and regarded as "a bit queer"'.[7]

Yet Tolkien managed to find a way to combine these contradictory natures when the story is finally written. Bilbo successfully rejoins hobbit society and participates in the community as much as ever; his journey does not change him so much inside that outwardly he cannot adjust again to life in the Shire. Unlike Frodo, who tries to participate more actively in the Shire's daily life (for example, by becoming Mayor for a short while, after he returns to the Shire post-War of the Ring) but ultimately is too broken to enjoy Shire life fully, Bilbo may be eccentric, but he is very much part of the community. His eccentricity, including writing poems and books, can be attributed to his ancestry and his wealth, both of which afford him leisure time and the public's expectation that he might do something 'odd'. His long-time friendship with Gandalf and his worldliness as a result of his early adventures in *The Hobbit* only reinforce Bilbo's true nature and (once untapped) potential. These quirks could also help readers justify Bilbo's comfort around large bodies of water and resolve an apparent contradiction in Tolkien's hobbit stories.

Tolkien's work to develop the best possible story seemed never-ending, and his keen attention to detail, while time-consuming when it comes to revisions, created a remarkably complete world in which hobbits live. In *The Annotated Hobbit*, Douglas Anderson revealed that Tolkien's corrections to the first proofs 'were considered somewhat heavy, and even though he had carefully calculated the length of the replacement passages, it was necessary to reset several sections'.[8] Many of Tolkien's changes throughout the revision process dealt with wizards, dwarves and a dragon, indicating that Bilbo may have been more clearly visualised even in the early stages of storytelling than the other characters who would emerge in the tale. Nevertheless, like Tolkien's later works, *The Hobbit* remained a published 'work in progress' for many years.

Revisions to *LotR*

As Tolkien wrote and revised chapters of *LotR*, he made important changes in everything from the hobbits' names to their characterisations. The many revisions today are kept among the manuscript collection at Marquette University, where the original pages clearly show the Professor's many corrections over time. The lines are frequently marked over as names are changed, and some typed pages have been labelled as rejections when the author decided the story should take a different turn, as in the following less important but interesting example.

Not only the hobbits of what would become the Fellowship changed greatly over time and many drafts – so did their relatives. When Bilbo disappears from his birthday party, in an early version of 'Concerning Hobbits', Rory Brandybuck tells daughter-in-law Pandora that 'mad Baggins' is probably off on another adventure.[9] The published version changes the name of Merry's mother from Pandora to Esmeralda. Name changes like these are common in these early drafts, and nearly all important hobbits in the story go through at least one or two before Tolkien finally decided on the published name; Sam is the notable exception to this pattern. Every revision, even to characters who do not have a large role in the book, came as a result of Tolkien's careful consideration of plot and character details and how they would fit together to form a much bigger picture of the Shire and of Middle-earth.

The Power of Naming

The Professor and lover of languages determined not only the name to appear in publication for each hobbit but noted differences between the published (our English) version and the original name in the hobbits' language and that of the Common Speech (also known as Westron, a standardised or common language understood by all races).

Most hardcore fans know that Merry's name as translated from the Bucklandish is 'Kali', short for Kalimac.[10] Before he was either Merry or Kali, however, he was written into the story as Marmaduke Brandybuck. Marmaduke later turned into Meriadoc, but he was always a responsible hobbit who liked to plan.

In the final volume of the *Histories*, the Tolkiens (J.R.R. and Christopher) discuss important differences between the hobbits' real names (in their own language) and the names by which they were known to others in Middle-earth. Merry's real name is Chilmanzar, whose diminutive form, Chilic, also means 'merry'. A further explanation of the choice of the 'high-sounding and legendary name' of Meriadoc linked Buckland to the Shire in a similar way that Wales is linked with England, and Meriadoc sounds appropriately Welsh.[11] Several fan-scholars have linked the names of Conan Meriadoc, a legendary king of Brittany in Gaul, with Meriadoc Brandybuck, and a modern variation of the name is Meriadog in Welsh.[12]

Similar explanations were given for the names of Bilbo, Frodo, Sam and Pippin, whose name is particularly interesting. Tolkien lists Peregrin's Shire name as Razanul, 'the name of a legendary traveller' that contains the root words meaning 'stranger' and 'foreign'.[13] The name is certainly appropriate for Peregrin Took, who becomes one of the best-travelled hobbits of the Shire and who amazes the citizens of Gondor upon his arrival and role in the Guard. Pippin truly seems foreign to those in Minas Tirith, who had never seen a hobbit before his arrival, and give him the presumed title of prince as if he were a visiting foreign dignitary.

The shortened form 'Razal' is a type of small red apple,[14] perhaps even kin to the modern Pippin apples, although they usually are green-, yellow-, or orange-skinned instead of red. Fans of Jackson's *FotR* remember a scene in which Pippin is tossed an apple, which inadvertently ends up bouncing off his head, and fanfiction writers frequently connect Pippin with apples as a possible source of his naming. Whether fans know of Tolkien's decisions behind the name, they often choose similar modern word associations to fit Pippin's name.

Differences in names turn up in the much-marked copies delineating the author's revision process. Tolkien reworked 'A Conspiracy Unmasked' many times during several decades. Of all the chapters in *LotR*, the first few have been most heavily revised in all respects: character, names, events and tone.[15] At one time in Tolkien's early drafts, Frodo Baggins is first called Frodo Took, but he is not the main hobbit in the story. That honour goes to Bingo Baggins, Bilbo's son. However, Frodo Took changes names and personalities before he finally becomes merged with Bingo to create the Frodo Baggins readers know and love. Frodo Took changes to Folco Took, who becomes one of the many variations leading to the Pippin character who finally emerges in the published version.

A character who might loosely be considered Pippin begins as Odo Took, then becomes, in turn, Odo Bolger, and later turns into Hamilcar Bolger and finally Fredegar, or Fatty, Bolger, and then becomes the stay-in-the-Shire hobbit. The personality of Odo Took, however, becomes more Pippinish when it merges with Folco Took. When the name Odo Took changes to Odo Bolger, the personality becomes more like that of Fredegar Bolger in the published work. Folco Took becomes a mixture of the Frodo–Pippin personalities for a while. Folco is next known as Faramond Took, and changes again in personality and name to become Folco Boffin, a lesser-known character.

The personality of Folco Took shifts with the name change to Peregrin Boffin, who is next Peregrin Took. Even with all these confusing name changes and shifts in personality as the hobbits became transformed into their final prose versions, the 'Pippin' character was firmly fixed in Tolkien's mind from the beginning. As a hobbit archetype, this character, according to Christopher Tolkien, is 'a very "typical" hobbit of the Shire ... [but is also] very distinct: cheerful, nonchalant, irrepressible, commonsensical, limited, and extremely fond of his creature comforts'.[16]

Bingo Baggins, an older hobbit very fond of his home and reluctant to leave the Shire, is revised as Frodo Baggins, an adopted hobbit who seems younger than Bingo and more eager to follow Bilbo into an adventurous lifestyle. Samwise Gamgee consistently accompanies Frodo as servant and companion, and he is the only one of the Fellowship hobbits originally meant to travel with Frodo past Rivendell.

Building Characters: Growth in the Hobbits of the Fellowship

At times during the revision process, Tolkien indicates what readers nearly a century later now come to expect from their hobbits. It may seem strange to think that the characters so well known today could have been very different. Sam, for example, seems even more interested in 'urban legends' than later adaptations give him credit for. Instead of merely being superstitious, he displays a genuine interest in the strange goings-on outside the Shire, both in a pre-publication draft and the printed version of 'The Shadow of the Past'.

During a discussion with Ted Sandyman at the Green Dragon, Sam mentions both dragons and Ents, or what he calls 'Tree-men'. He recalls Jo Buttons (eventually Sam's cousin Hal) seeing an elm tree walking in the North Moors of the Northfarthing. Early in the story, Sam's discussions indicate his interest in the extraordinary, especially if it involves races other than hobbits. For such a common hobbit, Sam displays an uncommon interest in stories and folklore and takes note of hobbits whose experiences fall outside the norm. Sam also recalls that Bilbo knows that elves are sailing west; he even thinks he saw an elf in the woods and attributes that to the likelihood that many elves are now leaving Middle-earth.[17] These characteristics are part of Sam's makeup even in early versions of the story.

Later revisions to this chapter provide a longer explanation of what Sam overhears while eavesdropping on Gandalf's conversation with Frodo at Bag End; the conversation between Sam and Ted Sandyman also remains longer than what ultimately ends up in print.[18] No matter how long the text, Tolkien's revisions give Sam an unusual curiosity about events taking place outside the Shire and indicate the future Ringbearer's ability to keep an open mind about the possible beings he might encounter beyond the borders of his homeland.

In the fourth phase of revisions of 'A Conspiracy Unmasked', around October 1939, Tolkien made several final decisions about other characters. At this stage Bingo is gone, and Frodo's friends Meriadoc Brandybuck and Peregrin Boffin, better known as Merry and Perry, are close in character to the final Merry and Pippin. Tolkien initially planned for Meriadoc to travel only as far as Rivendell, and Pippin to stay at Crickhollow, but the later revisions bring all four hobbits into the Fellowship for the entire journey.[19]

Key changes in the plot involve different characters going along on the journey and the level of Gandalf's involvement. In early versions, for example, Gandalf and Hamilcar (sometimes Gandalf and Odo) travel together and encounter Orcs. What turns out to be the Pippin character sometimes goes ahead with Marmaduke/Meriadoc to make preparations at Crickhollow at the time when Sam, Frodo/Folco and Bingo leave Bag End. In many early versions, Bingo knows that his friends will accompany him; there is no 'conspiracy unmasked' as in the final version.

As the revisions progressed, the 'conspiracy unmasked' chapter took final form, and Merry, Pippin and Sam set out from Crickhollow with Frodo, after revealing that they have been waiting for Frodo to leave the Shire and developing a plan to accompany him to whatever end. Fredegar Bolger stays behind at Crickhollow to avoid the suspicion of other hobbits – or anyone looking for Frodo – if they see an empty house; in addition, Fredegar prefers not to leave the Shire on such an adventure.

Smaller changes involve dialogue revisions, but even the substitution of a few words can indicate more significant shifts in meaning. After the conspiracy has been unmasked, Frodo is both surprised at how much the others know and worried that everyone will discuss his departure from the Shire. Merry reassures Frodo that this is not true: "'After all, you must remember that we know you well, and are often with you. We can usually guess what you are thinking. We know Bilbo, too.'" The rest of this drafted section matches what was ultimately published. Merry later admits that he even knows about the Ring and admonishes Frodo, "'My dear old hobbit, you don't allow for the inquisitiveness of friends.'" The last word, 'friends', replaced a crossed-out 'the young'.[20] Merry's initial speech reinforces the close friendship between Frodo and the conspirators and reminds him that, even though he was young at the time Bilbo left the Shire, the older hobbit is still well remembered. By replacing the more generic 'the young' with 'friends', Tolkien again emphasises the close connection between Frodo and his cousins, particularly Merry.

As Pippin reminds Frodo in the currently published version of 'A Short Cut to Mushrooms', both he and Merry are well known to Farmer Maggot. In fact, the names Took and Brandybuck, if not Pippin and Merry, are well known outside the Shire. In a draft of 'At the Sign of the Prancing Pony', Barnabas (later to be renamed

Barliman) Butterbur comments that he does not know any Mr Green (Frodo's pseudonym at the time), 'But Took I know, and Brandybuck, of course.'[21] The 'of course' indicates Breefolks' long-standing acquaintance with the more prominent families of the Shire, especially those who live relatively closer.

A few scenes later, Tolkien describes Merry as not being terribly sociable. After the hobbits eat dinner, Frodo, Sam and Pippin decide 'to join the company. Merry said it would be too stuffy.' Merry, however, seems to be in full responsible cousin mode; he reminds the little group that they are escaping in secret. He even warns them to 'Mind your Ps and Qs, perhaps mindful himself of Pippin's often-outgoing behaviour. Pippin immediately reminds Merry that it is safer indoors. Neither cousin seems to heed the other's advice. Soon Pippin tells a funny story involving the fat mayor of Michel Delving, who ends up looking like a chalk-covered dumpling. Merry, in this draft and the published version, encounters the Black Riders and succumbs to the Black Breath, a malady diagnosed by Trotter (later Strider), the hobbits' new protector.[22] Although the draft indicates the basic structure of what would become the published chapter, insights into the hobbits' relationships or bits of dialogue that did not seem terribly important to the story or character development were eliminated from subsequent versions. Nevertheless, they provide some interesting glimpses into the hobbits' character development.

These types of changes, in which one character's actions would be substituted for another or the order of events would be modified to better suit events elsewhere in the story, are common among the many drafts Tolkien wrote of each chapter. An excellent example of the ongoing changes, which continued through publication (in the Ballantine and Ace editions in the US), concerns a number of word alterations in two chapters: 'The Muster of Rohan' and 'The Ride of the Rohirrim'.

A Long Journey into Final Form:
A Brief History of Two Chapters

In the first phase of Tolkien's writing, an A outline for these two chapters indicates that Tolkien had Théoden agree that Merry may join the Rohirrim as they head to battle. In fact, he assigns a lighter, younger soldier to carry Merry on his horse.[23] This member of the guard was likely Éowyn, but Tolkien didn't name the warrior until a later version, and, typically, the character changed names many times before becoming Dernhelm in the published book.

A major change occurs in the B outline when Tolkien shifted from telling the story from Merry's point of view, as in the A outline, to return to a more standard narrative. In the A outline, Merry recounts the previous three long days of riding. Around this time, Tolkien also changed the way that Merry travels towards battle; in a later outline Théoden refuses Merry's request to join the Rohirrim as they ride towards Minas Tirith. The king adds that if the battle were closer, Merry could fight, but the ride is too arduous for the hobbit to be carried as far as the White City.[24]

The language in Éowyn's/Dernhelm's proposal for Merry to accompany her was also revised many times before publication. In one early version of 'The Muster of Rohan', Tolkien described the scene this way:

> Suddenly a Rider came up to him, and spoke softly in a whisper, 'Where will wants not, a way opens, say we,' he said. 'So have I found myself.'… 'You wish to go where the lord of the Eorlingas goes?'
>
> 'I do,' said Merry.
>
> 'Then you shall ride before me,' said the Rider. 'Such good will shall not be wasted. Say nothing more, but come.'
>
> 'Thank you indeed, thank you sir – I do not know your name.'
>
> 'Do you not?' said the Rider softly. 'Then call me Cyneferth' [later changed to Grimhelm].[25]

The current published version of Dernhelm's invitation is worded this way:

> '*Where will wants not, a way opens,* so we say,' he whispered; 'and so I have found myself.' Merry looked up and saw that it was the young

Rider whom he had noticed in the morning. 'You wish to go whither the Lord of the Mark goes: I see it in your face.'

'I do,' said Merry.

'Then you shall go with me,' said the Rider. 'I will bear you before me, under my cloak until we are far afield, and this darkness is yet darker. Such good will should not be denied. Say no more to any man, but come!'

'Thank you indeed!' said Merry. 'Thank you, sir, though I do not know your name.'

'Do you not?' said the Rider softly. 'Then call me Dernhelm.'[26]

The final version benefits from additional dialogue to establish the relationship between Dernhelm and Merry as well as to explain exactly how the pair will ride unobserved by other soldiers. Dernhelm seems to have thought about the plan, which makes it feasible to Merry, who desperately wants to find a way to ride with the Rohirrim but does not really want to go against the King's command.

Merry's depression and loneliness at being left behind by the rest of the Fellowship and then being unable to go to battle like his friends become the basis of another much-revised section in the 'Ride of the Rohirrim'. In most drafts, Éowyn in disguise acts remote and seldom talks to Merry, who is left on his own. In some drafts, Merry is ignored completely, but in others, he is stepped on or over, a description that supports his low sense of self on this journey. Merry feels unwanted and inadequate, too small to be taken seriously, but large enough to be in the way.

One scene in particular illustrates the increased emphasis on Merry's lack of stature and status. In the current published version, a Marshal of the Mark, Elfhelm, almost trips over Merry. When the hobbit complains that he is not a tree root, Elfhelm compares him to a piece of luggage.

David Bratman, in a published presentation first given at a conference at Marquette University, discussed how

Tolkien adds not one but three comparisons of him with what is said in the first instance as 'just another bag that Dernhelm was carrying.' This phrase is part of one of the longest additions to the book ... Merry is so small and insignificant in a large group that he is not even sure if Théoden knows that he is there; and the entire *éored* ignores him.[27]

Bratman further explained that in an important revision, Merry exclaims that

> 'I am not a tree-root, Sir, nor a bag, but a bruised hobbit.' The bit about the bag, not relevant to what Elfhelm is saying but obviously much on Merry's mind, is a second edition addition. And he [Tolkien] adds one more sentence than he does in the first, a final dismissive command: 'Pack yourself up, Master Bag!' No other such comparisons of a hobbit to a bag are made[28] [in any of Tolkien's other works].

To complicate matters further, in the mid-1960s Ace published an unauthorised US version of *The Lord of the Rings*. Tolkien was compelled to make some revisions to the existing British published version so that Ballantine, the official US publisher, could acquire the US copyright for an authorised edition of the work. The Ace and Ballantine versions differ in sometimes slight wording, but even those small variations and omissions change Tolkien's story.

In a 1996 article in the newsletter *Beyond Bree*, Robert Acker noted some differences between the Ace and Ballantine texts. Once again, the 'bag' scene was changed in the rival companies' paperbacks. The 1966 Ballantine edition describes Merry as 'just another bag that Dernhelm was carrying. Dernhelm was no comfort; he never spoke to anyone. Merry felt small, unwanted, and lonely.' In contrast, the Ace paperback only mentions that 'Dernhelm was no comfort: he seldom spoke a word.'[29]

A few lines later, in the Ballantine edition, Merry says to the marshal, Elfhelm, '"I am not a tree-root, Sir,... nor a bag,"' and the punctuation around and capitalisation of Sir differ from the British official text. In the Ace version, Merry says to Elfhelm, '"I am not a tree-root, Captain."' Whereas the Ballantine version concludes the scene with Elfhelm's line, '"Pack yourself up, Master Bag!"', the Ace edition omits this line.[30]

The events are similar – Merry steals away against Théoden's wishes to ride with the Rohirrim, but he is ignored by almost everyone, including Dernhelm. The nuances of language, however, create a different Merry–Dernhelm dynamic. Although Dernhelm/Éowyn recognises in Merry a kindred spirit who will find a way to fight for family and friends, Merry finds it difficult to overcome feelings of inadequacy. His loneliness and anxiety increase. Not only is he stepped on because he is too small to be seen as Elfhelm walks about the encampment at night, but when he is noticed, he receives little more consideration than an inanimate object. To the Rohirrim, Merry is inconsequential, which deepens his loneliness and worry that he will be ineffective in battle. The longer passages in Tolkien's later drafts and officially published books better illustrate the depth of Merry's isolation and despair.

'Scouring of the Shire': Tolkien's Changes

The scouring of the Shire is a significant part of the complete *LotR* story. With it, Tolkien shows that even the most out-of-the-way rural spots can be touched by war, but after the final battles fought in their homeland the hobbits can rebuild an even better land. Life goes on; it does not end with the last battle or even a great victory. Furthermore, Evil will return some day; the final battle is not the ultimate victory. These themes often are missing from adaptations, which ignore the 'Scouring of the Shire' chapter and skip it in favour of a streamlined ending to the War of the Ring. An exception is the recent *LotR* musical, but even that adaptation merged several characters and lost much of Tolkien's message.

Tolkien also changed characters and events in this chapter, sometimes significantly. The most important revision involves Frodo. In early drafts, Frodo is very much part of the action instead of an observer or the one who pleads for mercy instead of violence. Early-draft Frodo leads the returning hobbits in capturing ruffians and rousing the Shire to action. With later revisions, however, most of Frodo's words and deeds are given to Merry, who then becomes a more prominent character in the published book by acting as a strategist and one of the captains who leads the hobbits to victory over the ruffians. Such an emphasis well suits Merry's description as the planner and responsible leader of the band of hobbits who set out from the Shire. Sam and Pippin also serve as effective soldiers throughout the drafts, although their roles, too, are modified from one draft to the next.[31]

Specific Word Choices

These revisions emphasise Tolkien as an author who loved words and took care that the precise meaning was matched to a character, setting or event. It is no wonder that he would be offended by changes suggested in some later movie scripts trying to summarise his story or give new dialogue to his characters.

In 1987, *Mythlore* published a study of the verbs used by characters in *LotR*. The textual analysis hints at personality traits Tolkien developed for his hobbits, simply through his verb choice. Frodo and Pippin are the only two hobbits who *interrupt* another character.[32] Bilbo, in either *The Hobbit* or *LotR*, 'screams', 'sneezes', 'squeaks' and 'begs'; from these verbs, he seems to be one of the most dramatic hobbits. Although other characters also share these verb choices, Sam alone of the hobbits 'blushes', 'protests', 'ventures', 'grunts', 'whistles' and 'muses'.[33] In particular, 'ventures' and 'muses' indicate a more cerebral Sam who thinks things through, indicative of his 'good hobbit sense'.

Paul Noble Hyde, who conducted the research, found that Merry and Pippin share common speech patterns and concluded the following about their linguistic similarity:

> How [does] one tell Merry from Pippin? Both 'mutter', 'stammer', 'pant', 'whisper', 'gasp', and 'laugh'. Pippin, however, is the only character who 'hesitates' and 'falters'; Merry is the only one who 'proceeds', 'argues', and 'wonders.' Merry 'exclaims', 'smiles', and 'chuckles.'[34]

Whereas Hyde's patterns indicate that these two hobbits' character development parallels their similarity in speech – in fact, the two parallel each other in every way in this analysis – the verb choices can also be interpreted as showing some important differences between the two.

As the youngest hobbit on the journey, Pippin seems the one most likely to 'hesitate' or 'falter'. As the older cousin, one who likely feels in charge of Pippin because of their close friendship, Merry would be more likely to 'proceed' and 'argue', while Pippin would follow his lead.

Before and shortly after leaving the Shire, Merry displays confidence in his leadership abilities and has a tendency to plan, as evidenced in his preparations for Frodo's departure from the Shire. His sense of responsibility, no matter that it naively puts him into danger, requires him to check the ponies and see what the Black Riders are up to in Bree. These qualities would also make him confident to 'proceed', at least until his encounters later in the journey make him realise just how small he seems to the rest of the world. True to his curiosity and interest in learning (leading him one day to write books), Merry seems likely to be the one who would 'wonder' or 'exclaim'. True to his name, in whatever language of Middle-earth, he is, appropriately, the hobbit to 'smile' and 'chuckle'.

The verbs that describe both Merry and Pippin, but not other hobbits, seem typical of close friends who confide in each other, share asides, or try to communicate with each other under duress. They 'mutter', 'whisper' and 'laugh' when they are together.

Even something that might escape most readers' attention, such as the choice of one verb over another, or the repetition of that verb only by one or two characters, mattered to Tolkien. His attention to detail and careful reworking of his text, even past the point of publication, is the best guide to understanding just how important words were to this author/linguist, and how carefully those who adapt his works should consider his words before they decide to change them.

Proofreading and Publication Errors

Even when Tolkien submitted the manuscript he wanted to be published, and after editorial and authorial changes throughout the typesetting and publication phases, errors still appeared in the book. In part, these problems can be attributed to what Tolkien Society member Pat Reynolds identified as Tolkien's unique use of language:

> The difficulties induced by Tolkien's private grammar, albeit one often with good philological reasons, and phonetic tools not normally encountered in a novel were compounded by his use of invented names and the invented languages behind them, invented writing systems, and use of old words.[35]

To complicate matters, the 'correct' typeset version was not kept, and when the highly popular book needed to be reprinted, it had to be reset. As Reynolds noted,

> Allen and Unwin appear not to have been informed that it would be re-set, and Tolkien did not proof the new text. Jarrolds [the company in charge of typesetting] did incorporate some corrections given to them, but introduced new errors, including the description of a Silmaril as a 'bride-piece' where Tolkien had written 'bride-price' (vol. 1, page 206). Numerous reprints followed, without emendations to the text, but with minor typographical corrections.[36]

Errors were further exacerbated with the unauthorised Ace edition in the US and the corrected, authorised Ballantine editions that arrived soon after. Throughout the 1960s and until his death in 1973, J.R.R. Tolkien continued to make corrections, a task Christopher Tolkien then continued; an error-free *LotR*, however, is unlikely to be published.

With the book's publication in numerous languages, the possibilities for introducing new errors via translation and typesetting increase. The subtleties of Tolkien's word choice and the author's nuanced style add to the likelihood of different meanings being introduced into translated versions of the story. The translation of an English word into a non-English word with a similar denotative meaning may still introduce an inappropriate connotation or create a different impression of a character. Few bilingual readers will go to the trouble of comparing texts, and errors or misinterpretations introduced into one translation may persist in many editions. Furthermore, the cadence and rhyming scheme of the English songs and poems Tolkien inserted into the narrative are likely to be lost in translation.

The positive side to all this is that Tolkien's works, especially *LotR*, continue to be read. As long as new readers anywhere in the world want to read Tolkien's words, the need for new translations or editions continues. Tolkien's careful word choice and seemingly endless perseverance to ensure continuity among his stories are admirable and, as a consequence, offer linguists, literary scholars and textual historians immense riches of materials to study, simply because of the many revisions Tolkien began and corrections that others continue to make, especially to *The Hobbit* and *LotR*.

3

The Lord of the Rings in the Movies – Almost

A s early as 1957, enterprising filmmakers or screenwriters looked to the newly published *Lord of the Rings* as a possible film adaptation. One such entrepreneur was Forrest J. Ackerman, a science-fiction aficionado who wrote stories, worked as a literary agent, and made cameo appearances in B-movies like *The Time Travelers* (1964), *The Howling* (1981) and *Amazon Women on the Moon* (1987), among many others. An interesting bit of trivia is that he also appeared in Michael Jackson's *Thriller* music video. Even after his death in 2008, films in which Ackerman had a small role were released (for example, *The Dead Undead* in 2010 and the short film *Second Unit* in 2011). A 2010 biography includes a highly appropriate cover designed to look like a monster magazine, reflecting Ackerman's long affiliation with science fiction, movies and magazines.[1] When Ackerman turned his eyes to *LotR* as a possible screenplay in the 1950s, he had played brief, uncredited roles in two films in the 1940s and developed a reputation in science-fiction literature as an avid fan and promoter, roles he would continue to play for the rest of his life.

In September 1957, Tolkien wrote to his son Christopher that Ackerman had visited him, bringing pictures of possible filming locations, which impressed the author. Not so the proposed treatment for the film, but he still thought that they might do business.[2] Business was indeed done, and by 1958 Tolkien reviewed scriptwriter Morton Grady Zimmerman's treatment (an early version of a script).

Early in the treatment, after Bilbo and Frodo are introduced, Gandalf arrives in the Shire and 'is met on the road by two Hobbits, MERRY and PIPPIN, who take the white-haired old man's huge sack of fireworks and carry them for him. They tell him it is almost party time.' Already the story has strayed from the book's beginning, and, as promised, Tolkien found many objectionable features that he wanted to alter. Several 'T.O.' – or 'Tolkien objection' – notations indicated the author's displeasure. On only the second page of the screen treatment, Tolkien marked out the words 'flags' and 'hobbits' in Zimmerman's line: 'Gandalf treats them all to a spectacular fireworks display; one which includes flags, Hobbits, and a great whistling dragon.'[3] In a letter to Ackerman, he complained about this section: 'Why should the firework display include *flags* and *Hobbits*? They are not in the book. "Flags" of what? I prefer my own choice of fireworks.'[4]

Ackerman initially sought approval from Tolkien by emphasising Zimmerman's scriptwriting prowess. In a letter dated 6 December 1957, Ackerman praises Zimmerman as a 'new Mike Todd or Orson Welles in embryonic form'.[5] Tolkien, however, was rightly more concerned with Zimmerman's accuracy than reputation.

The situation further deteriorated. Tolkien initially thought that even this bad treatment could be turned into a suitable script, although the draft was muddled and erroneous and Zimmerman did not seem to understand *LotR*. Zimmerman's script features caricatures of Merry and Pippin as pesky younger cousins, without differentiating between the hobbits or offering any depth to their characterisation. Whereas Tolkien's hobbits have distinctive personalities, Zimmerman and later scriptwriters often presented one-dimensional hobbits instead of Tolkien's more complex characters. To complicate matters, Tolkien and Ackerman could not agree on a timeframe for producing an acceptable draft – or the money to be paid to the author.[6] Not surprisingly, the Zimmerman script was never produced, and *LotR* seemed rather unproducible as a film for many years. The next important attempt at a *LotR* adaptation is John Boorman's and Rospo Pallenberg's 1970 script.

Director John Boorman is today best known for films like *Deliverance* (1972) and *Hope and Glory* (1987), both of which brought him Academy Award nominations. In addition to directing films, Boorman also has written and produced them. He co-wrote the screenplay for *Excalibur* (1981) with Pallenberg, but he also directed the film. His attempt at making a *LotR* film, however, was far less successful.

In 1969 Tolkien sold the rights to *LotR* to United Artists, having sold them the rights to *The Hobbit* in 1966. United Artists brought in new scriptwriters. Boorman later explained that adapting Tolkien's story for film was difficult because 'the text is very visual, but at climactic points Tolkien would often resort to poetic evasion...as when Gandalf is vanquished. "He fell beyond time and memory" – how do you film that?' His vision included using boys to play hobbits, 'complete with glued-on facial hair and dubbed adult voices'.[7] United Artists later decided not to spend the money on a live-action *LotR*. Of course, the executives overseeing the project were not familiar with Tolkien's book, which did not help when Boorman's script proved to be difficult to understand, even for those who knew the original story. As one scholar later wrote of this script,

> Considering Tolkien's appalled reaction to the much lesser liberties taken by Zimmerman, it is unlikely he would have appreciated Boorman's script at all. Characters, events, locations, themes, all are changed freely with no regard for the author's original intent. Situations are sexualised or plumbed for psychological kinks that simply do not exist in the book. (Tolkien would not have approved of Frodo's seduction by Galadriel, for example, and Aragorn's battlefield healing of Éowyn is so blatantly sexual it's not surprising Boorman marries them immediately.)[8]

Again, *LotR* seemed like an impossible film to adapt successfully. The Boorman–Pallenberg script failed to meet United Artists' expectations, and Boorman's creativity obviously needed a different outlet. He was paid for the script, but it was never filmed.

The concepts Boorman hoped to develop for *LotR* were not discarded, however. Many ideas that worked beautifully in his later film *Excalibur* (nudity and an adult-audience level of sexuality, for example) simply were not right for Tolkien's *LotR*; working within the framework established by Tolkien's book proved more daunting than a script in which he could pour all his creative ideas that would later work well on screen.

In light of the *LotR* adaptations that were eventually made, Tolkien fans still question the wisdom of the proposed Boorman film and compare scenes from *Excalibur* with what might have happened to *LotR*. Discussions about the adapted films on TORN forums have not so fondly mentioned Boorman's work. Shortly after the release of *The Fellowship of the Ring*, Tolkien fan 'Gorel' provided a more positive (somewhat of a rebuttal) comment that

> the visual design in *Excalibur* makes a Boorman *LotR* potentially interesting; he was deliberately filming Arthurian myth, not reality. Except for the opening sequence, PJ has gone for a very historical feel for Middle-earth…But I also wouldn't mind seeing a more *Excalibur*-esque version, especially when I imagine Lorien or the battle of the Pelennor Fields.[9]

Gorel added that a one-film *LotR*, such as United Artists tried to develop, would be too short to include all the details that make the story worthwhile.

Although the Boorman film was never made, speculation about this adaptation continues, especially in comparison with the *LotR* live-action trilogy released three decades after Boorman's attempt. Given the difference in budget and technology afforded Jackson, perhaps Boorman's critics should not judge him too harshly, although his vision of *LotR* on film does present some areas of concern to fans of the book. For his part, Boorman credited Jackson's accomplishment during a *Salon* interview in 2001, saying that 'As for the Jackson epic, I think it was a brilliant idea to make three films…I'm glad *The Lord of the Rings* is being made now, and I'm looking forward to seeing it. I'm sure it'll be a big success.'[10]

In that interview, Boorman was also asked about his work on the *LotR* script. He explained that he had corresponded with Tolkien and understood that the author seemed reluctant for a film to be made from his book. When Boorman wrote that he planned to make a live-action film, the author wrote back that he was relieved because he had a nightmare of *LotR* becoming an animated film.[11] That statement would prove ironic.

A few years after Tolkien's death, *LotR* became a partially animated, partially live-action film. By 1976, the Saul Zaentz Company purchased the rights to both *The Hobbit* and *LotR* and began looking for a suitable script. Ralph Bakshi wanted to animate *LotR* and take a very different approach to the story than Boorman had done. (See Chapter 5 for more discussion of the Bakshi film.) During the next two years, a series of scripts was written, beginning with one by Chris Conkling.

When an initial draft again did not meet expectations, Peter S. Beagle was brought in to doctor the script. Beagle made a number of changes to streamline Conkling's script and get into the action more immediately, as appropriate for a film adaptation. Although Beagle knew and respected Tolkien's book, he also made a number of changes to it so that the story would be easier to film. Without Beagle's intervention to write a script quickly that could be filmed, Bakshi's *LotR* may not have been made. In the intervening years, Beagle and Zaentz have disagreed about Beagle's contribution to the film and ultimately what he should be paid for his work. Most fans agree that Beagle, the author of fantasy-fan-favoured *The Last Unicorn*, and knowledgeable about Tolkien, greatly improved the Conkling script, even if the resulting film may not have lived up to expectations. By 1978, Bakshi's *LotR* brought to the big screen the first *LotR* cinematic adaptation.

As will be shown throughout this book, characters perceived as lesser in importance, such as Merry and Pippin, are changed more often in adapted scripts. *LotR*'s structural balance between Merry and Pippin is usually destroyed during adaptation. Characters are modified to fit modern needs for shortening the story for media other than print, or creating peripheral characters more relevant to a modern audience, frequently as comic relief. Merry and Pippin are particularly subject to the adaptor's need or whim, whereas Frodo and Sam often appear younger and more sympathetic for a modern audience.

Most adaptations are humancentric, rather than hobbitcentric. Especially on film and stage, men, most noticeably Aragorn, are the most important characters. Hobbits become cute and childlike rather than adults who take on the same wartime roles given to men, elves and dwarves.

The Same Scene from Different Scripts

As in Chapter 2 describing Tolkien's revisions, the adaptations of events from a few chapters of Tolkien's *LotR* illustrate how much Zimmerman, Boorman, Conkling and Beagle changed the hobbits as they readied what they hoped would be camera-ready scripts. As discussed in the following pages, examples of scenes from unproduced scripts point out each writer's view of what is significant in the scene and how each character should be portrayed. In some unproduced scripts, hobbits receive less respect and are viewed merely as expediently 'innocent' enough to carry the Ring. As might be expected, among the four hobbits who travel from the Shire, at least one or two will have their integrity sacrificed for comic relief or wide-eyed superstition, and Frodo may become anything from a burdened 'child' to a forgotten character as humans take centre stage. The scriptwriters' visions for a *LotR* film frequently differ from Tolkien's book as well as from each other's ideas of what would make a suitable adaptation.

'A Conspiracy Unmasked': Cinematic Adaptations

In many adaptations, Merry and Pippin often become annoying or simply comedic characters whose contributions to the Fellowship are minimised. One good example of this trend is the development of Merry and Pippin in Zimmerman's unproduced film treatment. It suggests a very different version of roughly Tolkien's 'conspiracy unmasked' chapter. Many script pages laced with 'T.O.' show Zimmerman's unfamiliarity with Tolkien's book and problems in adapting such a long story for a single film.

Early in the treatment, Zimmerman had Merry and Pippin 'pester Frodo with questions' after his run-in with Lobelia Sackville-Baggins as she takes over Bag End. (Hobbit fans may remember that Lobelia always has an eye for Bilbo's fortune and believes that the Sackville-Baggins family, not Frodo Baggins, deserves Bilbo's wealth. She goes so far as to steal Bilbo's silver spoons when thwarted from inheriting Bag End after Bilbo suddenly reappears after his adventure with the dwarves.) In the Zimmerman treatment, Merry and Pippin ask Frodo why he sold Bag End to move near the Old Forest, and they wonder where Bilbo is. An irritated Frodo compares the inquisitive Merry and Pippin with irritating, single-minded Lobelia,[12] a not-so-nice comparison, considering Frodo's feelings for her.

Although Crickhollow is not specifically mentioned, when Merry, Pippin, Sam and Frodo arrive at Frodo's new house, Fatty Bolger tries to warn Frodo of danger. Poor Fatty is then struck down by a Black Rider. On Frodo's command, the other hobbits run into the Old Forest. Pippin surprisingly thinks to get a weapon; he 'grabs an axe first, then runs'.[13] In this version, Merry and Pippin continue to tag along with Frodo after this scene, preferring to follow wherever Frodo leads rather than going back to face the Black Rider.[14]

Sam and Frodo are chosen by Gandalf to begin the journey, but Merry and Pippin fall into a perilous situation and simply accompany Frodo; this pattern persists in many adaptations. Unfortunately, without the 'conspiracy unmasked' part of Tolkien's story, Merry and Pippin lose integrity. Their planning and forethought, as well as their steadfast loyalty to Frodo, are greatly diminished when they merely follow Frodo on a whim, instead of months of planning to accompany their friend and cousin. In addition, their relationship with Sam becomes less well defined; Tolkien made Sam a key informant in the conspiracy, a hobbit trusted by both Merry and Pippin and more than just Frodo's gardener. The subtleties of Tolkien's character development become lost when the story is shortened to meet the constraints of another medium (for example, film, television, theatre), one with stringent time limitations.

A subsequent revision of the 1957 film treatment still included troublesome details that change the hobbits' character. As Merry and Pippin load a wagon with Frodo's belongings in preparation for the move to his new home, they still plague Frodo with questions in, as

Zimmerman noted, 'their usual busybody, flippant manner'.[15] The cousins once again seem young and sarcastic, not the well-prepared if typically fun-loving hobbits of the book.

At Crickhollow, Fatty Bolger manages to escape a Black Rider already inside Frodo's house. He warns Frodo of danger, and Merry, Pippin, Frodo and Sam run into the Old Forest; this time there is no axe-wielding Pippin. When Frodo tells Merry and Pippin that they may return home, they admit that they are afraid of encountering the Black Rider. Frodo therefore lets them stay with him.[16] Again, Merry and Pippin fail to determine their own course of action; they seem more like victims of circumstance than proactive hobbits determined to help their cousin on a perilous journey.

Scripts leading to Bakshi's 1978 semi-animated, semi-live-action film went through many revisions, written by many combinations of screenwriters. These adaptations took the hobbits ever farther from Tolkien's original text. A 1970 script by Boorman and Pallenberg, for example, has Sam, Merry and Pippin smoke their pipes as they stagger away from Bilbo's birthday party. Sam walks with a pretty girl, who rests her head on his shoulder.[17]

Instead of a 'conspiracy unmasked', Sam, Merry and Pippin burst into Bag End just as Gandalf warns Frodo that the Ring is only safe with someone 'simple, like a Hobbit'. Gandalf amends this insult by assuring Frodo that 'goodness and innocence and pity are the only proof against its power'. Merry, described as the fat hobbit who, indeed, manages to eat his way through this screenplay, pants after his abrupt arrival at Bag End, but Pippin, the skinny hobbit, 'jumps for joy' when Gandalf suggests that Frodo take his friends on a holiday to Rivendell.[18] Thus begins what is a *very* loosely adapted journey from the Shire.

After Boorman had left the *LotR* project and Zaentz acquired the rights to *LotR*, Chris Conkling wrote the next script, this time for *The Lord of the Rings Part One: The Fellowship*, based on Tolkien's *The Fellowship of the Ring* and *The Two Towers* (*TT*). The screenplay, dated 21 September 1976, enhanced Merry's and Pippin's role as narrators. The two first appear on page 3, when they run into Fangorn Forest, encounter Treebeard, and begin to tell their story.

This innovative way of shortening the story also glossed over major characters and plot points in an attempt to get to the battle action more quickly.

However, Conkling at least portrayed the hobbits closer to the ages Tolkien gave them: Merry is an adult at 36, and Pippin notes that he will be out of his tweens in four years.[19] At 26, Pippin is a couple of years younger than his book counterpart, but Merry's age matches Tolkien's description. In many adaptations, the hobbits are portrayed as similar in age and generally younger than the adult or even middle-aged status (of Frodo) that Tolkien accorded them. The 1976 Conkling script does provide a short version of the 'conspiracy unmasked' chapter, although the language has been modernised for a 1970s audience.[20]

This screenplay was also not accepted, and in May 1977 Beagle developed a 191-page screenplay with Conkling. A major difference occurred when the writers deleted Merry's and Pippin's narration of the first part of the story and instead began with Bilbo's birthday party.

In this adaptation, Merry, Pippin and Sam move Frodo from Bag End to his new home. Along the way, Merry and Pippin play catch with apples, nuts and oranges, 'sometimes juggling the thrown and caught objects with their mouths'.[21] Pippin tells Frodo that he will love his new house, noting that 'Merry and I love it already. We can walk all the way from his house and just be getting hungry when we reach yours.'[22] The emphasis for these two hobbits is always on food; the pair seems much more frivolous, even for hobbits, than Tolkien's depiction of them. Even Frodo is reluctant to leave the comforts of the Shire. On the way to Bree, he tells Sam, 'I'm frightened. I'm not made for quests and Black Riders, Master-Rings ... I'm made for the Shire – the slow, sleepy, stupid Shire where nothing ever happens.'[23] Modernised language and streamlined characterisation and plot differentiate this adaptation from Tolkien's *LotR*.

'The Muster of Rohan' and 'Ride of the Rohirrim':
Cinematic Versions

In Zimmerman's unpublished treatment from 1957, Merry rides to battle with the Rohirrim; however, his horse stumbles, the hobbit pitches forward, and a nearby knight lifts him to safety. Merry then rides with the knight. This version features 'comic Merry', who whistles and comments on that close call, to be nearly killed before the battle even starts. When the knight remains silent, Merry shrugs and rides along.[24]

The revised Zimmerman script adapts 'The Ride of the Rohirrim' more closely to Tolkien's published text. In this adaptation, Théoden spots Merry riding with one of the soldiers and can only shake his head because he questions the wisdom of bringing 'such a small person along to such a big war'. Éomer, however, speaks up for Merry, saying he 'has already survived many adventures that would have killed a bigger man'.[25]

As is typical of the 1970 Boorman–Pallenberg unproduced script, Merry and Pippin are only loosely based on Tolkien's characters. In Minas Tirith, Pippin becomes a court jester who accompanies Denethor.[26] Merry rides to battle with an unnamed soldier who loses an arm to the Witch King before Merry 'jumps recklessly at the Nazgûl' and stabs him. The one-armed soldier still manages the killing blow. Merry falls lifeless to the battlefield, reviving only long enough to remove the soldier's helmet. The soldier, of course, is Éowyn. The gradual build-up of the ride of the Rohirrim is omitted in favour of the battle scene; this is the only time that Merry and Éowyn interact.[27]

Other 1970s screenplays seldom covered the 'Ride of the Rohirrim' or the 'Scouring of the Shire'. Most adaptations ended roughly around the middle of *The Two Towers*, sometimes as only a sample of what would, if approved, be a finished script. Bakshi, of course, did not make it this far in his 1978 film. His unfortunately titled *Lord of the Rings* really covers only the first part of the story, and the ride of the Rohirrim is never shown in his film. A second film to complete the story was never produced, in large part because the first film did not do well at the box office and further funding was difficult to find.

'Scouring of the Shire': Cinematic Versions

Most screenplays and treatments failed to show the second half of *LotR*. Although the Zimmerman 1957 treatment provides an ending, this adaptation is far removed from anything Tolkien wrote. After Frodo takes the Ring to Mount Doom, Gollum steals it, only to lose it and his life in fire. Gandalf directs the eagles to find Frodo and Sam. Aragorn wins the battle, turns to Gandalf with a smile, and says, 'Nothing remains now but return home and rule.'[28] When Frodo wakes up, he visits Aragorn and is cheered by the people under the new King's rule. Frodo then leaves with the elves, and Aragorn and Arwen go inside their castle to rule.[29]

The treatment provides a happy ending, but nothing is known of the rest of the Fellowship, much less how the role of Ringbearer affects Frodo. Sam survives, but he disappears from the story after being rescued by an eagle. A revised script retains most of this ending.

For fans of hobbits, these rather insulting changes not only alter the substance of Tolkien's story but also relegate hobbits to background players. Even Ringbearer Frodo receives few accolades for his sacrifice, and his continuing suffering as a result of succumbing to the Ring's Evil is never mentioned. Such depth of characterisation apparently detracts from many films' proposed happy ending, one especially written to emphasise human characters.

Even in later produced scripts, such as Jackson's, the scouring of the Shire is left out, which changes the focus of Tolkien's story and emphasises the roles of men rather than hobbits; the Shire seems outside the scope of war's ravages, which ultimately undermines the heroic roles of the returned hobbits of the Fellowship. They, just as much as Éomer or Aragorn, must fight for their homeland and sacrifice much in order to rid the Shire of Evil.

Radically changing or omitting, in particular, the conspiracy or the scouring of the Shire section of *LotR* drastically changes Tolkien's tale and themes. Without the conspiracy, the strength of the Merry–Pippin–Sam–Fredegar bond is diminished; these characters' individuality and determination are slighted. Without the scouring of the Shire, Merry and Pippin are not recognised as fully mature hobbits who will become the Shire's leaders (as symbolised in the book by their taller-than-normal stature, the result of drinking the Ent draughts). The scope of hobbits' contributions and sacrifices is typically all-too-briefly summarised in most adaptations.

The following chapters illustrate how the scripts of radio, television, film and theatrical adaptations differ from these unproduced treatments or scripts just discussed. The scripts that resulted in successfully produced adaptations may not share all the problems associated with these unproduced screenplays, but they also receive their fair share of criticism about what is or is not included in the story.

4

HOBBITS ON RADIO AND TELEVISION

A lthough Tolkien's works had already won fans in the decades since *The Hobbit*'s publication in 1937, *LotR*'s arrival in the 1950s furthered the Professor's literary reputation and awoke millions of readers to historic fantasy. As academics and fans have noted, succeeding generations of fantasy authors learned from the master, and everything from the type of protagonist to the scope of the story (often requiring an entire series of books) to the now-mandatory inclusion of detailed maps could be attributed to Tolkien's pervasive influence on the genre.[1] Some similar types of fantasy stories recommended by Tolkien fans include Lloyd Alexander's *Chronicles of Prydain*, Kristen Britain's *Green Rider*, Terry Brooks's *Shannara Trilogy*, Raymond E. Feist's *Krondor Riftwar Trilogy*, Alan Garner's *The Weirdstone of Brisingamen* and Nancy Springer's *Book of Isle Tetrology*, among many others.[2]

Although today readers still choose *LotR* as their favourite or best book of any genre,[3] not just favourite or best fantasy book, for generations many *LotR* or *Hobbit* fans have come to know Middle-earth not because of Tolkien's books but from on-screen or audio adaptations.

One of the most popular adaptations was the BBC's radio versions of both *The Hobbit* and *LotR*. *The Hobbit* was first broadcast in 1968 and later re-edited into a series of half-hour programmes. In 1981, BBC Radio 4 broadcast 26 half-hour instalments (later combined into 13 hour-long episodes) of *LotR*. In 2002, the BBC broadcast the series again, as well as re-issued it on CD. (Recordings of the 1956 13-part BBC radio series failed to survive.) In the US, animation specialists Rankin–Bass first introduced audiences to Bilbo in 1977. Following Ralph Bakshi's 1978 *LotR* film, in 1980 Rankin–Bass premiered an animated *RotK*, although critics largely prefer the animated *Hobbit*. With the resurgence of interest in *LotR* following Peter Jackson's films in the early 2000s, even the US children's series *Veggie Tales* produced their own version of Frodo and his quest that was eventually seen worldwide on DVD, thus reaching a wide audience.

In appearance, dialogue and action the hobbits heard or seen in these adaptations are a wide-ranging group; they have little in common beyond the label 'hobbit'. These diversely interpreted characters more often represent styles and popular culture in their own times. Each iteration of a character, whether Frodo-as-bean in a children's morality tale or a whinging, weakened animated Frodo requiring Sam to save him, bears some, however vague, resemblance to his literary ancestor, but each writer, animator, actor and director adds his own unique creative fingerprint.

LotR on Radio

Over the years, several radio adaptations (later turned into audiotape and CD recordings) of Tolkien's works have been produced,[4] but the most popular is the BBC's 1981 broadcast of *LotR*, now available in a number of boxed sets. Brian Sibley and Michael Bakewell's scripts proved that *LotR* could be successfully adapted for another medium. This dramatisation helped pave the way for Peter Jackson's films a few decades later by proving that audiences would sit still for a long adaptation that was more faithful to Tolkien's book. At the time, Bakewell was the more seasoned BBC dramatist, but Sibley was a Tolkien fan who was given an incredible opportunity by the BBC to develop *LotR* for radio.[5] Sibley was tasked with dividing the story into

26 broadcast segments, a job he later recalled as 'fascinating literary jigsaw work'.[6] The combination of writing skill and familiarity with Tolkien's work certainly helped this radio adaptation succeed.

In hindsight, launching a radio adaptation of *LotR* penned by Sibley and Bakewell and starring a high-calibre cast including Ian Holm (Frodo) and Bill Nighy (Sam) would seem a predictable success. When the serial debuted in 1981, however, not all Tolkien fans or critics were immediately enamoured. A late-1980s *Mallorn* article recalled the 'spate of patronizing reactions in the media and in Tolkien Fan circles…As the serial progressed, its true scale and achievement was more widely appreciated.'[7]

Perhaps Tolkien fans were still upset by plot changes – or the unfinished story – in Bakshi's 1978 film. As the then-president of the Tolkien Society, Jonathan Simon, told a reporter enquiring about the upcoming BBC radio adaptation, 'The [Bakshi film's] technique was reasonable but the treatment of the plot was abysmal – and it was much too Americanised.'[8] Given this anxiety over recent *LotR* adaptations, it is no wonder that Simon reminded the BBC that Tolkien Society members would be listening rather critically to the weekly half-hour episodes.

Even Sibley later noted regretfully, if humorously, that some characters and scenes had to be cut. More than a quarter century after the BBC radio adaptation, Sibley reminisced about his early love of Tolkien's works, including the time he wrote a fan letter to Tolkien and asked him to autograph his copy of *The Adventures of Tom Bombadil.* Tolkien graciously complied. Even with this memorable fan experience, Sibley noted that 'poor Tom was one of the casualties' when the radio script was written.[9] Changes are inevitable in an adaptation, especially one that needed to be divided into equal sections carefully timed for broadcast, and not even the scriptwriters could include everything they might have wished they could save from the original text.

One big change from the book is the scriptwriters' organisation of scenes, which did not seem unnecessarily to perturb fans, including Tolkien Society members, who understood that a radio drama needed to make a powerful first impression as well as keep listeners tuned in from week to week. The radio version presents scenes in chronological order, instead of skipping among groups of characters – a much easier way for listeners to keep track of who is doing what, not to mention where and when – once the Fellowship breaks. Telling the story without changing the plot or characters seemed to be hardcore fans' greatest concern, one mostly allayed by the BBC's treatment of Tolkien's text. Over the years, as the BBC rebroadcast the radio version, it gained more popularity, so that by 'its fourth broadcast, in the Spring of 1987, this radio dramatisation [became] regarded as one of the finest of the decade, surpassing past productions in scope and ambition'.[10]

What makes audiences return to the radio version more often than most other adaptations? One likely reason is the actors' vocal qualities, which ensured listeners could easily distinguish among characters. Although some scenes were removed (most controversially, Tom Bombadil – who seldom makes an appearance in an adaptation – and Gildor, whose scenes with the hobbits were cut),[11] many of Tolkien's words remained intact in this script, and fewer book scenes were omitted. After all, in 13 hours of broadcast time, quite a bit of Tolkien's story – and better yet, emotional impact and atmosphere – could be transferred into a radio adaptation that was far more than a simple reading aloud of the text. The BBC radio adaptation captured the best of the book but turned it into the sounds of Middle-earth, bringing the story alive to listeners who then used their imagination to fill in the visuals.

The Radio Cast of Hobbits

The entire cast received accolades for their performances, and the hobbits presented in the BBC adaptation remain true to Tolkien's textual descriptions of their speaking patterns and actions. If anything, this adaptation, coming in the early 1980s after many Tolkien fans had seen the 1970s Rankin–Bass animated specials and Ralph Bakshi's 1978 film, renewed their faith in the capacity to adapt Tolkien's work into another medium. The nature of radio undoubtedly helped; it presented the story in an easy-to-digest fashion (and, even at 13 hours, much faster than many listeners would take time to read the book) while allowing listeners to decide for themselves just how characters or places looked. The minimal sound effects – such as the crunching footsteps of the Orc army – neither helped nor hindered audience 'participation' in creating the story, but the actors' often emotion-laden voices brought the story alive.

At the time of the BBC's original *LotR* broadcast, some cast members were relatively unknown, given their later stature in worldwide theatre and film. In addition to Holm and Nighy (then billed as William), the cast included Richard O'Callaghan (Merry), John McAndrew (Pippin) and John Le Mesurier (Bilbo). For many (older) *LotR* fans, these are the definitive voices of Tolkien's characters, much as (younger) fans in the 2000s picture Jackson's film actors as 'their' Frodo, Sam, Merry, Pippin and Bilbo.

In *Mallorn*, author James Kearney fondly reviewed these portrayals of hobbits:

> In Ian Holm's voice, I heard Frodo the cheery hobbit suffer and mature under a heavy burden. That was as much as Tolkien had provided for him but the character was developed still further – in small ways, when the voice cracked and weakened after the climbing of the stairs to Cirith Ungol, the ferocious selfish passion when Frodo snatched the Ring from Sam in prison, and the irritable outbursts on the first stage of their Mordor trek.[12]

Sam, as voiced by Nighy, received a similarly warm review from this fan/author, who noted the gradual change in Sam's demeanour, from subordinate servant 'whose courage and support grew in the Quest, and the patronising Master–Servant relationship gradually dissolved into a friendship of two equals'.[13]

In the action-packed *RotK* segment of the serial, the actors' dramatic emphasis reaches the necessary climax, and each hobbit is featured as his part in this great story is highlighted. A plus in this *RotK* is the scouring of the Shire, which, although abbreviated, takes the story back to the Shire, where it began, instead of leaving it in Minas Tirith, as in many adaptations. The BBC adaptation retains emphasis on the hobbits, even when other characters meet once again at the Grey Havens for their farewell. Even Sam's final line from the book, 'I'm back,' becomes the final line of this radio adaptation.

Hobbits of Middle-earth on the BBC

When the 'Road goes ever on' theme appears in an adaptation, it typically represents Bilbo and his legacy to Frodo and the other Fellowship hobbits. Where the road leads, they cannot tell, but these atypically adventurous hobbits feel compelled to follow. In some adaptations, such as the *LotR* musical (see Chapter 6), this theme is given a bouncy tune. The BBC radio series, however, takes it very seriously, presenting an almost dirge-like tune. This sombre atmosphere is especially appropriate at the beginning of *RotK*, when the lyrics preface the darkest of the three parts to the story. The road ironically leads once-carefree hobbits to a desperate, dark place, not just for Frodo and Sam, but also for the separated Merry and Pippin. At the beginning of *RotK*, Frodo reminds listeners just where the story left off; he awakens within the tower at Cirith Ungol and retells his emotions at being captured by Orcs and separated from the Ring. Sam is discussed, from Frodo's perspective, long before listeners hear him and learn how he comes to the tower and what he does.

The particularly 'hobbity' aspects of Sam finding Frodo, taken directly from Tolkien's book, are well preserved in this adaptation and illustrate the strength of Holm's and Nighy's characterisations as, respectively, Frodo and Sam. To locate Frodo within the vast tower, Sam sings. Hearing a Shire song, but, more importantly, hearing someone sing, reminds Frodo of who and what he is at a time when he has been driven almost mad with torture and doubt.[14] Sam chooses a most hobbity way to get Frodo to indicate where he is. Sam's voice in this adaptation sounds common or 'homespun' – good enough but not trained, clear and sure but practical – he sings because hobbits sing, without being self-conscious or proud of his voice. Sam knows that Frodo, if he is able, will respond. (In contrast, only Pippin sings in Jackson's adaptation, and Billy Boyd's lovely tenor, which captures the hobbit's wistful sorrow in the scene, is that of a professional singer.) When Frodo joins in the song, Sam determines his location while the Orc guarding Frodo merely assumes the prisoner is out of his mind with fear and pain. Including the song as part of this adaptation preserves a minor, yet important detail in the story and indicates how closely Sam and Frodo are linked to each other, as well as to the Shire.

Throughout this adaptation, Holm's sturdy voice makes Frodo seem an older, stronger character than the Frodo Elijah Wood portrays in the Jackson films. Nevertheless, there still comes a breaking point for poor Frodo. Once Sam has dispatched the last Orc guarding Frodo, the former servant very practically takes charge of the situation. He tells Frodo that he has taken the Ring to keep it safe. Frodo becomes almost hysterical in describing how the Orcs' questioning nearly drove him mad. When Sam shows Frodo the Ring and tells him, quite practically, that he could continue to help carry it, Frodo becomes irrationally angry.[15] Sam knows how difficult it is to carry the Ring, and he hopes to save Frodo from this burden.

Sam, as voiced by Nighy, seems to offer a fair alternative; he only wants to help dear Frodo and is not interested in keeping the Ring to increase his own power. Frodo, however, has been Ringbearer long enough that the Ring's presence, more than an Orc interrogation, has brought him closer to madness. He calls out for the Orc chief to help him retrieve the Ring from Sam, something he never would have done in his right mind. Once reunited with the Ring, Frodo comes to himself and apologises to Sam. He wants to spare Sam from the type of madness he only belatedly recognises in himself. Whereas in the Jackson film wide-eyed Sam seems briefly mesmerised by the Ring and Frodo angry, although impotent to take it from him, the dialogue and actors' delivery fire up emotions in the BBC adaptation. Once Sam has been replaced as Ringbearer, he once again takes charge of the practical aspects of their journey, first finding clothes for Frodo.

Pippin also makes an early appearance in the BBC *RotK*, and he often talks with Denethor, as well as becoming privy to conversations between Mithrandir/Gandalf and Denethor, once the steward learns that Osgiliath has been taken and his son Faramir is badly wounded. In Jackson's version, Denethor does not seem to know what to do in his despair; this BBC Denethor, voiced by Peter Vaughan, only gives up when he feels Minas Tirith is doomed to defeat and simply wants to spend his final hours with his son, an interpretation much closer to Tolkien's prose. In the BBC adaptation, Denethor gives Pippin more to do, and listeners have a much better idea of the hobbit's duties at court prior to battle. He prepares Denethor's chambers for the wounded Faramir; he tells others of Denethor's commands;[16] he learns a great deal and has much more interaction with Denethor than in other adaptations. This amount of interaction gives Pippin a clearer sense of what will happen in the city and instills urgency to his actions. He reports directly to Denethor, rather than being part of the regular guard. The scenes between Denethor and Pippin are well developed in this adaptation.

Denethor decides to immolate himself and his son, to choose the time of their deaths rather than allow themselves to be killed at the hands of the invading army. He even seems to show belated concern for his son, which Pippin observes. Even when Denethor releases Pippin from his service, the hobbit explains that he wants to earn the arms given to him and will return, after relaying Denethor's orders, to protect the steward and fight to the last man, or hobbit. Pippin does not accept the inevitability of their defeat, telling the steward he will only lose hope if Gandalf abandons the fight. This Pippin is a strong character and knows exactly what he needs to do in order to help Denethor in his great despair.

What is striking about the BBC adaptation is that Pippin is such an assertive character. He finds Gandalf to persuade him to stop Denethor, not because he is frustrated at having been physically thrown out of Denethor's service and thus being unable to save Faramir, as in Jackson's adaptation, but because he is worried and logically takes the next step of finding Gandalf to intercede. Interestingly enough, although their emotions and motivations may be different, the intonation and inflection of the two best recognised Pippins – Boyd in Jackson's films and McAndrew in the BBC radio version – are remarkably similar when they beg for Faramir's life. Boyd's dialogue with Denethor matches McAndrew's internal dialogue, provided as an 'aside' to listeners.

Merry turns up in scenes shortly thereafter, much of the battle having been compressed by the Sibley–Bakewell script. Battle scenes are enacted during brief action sequences or vignettes between stanzas of song; the Battle of the Pelennor Fields is heard mostly as a lay for Théoden, with pauses for dialogue and action to be inserted as highlights of the battle.

Merry's role is very different from that in other adaptations. Théoden asks Dernhelm to accompany him as he stands before the Witch King, but once the king has fallen, Dernhelm stands alone between them. Listeners hear Merry's internal dialogue as he decides he must help Dernhelm in this fight. The Witch King, however, scoffs at Merry's effectiveness; he compares the hobbit's attack to the buzzing of a gnat. Merry then tells the newly revealed Éowyn to slay the Witch King quickly, which she does. When Éowyn falls after killing the Witch King, Merry, as in the book, goes to Théoden and hears his final commands. The hobbit also observes the transfer of power between Théoden and Éomer.

More important to the hobbit's peace of mind, Merry asks Théoden's forgiveness for going against his wishes, especially because he has not been as effective a soldier as he hoped to become. Théoden gives Tolkien's speech of remembering the king in times of peace. Merry directs Éomer both to Théoden and Éowyn, which motivates Éomer to call for the remaining Rohirrim to continue the fight.[17]

Of all the hobbits portrayed in the BBC's *RotK*, Merry is less self-directed. Dernhelm/Éowyn asks Merry to help her defend the king; she tells him to attend to the king when she is wounded. Although Merry wants to help in whatever way possible and, indeed, directs Éomer to his fallen kin, he seems overwhelmed by the battle. He knows what he should do, but he seems to feel inadequate as a warrior once he is confronted with battle. What motivates Merry is love for Théoden and Éowyn; he only fights because of those he loves and is far from being a natural fighter, a theme not clearly presented in other adaptations. This interpretation, however, makes Merry a richer, unique character, not a 'generic' hobbit.

In another break from other adaptations, the Houses of Healing section of the book is reproduced, almost verbatim, in the BBC adaptation. Unlike other versions, before and since the BBC's, the Witch King scene is usually Merry's finest hour and gives him as much honour as he is likely to receive. The Sibley–Bakewell script instead emphasises many of Tolkien's later chapters, in which Merry's heroism is recognised and honoured by others. When Éowyn awakens in the Houses of Healing, she reminds her brother that Merry must be recognised as a Rider of the Riddermark for his great service to Rohan. Pippin's and Merry's scene following the latter's healing also indicates the younger cousin's admiration for his older relative's great deeds, and even a usually harsh Gandalf tells Merry 'Well done.'[18] Stabbing the Witch King, although important, is not the sum of Merry's bravery in this adaptation. He truly displays the 'great heart' for which Théoden commends him, not just during one moment in battle.

As a self-proclaimed fan of Middle-earth since 1977 wrote in a review of the BBC radio series,

> Merry (Richard O'Callaghan) and Pippin (John McAndrew) are especially good. The former is an earnest, dependable, and sweet-natured portrayal which suits the sentimental side of the character and highlights his affection for Théoden, and Pippin is eager, young, but determined rather than simply comical.[19]

In this adaptation, Merry and Pippin have separate but equal experiences and emerge as heroes as much as Sam or Frodo. As in Tolkien's book, each hobbit has an important role to play in the overall story, and each accomplishes his task in his own inimitable way.

The BBC radio adaptation not only most successfully transfers the majority of Tolkien's story to another medium, but it compels listeners to continue the journey alongside the hobbits. At 13 hours, the journey is indeed long, even broken into half-hour or hour segments, but the story retains its richness. In part because radio allows listeners to add their own visuals, this adaptation can more easily and successfully open up the story. The radio adaptation is technically simpler and far less risky than a film project, which must both compress the story due to time constraints and determine what audiences see.

The 1981 BBC radio adaptation, however, succeeds not only because radio is a less technically demanding medium, the actors are vocally superb, or the script could be long enough to remain more faithful to Tolkien's original. In part, its success lies in its varied depiction of hobbits, producing a story in which each hobbit sounds and acts differently from the others and is true to his book character. The love and compassion the hobbits feel for each other, as well as their new friends specifically and Middle-earth more generally, clearly come through, and the hobbits as a group reveal a complete range of emotions. These characters are complex but easily understandable; this adaptation refuses to reduce any hobbit to a caricature or type, deservedly making the BBC radio adaptation one of Tolkien fans' perennial favourites.

Since its initial broadcast, beginning on 8 March 1981, the BBC has replayed the 13-hour adaptation in 2002, shortly after Jackson's adaptation of *FotR* premiered in December 2001.[20] The connection between the BBC's *LotR* and that created by Jackson's cast had been made much earlier. Most prominently, Ian Holm, Frodo in the BBC radio production, became Bilbo in Jackson's films. Even peripherally, the radio series may have influenced other film cast members; BBC Radio 4 controller Helen Boaden noted that those in Jackson's cast unfamiliar with Tolkien's book received copies of the BBC's version.[21] Dominic Monaghan (Merry) mentioned in early interviews about the films that his father played the BBC version in the car during family trips.[22]

Of course, the BBC also profited from its association with the release of the Jackson films. It re-released the series in three parts, further enhancing the radio serial's popularity. By 2001, the *LotR* radio adaptation had already sold 100,000 copies worldwide and become the most popular spoken-word recording in the BBC's vast collection. Many fans, old and new, agreed with the BBC's Boaden that the series is a 'completely memorable experience'.[23]

The BBC's faith in *LotR*'s continuing popularity paid off in high ratings for the 2002 broadcast, taking place on Saturday afternoons between January and March. In a 9 May 2002 press release, Boaden thanked the Radio 4 audience, more than 800,000 stronger since the previous year, for listening, adding that the record Saturday afternoon audience 'clearly relished this remarkable dramatisation'.[24]

Hobbits on Television

Rankin–Bass created two animated specials – *The Hobbit* and *Return of the King* (*RotK*) – just for television, and the children's programme *Veggie Tales* introduced a version of *LotR* involving its own cast of vegetable characters. These programmes are the most culture-specific adaptations of Tolkien's hobbits; although they often stray far from the original, they have become a primary way for children, in particular, to meet Tolkien's characters and have played an important role in bringing hobbits into mainstream popular culture.

The Hobbit

For five years in the early 1970s, US and Japanese production companies worked together on an animated version of *The Hobbit*. The reported production cost was $3 million (US).[25] Finally, on 27 November 1977, Rankin–Bass presented their first Tolkien adaptation, *The Hobbit*. Arthur Rankin, Jr., and Jules Bass produced and directed; Romeo Muller adapted the story, with music by Maury Laws and lyrics by Jules Bass. US network NBC broadcast the highly anticipated 90-minute special during prime family viewing, at eight o'clock in the evening. In succeeding years, this adaptation would travel the world when released on video, and its soundtrack sold on vinyl (accompanied by a follow-along storybook), later gaining an even larger audience when *The Hobbit* became available on DVD and soundtrack CD.

Many now-adult Tolkien fans fondly remember this adaptation as their first real introduction to the Professor's stories, and children who saw the Rankin–Bass TV special often went on to read *The Hobbit*. As a first introduction to Tolkien, this adaptation does a good job of presenting Bilbo as an initially reluctant adventurer who becomes a hero by default; the television special even begins with Tolkien's first line: 'In a hole in the ground there lived a Hobbit.'[26]

Nevertheless, the programme is very much a product of its time. In a *New York Times* interview published on the day of *The Hobbit*'s

TV premiere, Rankin noted that the popularity of *Star Wars* (1977) could be traced back to Tolkien: 'Maybe the new fantasy market – the popularity of movies like "Star Wars" – has come from Tolkien…The old wizard with the Force in "Star Wars" – that's Gandalf, the wizard of "The Hobbit".'[27] Tying his TV special to a popular new film was an effective way to promote the programme to older adolescents or adults who might not watch a children's special.

Another reminder of *The Hobbit*'s 1970s style is folk singer Glenn Yarbrough's song 'The greatest adventure', which not only takes lines from the book ('Roads go ever ever on') to provide a musical bridge between scenes throughout Bilbo's adventure, but contains lyrics full of uplifting advice for young audiences. Representative lines are these: 'The greatest adventure is what lies ahead…The chances, the changes are all yours to make. The mold of your life is in your hands to break.'[28] (Yarbrough's contributions to the soundtracks of *The Hobbit* and Rankin–Bass's *Return of the King* are discussed in greater detail in Chapter 6.) A male chorus harmonises with Yarbrough in a style familiar to families who watched a long line of Rankin–Bass holiday specials, such as *Rudolph the Red-Nosed Reindeer* (1964), *The Little Drummer Boy* (1968), *Frosty the Snowman* (1969), *Santa Claus is Comin' to Town* (1970) and *Here Comes Peter Cottontail* (1971). The Rankin–Bass *Hobbit* provided wholesome family entertainment, which, of course, was its aim rather than being an entirely faithful TV adaptation of Tolkien's book.

Bilbo (voiced by Orson Bean) is first shown living a quiet, domestic life: he washes the dishes and enjoys a pipe. Cartoon Bilbo has broad features that easily distinguish him from a typical man. Lester Abrams's and Tsuguyuki Kubo's child-friendly design creates a round-faced Bilbo with huge brown eyes looking wonderingly at the world outside the Shire; he seems harmless, a short, chubby character with very furry feet. He wears what becomes 'typical' hobbit fashion: a golden brown vest, white shirt and knee-length trousers; he adds a green cape when he leaves home. During his dinner party for Gandalf and the dwarves, he constantly frets about his plates and silverware; his world seems bound by the comfortable confines of Bag End. In fact, Bilbo is the only hobbit in this adaptation. Bag

End exists in isolation, and all that audiences learn of hobbits comes from Bilbo.

Gandalf's understanding of who Bilbo is certainly differs from the hobbit's idea of himself, especially when the wizard barges into Bag End to introduce Bilbo as the dwarves' new 'burglar' to regain their treasure from the dragon Smaug. Although he often speaks harshly, Gandalf (voiced by John Huston)[29] nonetheless harbours a special fondness for Bilbo. The wizard assists him and the dwarves, but he will not solve all their problems or interfere with their quest to be rid of Smaug and retrieve the treasure. At one point Gandalf tells Bilbo, 'There's more about you than you guessed,' and the hobbit's first adventure beyond the Shire clearly supports Gandalf's assessment.

Unlike other portrayals of Gandalf, the Rankin–Bass character is magical, often resorting to using special powers, for example, to hurry the dawn so that the sun turns trolls to stone or to create fireballs to attack wolves; he converses with the eagles; he mysteriously comes and goes throughout the story. Gandalf's knowledge, however, has limits, as shown when he cannot read the runes on a sword Bilbo and the dwarves find. In these scenes, Bilbo represents the audience by asking questions they would likely ask if they were in his position. While Gandalf gazes at the ancient elven sword and tries to understand the runes, Bilbo asks, 'What are runes? What are moon letters?' He even voices a modern 'Huh?' (a break from his formal 'Middle-earth' speech pattern) when Gandalf's replies become too cryptic. Throughout this adaptation, the audience, especially children, is meant to identify with Bilbo on his grand adventure.

By title and reputation, however, Bilbo is a strange role model; throughout the story he is called a thief or burglar. Gollum first considers him a thief. The Rankin–Bass version of the way Bilbo acquires the Ring is similar to Tolkien's revised tale of the riddle contest. The hobbit, lost from the dwarves, finds the Ring in Gollum's cave. He utters a strangely Christian line, 'Bless my soul,' when he finds it, noting that it would make 'a nice souvenir to show the neighbors back home'. Bilbo reluctantly accepts Gollum's riddle challenge as a way to be shown the way out, but the hobbit cleverly manipulates the rules to his own advantage. When Gollum realises that Bilbo has the

Ring and attacks him, the hobbit quickly escapes. Upon sliding the Ring onto his finger, Bilbo discovers he has become invisible, which allows him to follow Gollum out of the cave and leap-frog over him. This series of events makes Bilbo seem more clever than thieving.

Even without experience as a 'burglar', Bilbo seems to fall into that role after Gandalf brings the dwarves to Bag End to hire him as such. After protesting that he does not know how to burgle, the hobbit nevertheless tries to act like a professional burglar during the journey to the Misty Mountains. He gets caught on his first attempt to steal dinner from trolls; he enrages Smaug, who also calls him a burglar, when he confronts the dragon among his treasures.

Bilbo's greatest skill, however, is cleverness. Bilbo observes the Mirkwood elves who capture the dwarves; he determines that the best way for them all to escape involves hiding in empty wine barrels floated down river. He figures out a riddle to open the back door to Smaug's lair. He remembers Smaug's vulnerable spot, an important fact when Smaug attacks a nearby village and only Bilbo can save more lives by telling an archer where to shoot the dragon. No matter what the danger to ensnare Bilbo or his companions, the hobbit becomes ever better at figuring out ways to escape, avoid enemies, or solve puzzles. Bilbo must use his mind rather than physical strength because hobbits are small creatures and can easily be preyed upon by larger, more fearsome beings in the outside world. *The Hobbit* shows just how many dangers await little hobbits: trolls, goblins, wargwolves and a giant spider all want to turn Bilbo into dinner. Bilbo's reliance on brain rather than brawn gradually turns this 'burglar' into a children's character worth emulating.

The hobbit also has trouble understanding other characters' greed. 'Big people', including dwarves, elves and men, are often quarrelsome or downright warlike and greedy. Bilbo initially refuses to take part in what becomes the Battle of Five Armies because he does not see the need for bloodshed over gems or territory. After the battle and just before his death, dwarf king Thorin makes peace with Bilbo, admitting that 'If more of us valued your ways, food and cheer above hoarded gold, it would be a merrier world.' *Hobbit*-loving parents (especially those who believe in the themes presented in this folk-music-laden

TV adaptation) likely approved of this message of peace, especially in a late Cold War, Vietnam-era family programme.

In contrast to Bilbo, Gollum receives a great deal of fan criticism for the way he looks in the animated special. Smeagol is very like hobbits until the Ring corrupts him, according to Tolkien, and in the long years he keeps the Ring close, he turns into the creature Gollum. In the Rankin–Bass *Hobbit*, that means he becomes green and frog-like, not remotely resembling hobbits. As one fan put it, Gollum is a 'slimy little frog-man that is more annoying than anything else'.[30] His connection with hobbits, and the Ring's power to transform a hobbit-like character into something more malevolent, become muted. This portrayal of Gollum can alter the way viewers even think of Bilbo, if they realise that new Ringbearer Bilbo might one day become like Gollum. The transformation seems unlikely, even in the presence of a powerful Ring, when the result might mean that Bilbo becomes, in essence, a frog.

Like the contrast shown between Bilbo and Gollum, positive characters like the eagles and thrush are shown as opposite characters like warg-wolves. Appropriately enough, this adaptation also shows Nature, through the helpful characters of the eagles and thrush, as honourable and truthful; only the warg-wolves, as animals corrupted by Orcs, attack ferociously and mindlessly. Such oppositions can be used to show children the difference between Good and Evil.

This late-1970s adaptation emphasises popular themes arising in the US during the 1960s, when Tolkien's *LotR* became a revered text among university students and counterculture hippies. Although *The Hobbit* may seem simple and innocent compared to current children's programming, it reinforces many of Tolkien's ideals, including respect for nature.

The Hobbit was well received on US television. Xerox paid more than $1 million (US) to sponsor the programme for two TV broadcasts, but, as then-Vice President of Advertising and Communication David Curtin explained, Xerox's educational division expected additional dividends from products and materials related to the TV special.[31] The company's initial investment not only attached Xerox to a respected literary work and the first time the story had been told on screen (and by well-known Rankin–Bass

Productions), but it also promised long-term payoffs when *The Hobbit* was used in the classroom.

Rankin–Bass's success with *The Hobbit* made a follow-up Tolkien feature inevitable. At the end of the special, Gandalf even prefaces the coming of *LotR* by telling Bilbo that this story is only the beginning. Within a year, the Bakshi version of *LotR* would make it to the big screen, and, soon after that, Rankin–Bass's *RotK* would premiere on US television network ABC.

The link among these three adaptations debuting within such a short time helps audiences to bridge gaps in any one TV special or movie. Critic Richard Scheib, writing in *Moria*, New Zealand's online review of science fiction, fantasy and horror films, elaborated on the connection:

> Almost certainly *The Hobbit* was made to capitalise on the interest sparked by Ralph Bakshi's planned two-part animated adaptation of the *Lord of the Rings*…Rankin and Bass later returned to Tolkien with *The Return of the King/Frodo: The Hobbit II* (1980). This is not a sequel to *The Hobbit* but an unofficial sequel to the Bakshi film, with Rankin–Bass adapting the third book in *The Lord of the Rings* and essentially finishing telling the saga that Bakshi never managed to complete.[32]

The Return of the King

As Scheib noted, Rankin–Bass's *RotK* (1980) is widely believed to be meant as a follow-up to Ralph Bakshi's partially live action, partially animated *LotR* (1978), a film that never made it into the final third of the book's story. Instead of being merely a follow-on to Bakshi's film or the last in a decade's worth of animated Tolkien tales, however, in tone and use of animation Rankin–Bass's *RotK* seems more of a continuation of their *Hobbit* (1977). In fact, the early portion of *RotK* provides a flashback of sorts to *The Hobbit*, as the story of Bilbo's encounter with the One Ring is retold, not only for the group of friends gathered for Bilbo's hundred-and-twenty-ninth birthday but for any viewers who missed the earlier TV special. By jumping directly into *RotK*, the Rankin–Bass story must also quickly summarise key plot points from *FotR* and *TT*, which it does by having Frodo's story briefly told at the party.

Instead of being a more 'adult' than children's version of *LotR*, as the Bakshi film seems to be, the Rankin–Bass *RotK* returns to a kinder, gentler type of animation. Certainly there are battles in this animated version, but the way the story is told minimises graphic violence and emphasises such wholesome values as family and friendship. The Rankin–Bass *RotK* more closely resembles the style of such popular animated series as *The Smurfs* (1981) or *The Berenstain Bears* (1985), with cute characters that mimic human characteristics, more than equally popular animated series based on heroic human characters, such as *GI Joe*, *Rambo*, or even *The Real Ghostbusters*, popular later in the decade.

Despite the cuteness of the animation or the genial nature of the musical elements of the story, the Rankin–Bass adaptation of *The Lord of the Rings* compresses many details to the point of creating an entirely different story. Frodo and Sam arrive in Rivendell to celebrate Bilbo's birthday with the old hobbit, here called 'the renowned tormentor of dragons',[33] an obvious reference to key scenes from *The Hobbit* to help audiences connect elderly Bilbo to his adventurous younger self. Frodo and Sam encounter Gandalf and a minstrel from Gondor, whom the wizard thoughtfully brought along to sing the backstory. The ballad 'Frodo of the nine fingers', sung by folk singer Glenn Yarbrough, fills in the details of *LotR*'s earlier chapters and allows Frodo to tell the rest of the story well in progress. Merry and Pippin also turn up for the party, but they seem more preoccupied with slicing the birthday cake than hearing stories. Other points of contention are the characterisations of the hobbits and the story's ending, which takes Tolkien's work in an entirely different direction.

The well-known cast who voiced this animated version included Orson Bean (Frodo and, as in *The Hobbit*, Bilbo), William Conrad (Denethor), John Huston (again playing Gandalf) and Roddy McDowell (Sam). Two radio personalities, Sonny Melendez and the more nationally famous Casey Kasem (*America's Top 40*) provided the voices for Pippin and Merry. In typical 1970s style, Yarbrough's ballads link not only story elements but provide a folk-music soundtrack popular in earlier animated and stop-action children's features. (*Frosty the Snowman* and *Rudolph the Red-Nosed Reindeer* both feature folk-singer-turned-actor Burl Ives; Yarbrough's music continues that tradition.)

This *RotK* adaptation focused on humans (more precisely, men), rather than hobbits. Even the human-free Rankin–Bass *Hobbit* introduced audiences to the concept of hobbits via a map of Middle-earth, itself introduced as coming from a time before man's history. Particularly in *RotK* but at times in *The Hobbit*, hobbits are compared with humans (usually with men). In most comparisons, men become more physically dominant and heroic in the story; hobbits are more child-sized (and cuddly) and less threatening.

Tolkien's story clearly delineates different categories of sentient beings, not all of them human. Characters categorised as elves, dwarves, hobbits, wizards, Orcs or Ents, for example, have specific appearances, history, homeland etc., that make them unique. Hobbits are equal to other groups, not relegated to second-class Middle-earth citizenship because they are not human (or, specifically, men). For Bilbo, as well as the later hobbits of the Fellowship, to be merely deemed 'little men', not only in stature but in ability to be heroic, is one typical problem with adaptations. In an animated version, hobbits may be drawn to look different from men – a problem not so easily solved in live-action adaptations. However, perhaps an even more serious problem with many adaptations is the propensity to make hobbits less important than the men (or women) in the story, as if humans should automatically be the most important characters. Tolkien does elevate Aragorn (and to a lesser extent Éomer) as leaders of men, but he does not do so at the expense of hobbits.

As noted above, animated hobbits can easily be drawn to look very different to men, and the Rankin–Bass hobbits retain some characteristics – like furry feet – described by Tolkien and easily used in these specials as a way to differentiate hobbits from other characters. Strangely enough, Frodo, usually the 'cutest' hobbit in adaptations (perhaps as a way to gain audience empathy early in *LotR*), is decidedly less attractive in this version. Although his big brown eyes mark him as kin to Bilbo, Frodo's bulbous nose and well-rounded body make him look like an average hobbit.

Other than the much thinner Pippin, all hobbits in this adaptation look extremely well fed, with Sam and Merry the most rotund. Sam's hair colour may match Frodo's, but he is rounder and has a larger nose. Merry resembles Sam in body size, but his personality is bossier, and he frequently tells Pippin what to do. Pippin looks distinctly different from Merry, a plus for those viewers who have trouble distinguishing between the pair. This Pippin is taller than the other hobbits (although no mention of Ent draughts – or Ents, for that matter – is made); he is much thinner overall, with a small nose and slight features. All hobbits have pelt-like foot fur, which further removes them from other characters. *RotK*'s hobbits meet audience expectations of what they should look like, based on Bilbo in *The Hobbit*, but their hairstyles and language make them relevant to a US audience watching television at home in 1980.

The hobbits look like they stepped out of 1970s California (a style popularised in television series filmed in Los Angeles and one easily recognisable to audiences just beginning a new decade).[34] Pippin sports wide sideburns, and the younger hobbits have long, wavy hair, not the curlier variety of which Tolkien writes. Frodo's shaggy brown hair is more rock singer than hobbit fashion. When Sam dreams of the 'small things that life is all about' (a song lyric from the animated *RotK*), he envisions hobbit children playing in the garden, his wife carrying a baby and being surrounded by youngsters, and himself smoking a pipe as he oversees his humble home. The 'hippie' virtues of a communal rural lifestyle were popular in the 1960s and early 1970s among the young seeking an alternative lifestyle to that of what they perceived as a materialistic technological society. These values found a home in Rankin–Bass's Shire, making the different-looking hobbits seem very human.

The hobbits' manner of speaking, yet another way to differentiate them from men, is less consistent than their appearance, even if it was more consistent with US fashions of the recent past than with Tolkien's story. One criticism of the Rankin–Bass *LotR* is that the language, not only word choice but an actor's accent, changes from scene to scene. Although Sam frequently sounds 'British', his speech patterns make it difficult to know exactly from which region he might hail; British actor Roddy McDowell should have been able to keep the accent consistent, but Sam at times sounds American. The other actors sound very American (and, indeed, were prominent US actors), but Pippin in particular often resorts to modern language that seems as out of place as the inconsistent diction. 'Do these palantir things ever lie?' he asks Gandalf, later proclaiming that Denethor has 'gone loony, I tell you!' In contrast, Sam's word choice comes from another time. At key moments he makes grandiose statements like the following, when he envisions what he might do if he possessed the Ring: 'Let [this Orc-infested] desert blossom and live...for Samwise the Strong!...So shall I transform the world!'

Sam certainly transforms this adaptation, in which he is much stronger than Frodo and often carries the action sequences. Rankin–Bass summarises Frodo's early 'adventures' with narration and shows only Frodo's capture in Cirith Ungol, where the Ringbearer lies beaten and unconscious after losing the Ring – and the story breaks for a commercial. Sam, although not portrayed as terribly smart, still becomes an action hero. He travels into the tower alone, throwing himself against the gate separating him from Frodo until he finally knocks himself out. Soon after awakening, he just happens to find the missing Ring, as well as Frodo's cloak and Sting. Although Sam decides to wear the Ring for 'my sweet master Frodo', he then leaves Frodo in the tower, and instead of destroying the Ring himself, chooses to do so in Frodo's name.

Along the road to Mordor the Ring tempts Sam, and throughout a long song Sam sees what type of conquering war king he would become, leading a mounted attack of men on Barad-dûr. He would turn the barren plains full of Orcs hiding in holes into a blossoming valley. Sam as saviour is not a new interpretation of this hobbit's role in the story, but in this adaptation Sam envisions himself wielding a god-like power to change Orcs into benign, if exotic, forest animals. At the moment Sam decides to put on the Ring instead of merely carrying it, however, his 'plain hobbit sense' returns to save him, and he realises that he only needs a small garden plot to keep him busy and happy. A 'happy song' ensues, praising the virtues of a 'small' life.

Of course, the Rankin–Bass *RotK* presents a child-friendly version of an adult, often violent plot. Although children might enjoy being scared by stories, the Rankin–Bass specials present benevolent, non-threatening depictions of life. Earlier holiday specials like *Rudolph*, *Frosty the Snowman* and *Santa Claus is Comin' to Town* might introduce dramatic conflict, but the good characters are never really in any danger, and a happy song indicates that a problem has been solved. *The Hobbit* and *RotK* continued this trend. Sam only briefly succumbs to power madness, for example, before he returns to being the benevolent hobbit who only needs home and family to be complete.

Drawings of the Shire, highly reminiscent of Tolkien-the-artist's illustrations, introduce the following segment showing what the 'small things that life are all about': a child (looking more human than hobbit) on a rocking horse, butterflies, an open smial door, a woman with babies, a family playing together – everything important to Sam's life in the Shire. By the conclusion of this song/fantasy sequence, Sam decides that only Frodo is capable of destroying the Ring and returns to Cirith Ungol to rescue him.

Such diversions not only shift Tolkien's emphasis but also keep audiences from focusing on the Ring's journey. Instead, Sam becomes the poster hobbit for family values, and his temptation, emphasised through a long musical sequence, offers a 'moral' to the story. Poor Frodo, however, fails to enter the story even at this point. The story next skips to the siege at Minas Tirith.

Without any further explanation of how he came to be in Minas Tirith or what has happened to Merry, Pippin mysteriously turns up to read mad Denethor's command for someone to kill him. The armour-clad Pippin hurries to find Gandalf, and Gandalf-as-narrator explains to the audience that 'the hobbit Pippin...had proved a most valuable assistant for me'. In this adaptation, Gandalf apparently waits around for Théoden and his army to rescue those in Minas Tirith. Later dialogue indicates that Gandalf had dispatched Merry to fetch Théoden; Merry brings an arrow to Théoden to indicate his assistance is needed. The hobbit then rides his own brown pony as part of Théoden's army and, indeed, helps to lead the charge, greatly elevating Merry's role and allowing him to become an equal warrior in Théoden's army, not Tolkien's left-behind hobbit who secretly rides to battle with a disguised Éowyn.

Back in Minas Tirith, after Denethor's death, Pippin encourages Gandalf to take charge until Aragorn arrives to take the throne. The wizard, in this mancentric adaptation, passively succumbs to his vision of the black fleet's arrival. 'Is there no hope?' Pippin demands. 'None,' intones Gandalf, who pessimistically believes that Frodo – and all possibility of salvation – is gone.

Just as the roles of some hobbits (usually Merry and Pippin) are minimised in many adaptations, so is Sam's role sometimes elevated and his devotion to Frodo rewarded with more screen time. In this adaptation, Sam's role is made much more important, perhaps to emphasise that other 'little people' (children) can succeed or save the day if they remain hopeful and do their best to help others. If they value their home and family above power or wealth, they will be able to succeed. By saving Frodo, Sam in effect saves Minas Tirith, or even the whole of Middle-earth.

Despite his significance to the story, Sam is not clever enough to figure a way into Cirith Ungol. He frequently does not have to solve problems on his own; magic intervenes. He discovers a phial in Frodo's cloak, and the suddenly radiating vessel magically opens the gate for him. Because the Orcs once guarding Cirith Ungol are already dead when he enters, Sam confronts a lone Orc, who provides him with the information he needs to find Frodo. The hobbit next sees an Orc whipping Frodo, but even then Sam does not need to fight Frodo's tormentor: the Orc falls through an open trapdoor to his death. Although much of the story elevates Sam, he still seems to have more luck and less intelligence than men; his successes seem to be magical rather than by his own design.

Sam's and Frodo's relationship is still highlighted in this adaptation. Sam looks after Frodo even as he cries over his master and kisses his brow. Frodo says he feels like a child comforted from a nightmare by a beloved voice. Although Sam clearly loves his 'dear master', the Rankin–Bass version portrays his devotion purely, with no possible homoerotic overtones (which fans have looked for in later adaptations), as befitting family entertainment of that decade.

What is striking about the Cirith Ungol sequence is the elevation of Sam as a hero and Frodo's demotion both as Ringbearer and main character. In this adaptation, Frodo seems weak and ineffectual. Pessimistic Frodo worries that Evil has overtaken the world and comments that only the elves can sail away (leading to another song about elves taking a white ship to their homeland). Even in the short Mount Doom scene, Gollum (the only time he is shown on screen) arrives just in time to struggle with Frodo for the Ring; the hobbit's climactic scene is told more than shown. After the story shifts to the battle at Minas Tirith, Frodo's part in the story seems much less dramatic and important. The hobbit calmly announces the Ring's destruction and seems rather ambivalent about the loss of his finger (a bloodless loss, because the action takes place off screen). Frodo again acts fatalistically; his parting words to Sam as lava overtakes them on the disintegrating mountain are 'Die well, Samwise.'

Frodo does not physically change; his burden does not seem to alter his appearance. Nevertheless, his role in this adaptation diminishes as Sam's role increases. Without Sam's intervention throughout the story, Frodo would not last long. He becomes more of a pessimist and doomsayer than a valiant, sacrificial hero. Because Sam is portrayed throughout this adaptation as a loyal homebody who only desires a simple, family-oriented life, he is a good role model for children to follow. Parents and children watching this TV special together would likely approve of the family values, best portrayed by Sam, being the foundation from which he can complete heroic deeds. However, as mentioned earlier, Sam is not the smartest character in the story. Thus, viewers' overall impression of all hobbits may be that they 'win' – whether as Ringbearers or soldiers – more by luck and magic than intelligence. They may be loyal and persevering, but they need others' help. Not even Sam can save Middle-earth on his own, and this hobbit is far less of an action hero than humans. The battle scenes quickly show that the true action heroes of the Rankin–Bass version are men (and one woman, when Éowyn arrives, wearing form-fitting armour and with her blonde hair flowing to her shoulders). Hobbits cannot compete with humans in battle.

While Sam is saving Frodo, Merry, back on the battlefront, fights an Orc more than twice his size. He is saved from impending death when Pippin shoots an arrow into the Orc, and the hobbits are reunited in the middle of battle. Of course, they take time to link hands and dance in a circle while exclaiming their joy at seeing each other again. (Fortunately, the battle ignores them.) Pippin and Merry each get credit for saving the other; Pippin cries, 'Bless you for bringing Théoden and his army. You've won the day for us!' Hobbits seem to exist in their own little world; they may save each other from harm or bring human reinforcements to fight, but hobbits are largely removed from the bigger battle going on around them.

Merry and Pippin's happy reunion is soon shattered. Théoden's horse bucks when the lead Nazgûl turns the skies eerily dark. Théoden falls off his horse, dead, causing Merry to rage at the skies, 'Hear me, Oh Darkness! I will avenge my lord!' After this outburst, however, Merry breaks down, and Pippin comforts him. During the confrontation between Éowyn and the Nazgûl, the action is again averted while the hobbits discuss what happens. Merry explains to Pippin how Éowyn came to the battle, and the two hobbits discuss her attack on the Nazgûl. Just when Éowyn is about to be zapped by her enemy's evil power, Merry screams 'No!' and rushes forward to stab the Nazgûl in the back. After the empty body twitches and deflates, Merry and Pippin accompany Théoden's body into Minas Tirith. The pair again hug each other in joy when Aragorn arrives with the black ships; the returning king chases the Orcs away to the Black Gate.

Like Frodo and Sam, the primary significance of Merry and Pippin is their friendship. Although each has brief, separate scenes, most often they are shown together, whether bickering, discussing recent events, or providing comfort to each other. They value family and friendship and are shown as having little interest in politics – certainly not war. They fight in order to preserve the lives of their friends and kin. In this adaptation, men (and Éowyn) are action heroes with little time for open displays of affection. Hobbits, on the other hand, take the time to embrace and celebrate being alive and together, even when deadly dangers surround them. This depiction reinforces the idea that hobbits are lucky, or that magic protects them, because they do not seem to worry about taking time out for happy reunions in the middle of mortal combat. Their role in the story is limited, as evidenced in the scene at the conclusion of battle.

While Aragorn triumphantly enters a restored, blossoming Minas Tirith as the returned King, the hobbits and Gandalf watch his entry into the city from a tower high above the gate. Their part in the story is over, and the hobbits never receive recognition, much less acclaim, for their actions. Somehow Frodo and Sam survive their ordeal and are able to return home, but once the Ring is destroyed, no further mention is made of it. Aragorn becomes the traditional war-hero-king welcomed into Minas Tirith. Humans, represented here by Aragorn, are the true heroes and saviours who receive their due glory. Hobbits, unfortunately, become an afterthought to everyone but themselves.

Even when the story comes full circle back to Bilbo's birthday party and departure, along with Elrond and Gandalf, to Valinor, the hobbits are diminished by changes in the story. In this version, the Shire never changes, and the Travellers' journey apparently has had little impact on their lives or community. Frodo, Sam, Merry and Pippin are not radically different hobbits after their outerworldly experiences. Bilbo's nap during the telling of the Ring story may be the result of boredom as much as old age; even he does not seem moved by his kin's ordeal.

Gandalf conveniently explains that the Age of Men is beginning, and his work, as well as that of the elves (represented by Elrond), is done. Bilbo is accorded passage across the sea not because he was a Ringbearer but, as Gandalf says, he 'served us well', and Elrond assures him (and the audience) that 'there's always room for a friend'. Frodo wants to accompany them, and Gandalf merely agrees; Frodo's need for healing or his ability, through Arwen's grace, to travel to the Blessed Realm has no place in this simplified version.

Although Sam does not want to be parted from Frodo, his former master assures not only Sam, but Merry and Pippin as well, that they can have good lives in the Shire, with wives and babies, food and tobacco.[35] What more could they want? At the end of the tale, despite the emphasis on men as the real heroes, Rankin–Bass attempt a last-minute nod to hobbits as role models and ideals for the future of humanity, perhaps because of their family values and deep friendships highlighted in this adaptation. Gandalf answers the question 'Is there room for hobbits in the Age of Men?' The wizard assures Sam (and the audience) that hobbits are closer to men than they realise and will be a part of the future. Elves, dwarves, wizards and even Orcs fade away, but men (and hobbits) endure. This shift from a humancentric to hobbitcentric focus attempts to make Tolkien's story relevant to the next generation. Gandalf promises, 'One day you will be as men,' noting that each generation of hobbits stands taller than the previous, Pippin being an excellent example. Thus, according to Gandalf, hobbits survive only because they can evolve to become like men.

Gandalf talks directly to the audience as he 'looks' into the 'camera'. Children may wonder if they, too, are part hobbit, and thus share the positive hobbit traits shown in this story. In this way, Rankin–Bass tries to have it all within a shortened, less violent *RotK* plot – battle action with clear heroes (and a heroine), friendships between lovable hobbits, and an emphasis on the joys of family and rural living. The darker elements in Tolkien's story, such as an exploration of Evil and its effects on those who challenge it, may have been deemed inappropriate for children, but turning the more adult *LotR* into a *Hobbit*-sized programme necessarily poses problems. What stands out in this adaptation is the hobbits' gentler qualities; hobbits still seem innocent and need the protection of others, even after their quest. Nevertheless, they can some day 'grow up' to become as heroic and well recognised as adult human characters. Perhaps that truly becomes the moral of the story for children.

Veggie Tales: Lord of the Beans

A much later television adaptation designed for children takes its themes from yet another *LotR* adaptation, Jackson's cinematic trilogy, but puts a spiritual spin on the story. Big Idea produces a series of stories designed specifically for children; each has a moral and can be illustrated with a Bible verse. This wholesome programming goes well beyond the family values the Rankin–Bass animated adaptations only hint at. Each *Veggie Tales* story promotes a virtue and illustrates a lesson to be learned by a familiar vegetable character who plays a role within a popular recent television series or movie. Recognising that children, as well as their parents, are highly familiar with popular culture, the company often parodies popular stories, with all major roles going to talking vegetables. Audiences who have seen instalments of the series easily recognise the *Veggie Tales* characters playing these roles, but viewers are also familiar with the story being very loosely adapted to fit the *Veggie Tales* format.

Veggie Tales references only a few ideas from *LotR*, in this case Jackson's movies more than Tolkien's book, and makes them palatable for children and their parents. In *Lord of the Beans*,[36] the familiar movie-version characters Bilbo, Frodo, Gandalf, Aragorn, Gimli and Legolas are turned into Billboy Baggypants, Toto Baggypants (borrowing from *The Wizard of Oz*), Randalf, Ear-of-corn, Grumpy (borrowing a name from a Disney dwarf) and Leg-of-lamb. The 'other elf' in this fellowship, Leg-of-lamb's cousin, is unnamed but bears an uncanny resemblance to a cooking-baking Keebler (very familiar to children who have grown up seeing Keebler elves baking cookies in trees in the many cookie-company advertisements. The reference, however, is more popular culture than product placement). This elf finally turns the Sporks – Scaryman's (Saruman's) evil blend of spoons and forks – into friends by tempting them with the cookies he bakes in a convenient tree.

The plot very loosely follows scenes from *LotR*: Gandalf's/Randalf's arrival in the Shire, Bilbo's/Billboy's birthday party, discovery of the One Ring/One Bean at Bag End, a visit with talking trees, a riddle before opening a door into a mountain, the Ringbearer's/Beanbearer's journey after the breaking of the Fellowship. The presentation of these scenes, however, primarily parodies Jackson's version of the story and mimics key scenes.

When Randalf tells Toto to hold the magic bean in the fire, it reveals an inscription: 'If you can read this, you're too close.' Bumper-sticker readers everywhere understand and laugh. The bean's other side, however, provides a more prophetic meaning: 'Use wisely.' Toto realises that he has been given a great gift, but, unsure what to do with it, he must decide wisely how best to use it.

Along the way Toto meets Randalf's friends, Ear-of-corn, Leg-of-lamb and Grumpy. These characters, just like Aragorn, Legolas and Gimli in Jackson's film, pledge their weapons to help Toto on his quest. They even use the same dialogue: 'You have my sword,' 'And my bow,' 'And my axe.' Dialogue taken from the recent films makes this *Veggie Tale* more enjoyable for parents, who well know the films, as well as to their children. Although *Lord of the Beans* was released in late 2005 in the US, two years after the theatrical release of *RotK*, the films would still be familiar to parents, who had probably seen them at the cinema. Children too young to have seen the films on a big screen might be old enough, two years later, to have seen the trilogy on DVD. Because of the continuing popularity of the Jackson adaptation, parents and children who buy this particular *Veggie Tale* are likely very familiar with the *LotR* trilogy. They recognise lines of dialogue, and the animated scenes closely drawn to resemble the camera angles used in the films make some scenes look more like an animated re-enactment or adaptation than a simple parody.

The fact that so many adaptations (for example, the Jackson films, *Lord of the Beans*, television and film references to *LotR* – such as those mentioned in the Introduction – *The Hobbit* children's opera, musical parody *Fellowship!*) all took place in the 2000s speaks not only to the continuing popularity of Tolkien's stories but the pervasive appeal and marketability of the Jackson films.

The conclusion of this *Veggie Tale* differs the most from either the Jackson adaptation or Tolkien's story. Toto tosses the magic bean into a dusty well, which, rejuvenated by his wish to help people, shoots a geyser over the parched countryside and brings prosperity again to a forgotten people. Toto is revered as the sharer/bringer of the 'lord of the beans' – the magic bean with all the properties of four lesser magical beans; he alone knows how to use the power of the One Bean to bring life back to the barren landscape, and thus how to restore its people. The moral of the story is for children to use their talents wisely to help others.

LotR's great struggle between Good and Evil is simplified as Toto's personal choice of how best to use what Billboy leaves him – his physical but also spiritual inheritance. Scaryman simply wants to own the bean because it can give him whatever he wants, rather like a genie's magic lamp, only with unlimited wishes. Grumpy tries to persuade Toto to use the bean to make burritos when he is hungry, but Toto steadfastly keeps the bean safe until he knows exactly how to share its use with others. This simplification waters down Tolkien's story and turns it into more of a general coming-of-age tale as defined by literary critic Joseph Campbell. In Campbell's description of the hero's journey,[37] he explains that the hero must travel from home to learn about the outside world (here called Center Earth) and determine his role in society. Thus, *Lord of the Beans* thematically pays tribute as much to Joseph Campbell as J.R.R. Tolkien.

LotR is an interesting choice for parody. Of course, given the films' wide recognition factor and popularity, the *Veggie Tales* parallel attracts children, who watch the TV programme or get their parents to buy the DVD. Such a dark story is not typically a likely plot to parody, but Tolkien fans are noted for taking the Professor's works very seriously. Parodies like *Lord of the Beans* (or Harvard Lampoon's *Bored of the Rings* or stage productions like *Fellowship!*) poke fun at *LotR*'s and fans' seriousness while paying a fond tribute to a beloved classic.

This parody is not meant to re-create Tolkien's complex story but to provide audiences with readily identifiable characters who can teach children a lesson. In this regard, Peter Jackson's Frodo, as played by teenaged Elijah Wood especially in *FotR*, is a good choice as role model. *Lord of the Beans*'s Toto (played by *Veggie Tales* 'actor' Junior Asparagus) sports wavy hair the same colour and style as movie Frodo's. He wears a similar outfit, down to the colours of his vest and cloak, which is clasped with a leaf brooch. In a departure from either film or book, Toto's voice is clearly a child's – high pitched, innocent, often giggling. Frodo is turned into a childlike protagonist who needs no other 'flobbits' to help him on his journey; the larger (with the exception of grape Grumpy) vegetables shepherd him. Like Tolkien's canny Frodo, Toto solves the riddle needed to open the Blue Gate, a door leading into a mountain with a 'back door' too small for anyone but Toto to walk through; thus he continues his journey alone when the 'big vegetables' cannot fit through the door.

Perhaps the irony of *Lord of the Beans* for hobbit lovers is that there are very few 'flobbits' in this story; they only get one important early scene. Billboy's birthday party parodies Jackson's vision of the Shire, with the party field and Bag End close cousins of the cinematic version. Billboy's speech is a short jibe at the other flobbits, and Randalf provides the fireworks.

The fireworks scene is the only time that – perhaps – other Fellowship hobbits are parodied on screen. A chubby flobbit (Sam?) runs through the crowd, his hair aflame, presumably from being too close to the fireworks. The unnamed flobbit runs towards Toto and Randalf, who seem oblivious to what is going on and comment about the beauty of the fireworks and how much the flobbits enjoy them. The fiery flobbit wears clothing similar to Sam's attire in Jackson's *FotR*. If this is indeed supposed to represent loyal, loving Sam, *Veggie Tales* returns him to Bakshi-style comic relief: silly, clumsy, simple.

The audience's only glimpse of 'Merry' and 'Pippin' also takes place during the fireworks scene. Clothing again provides the only clues about who these unnamed flobbits are supposed to be. 'Merry' wears a white shirt and yellow vest, just as in Jackson's *FotR*; 'Pippin' is best known by his green scarf (but his jacket is brown, not the blue coat movie Pippin wears when he leaves the Shire). The two stand next to each other during Billboy's birthday speech and understand each other's body-language comments on the nonsense he spouts. *Veggie Tales* perhaps inadvertently winks at the critics who find it difficult to distinguish Merry from Pippin in either the book or the films; other than their costumes, the flobbits look alike in size, build and matching greyish hair. They identically shrug after one of Billboy's strange statements and raise eyebrows as they glance at each other a second time. At least the well-known friendship between Merry and Pippin survives even in this parody, evidenced by their close proximity and mirrored actions. Only astute fans of the *LotR* films, however, might recognise 'Merry' and 'Pippin' in the crowd.

Although the flobbits may seem unaware of the outside world, Billboy tries to provide a warning for them before he disappears from his party. In one of the two songs (Toto sings the other), Billboy explains that his travels and wealth have provided only momentary happiness. In a parody of Bilbo's line about feeling like too little butter spread across too much bread, Billboy says that his life now is like 'chocolate pudding scraped across too much ham'. Toto alone heeds this warning and learns that sharing what he has with others can bring him true happiness. The good news for hobbit lovers is that the flobbits are the moral centre of this story. Bilbo's materialism/consumerism is not as spiritually fulfilling as Toto's selfless good deed. The flobbits *are* the story, and Toto best illustrates their virtues.

Toto leaves the Shire and discovers how to use the bean without the help of another flobbit. He does not need much assistance beyond minimal guidance from Randalf; Toto is never tempted by the bean and decides how best to use this gift all by himself. He is the undisputed hero of the story, which is appropriate because the young, short, innocent Toto is the perfect role model for children.

People who bought this DVD through Amazon.com seemed highly enthusiastic about their purchase and favourably compared the *Veggie Tales* adaptation with Tolkien's original as well as Jackson's trilogy. Most reviewers noted that adults would find the story just as humorous as (if not more so than) their children would and appreciated Big Idea's mesh of the popular *LotR* story with a Christian message for children. These kinds of comments were common among the more than sixty reviews posted online: 'It is both an entertaining spoof of the *Lord of the Rings* movies, with a theme reasonably close to Tolkien; using great power for selfish ends is ultimately destructive';[38] 'Not only is the novel spoofed – but so are the movies. [A]dults familiar with either version of the story will find much at which to laugh';[39] 'My own children … love LOTR and get a huge kick out of this parody … [W]hy not take what Hollywood has done and make something that kids can remember and relate to as they get older. I know my kids will always think of Sporks and "the other elf" and chuckle as they're watching

LOTR.'[40] As these grown-ups attest, watching *Lord of the Beans* is more enjoyable for fans of the movies in particular, and book readers do not seem to be offended, but rather amused, at the connections between the stories.

The negative reviews also refer to the enjoyability or appropriateness of a parody of Jackson's *LotR*. One critic summed up the key problem with such a parody: viewers 'with no knowledge of LOTR wouldn't get most of the jokes'.[41] As with many adaptations, the length of *LotR* proved daunting: 'The Lord of the Beans was a 100% knock of Tolkien. Which would be fine, except that they chained themselves to a 9-hour movie and tried to parody it into a 45-minute cartoon.'[42]

Despite this appropriate criticism, *Veggie Tales* adds yet another layer of meaning to fans' enjoyment of Jackson's *LotR* and Tolkien's original, although the differences between these (sometimes very loose) adaptations and Tolkien's work are generally not perceived by fans who primarily entered *LotR* fandom because of the movies.

* * *

These radio and television adaptations have had a tremendous impact on Tolkien fans, and many who grew up listening to and watching them used them as inspiration for their own Tolkien-themed artistic expressions later on. Perhaps more important, the young children who learned about *The Hobbit* or *LotR* because of these adaptations often decided to read the books.

Some adaptations may reach a wider audience, and therefore have more global influence, than others, simply because of their target audience. The BBC radio adaptation, for example, initially reached a UK listening audience, but the sheer number of times, even more recently, that the radio dramatisation has been rebroadcast has increased its listenership. With the transference of the radio drama to CD, this adaptation became more marketable and could be purchased by audiences worldwide. Positive reviews and word-of-mouth promotion throughout Tolkien fandom also helped make this adaptation one of the most popular and influential, not only in its day but in the decades since its first broadcast.

In comparison, an adaptation like *Veggie Tales* probably draws a smaller, if equally devoted, audience than a nationally broadcast radio or television special. Although popular with families with young children, older potential buyers of the *Lord of the Beans* DVD may not have seen the original television broadcast and may only have learned of this particular *Veggie Tale* because of its *LotR* content.

Some adaptations, including this *Veggie Tale* as well as the Rankin–Bass *RotK*, reflect the styles of the time when they were produced, instead of an indeterminate 'Middle-earth' time; they may not present hobbits as heroic characters true to the book instead of creating characters that look or sound more like the target audience. A mutton-chop-sideburned hobbit may be recognisably in style in 1980 (simply because people watching the first-run special would remember that recent style, even if it was not currently in fashion). Later audiences watching long-haired 'hippie' hobbits or listening to a Glenn Yarbrough soundtrack (or watching a flobbit patterned after Elijah Wood's appearance in the Jackson films) may feel nostalgic for the era in which the adaptation was made but will likely not relate to it in quite the same way as the audience first watching the adaptation years before.

Whether an adaptation becomes a nostalgic reminder of some viewers' first exposure to hobbits or retains its Middle-earth integrity and seems less glaringly dated when fans return again and again to watch (or listen) to it, these *Hobbit* and *LotR* adaptations have a long-lasting impact on individual hobbit fans as well as popular culture in general. They are also important because they generated – and continue to generate – a greater awareness of Tolkien's stories, especially among children and adolescents who missed out on the Tolkien fan frenzy of the 1960s.

5

HOBBITS ON THE
BIG SCREEN

I n the middle of *Simpsons* episode 'That '90s Show' from 2008, in
which Marge reminisces about her days at Springfield University,
young Comic Book Guy pontificates in the outdoor quad. As
Marge passes by, she overhears him conclude, 'And *that's* why *The
Lord of the Rings* can never be filmed.'[1] Tolkien likely would have
agreed, perhaps one factor in his decision to sell the film rights to his
epic. Saul Zaentz, who acquired the rights,[2] has had other ideas about
the story, as evidenced in his involvement with Ralph Bakshi's 1978
film, Peter Jackson's 2001–3 trilogy, and long negotiations eventually
leading to the *Hobbit* films.

Not only has *LotR* been deemed difficult to film because of the
length and complexity of the story, but it, and as a result *The Hobbit*,
has also been embroiled in studio disputes that brought nearly as
much attention to the legal issues as to the quality of the cinematic
storytelling. Zaentz is one of the interesting characters in the filmed
LotR's and *Hobbit*'s backstory, with a lifetime devoted to the record
and film industries. As a film producer, his successful films include
Academy Award winners *One Flew Over the Cuckoo's Nest* (1975),
Amadeus (1984) and *The English Patient* (1996).[3] As the owner of
Tolkien Enterprises, Zaentz, more importantly to Jackson's adaptations,

has the rights to *LotR* and *The Hobbit* and produced Ralph Bakshi's 1978 *LotR* film. He did not produce Jackson's *LotR* but granted permission for it to be made by New Line Cinema.

After the successful Jackson trilogy apparently made a lot of money, the director and New Line got into a lengthy dispute over the final accounting, leading to Jackson's lawsuit against New Line. In the fallout, New Line did not seem likely to bring back Jackson to direct *The Hobbit*, and time was of the essence because the company would soon lose the rights to make the film. Zaentz, however, had no complaints with Jackson and assumed that, one way or another, the legal issues would be worked out and that some day, by some studio, the film would be made. In a 2006 interview in Germany, soon republished in English on the TORN site, Zaentz commented that Jackson was his choice for director whenever *The Hobbit* could be made. He noted that

> Next year the Hobbit-rights will fall back to my company. I suppose that Peter will wait because he knows that he will make the best deal with us. And he is fed up with the studios: to get his profit share on the Rings trilogy he had to sue New Line. With us, in contrast, he knows that he will be paid fairly and artistically supported without reservation.[4]

To summarise many years of negotiations briefly, Jackson ended up as the director of three *Hobbit* films produced by MGM, New Line Cinema, 3Foot7 and WingNut Films (the latter two being Jackson's companies).

Although some Tolkien fans and critics find lots to dislike about cinematic adaptations, no matter who directs or produces them, the fact remains that Jackson's trilogy has brought plenty of new fans to Tolkien's story and, unless some day a more definitive screen adaptation is made, will likely be *the* cinematic adaptation by which all others are measured. Because Jackson's three *Hobbit* films not only adapt *The Hobbit* but include background information from other Tolkien books, the six-film *Hobbit-LotR* 'history', as told by Jackson, should prove a difficult combination to beat. *The Hobbit: An Unexpected Journey*, *The Hobbit: There and Back Again* and the third film are not only linked stories in their own right, they also create a prequel to characters and events in Middle-earth shown in the three *LotR* films: *The Fellowship of the Ring*, *The Two Towers* and *The Return of the King*. The *Hobbit* films also provide insights into Middle-earth that may cause audiences who then return to the *LotR* trilogy to view the earlier films (but later-in-time stories) in a different light. It is doubtful that anyone in the foreseeable future will try to tackle all these stories in a similar series. Thus, in a little more than a decade of film production (plus more years in wrangling rights and settling studio disputes), Peter Jackson has accomplished what, even a few years ago, few Tolkien fans thought could be done, and, according to the verdict of *LotR* fans and the anticipation for *The Hobbit*, he has done it well. Directorial wisdom decrees that if *LotR* can be presented as an understandable, inventive entertainment palatable to audiences seated for a reasonable number of hours in a cinema, then any epic is fair game.

LotR has long served as a cinematic proving ground not only for the scope of stories told on film but the artistic direction needed to tell them. Bakshi experimented with rotoscoping, a technique combining live action and animation. Jackson's vision required innovative computerised graphics (computer-generated images, or CGI, and motion-capture technology) to be created in order to render Gollum, in particular, a live-action character. Innovative special effects also created a 'real' Balrog, flying Witch King and Army of the Dead. Even newer filmmaking and special-effects technologies available by 2011–12 have made *The Hobbit* more innovative than *LotR*. Not only has the story been adapted for film, but this particular story has led to leaps in the technology of filmmaking and therefore had an effect on the entire film industry.

Bakshi's *The Lord of the Adaptations*... Not Quite

After many potential scripts (see Chapter 3), one was finally accepted for Ralph Bakshi's 1978 feature film, entitled *The Lord of the Rings*, even though it ended abruptly after material from *The Two Towers*. Bakshi 'designed every foot of the film, with its 250,000 separate images', while 'more than 150 artists did the actual animating'.[5] Bakshi's interpretation of the source material often put a dark spin on the film; he revealed that his version of Mordor 'is very much like Auschwitz. It's ashes. It's cold. It smells of the decay of humanity. The dead die and stay unburied.' In contrast, Rivendell is 'rich, old wood, very Victorian, turn-of-the-century Vienna'. Although these allusions made sense to the director, they were not obvious to audiences in the late 1970s, and the historic comparisons to World War II death camps or the even earlier Victorian era certainly may be far less familiar to audiences today who see the film.

The director thought of the story as 'totally realistic. But it wouldn't be believable either in live action with people dressed up in Orc suits, or as a standard cartoon.'[6] Therefore, through rotoscoping, the Bakshi film became a mixture of live-action sequences turned into animated images and true cartoon animation; the credits and many battle sequences played against a bright-red background that emphasised shadowy characters embroiled in conflict. This experimental style and the requisite cutting to adapt the story for the screen became two focal points for many fans' and film critics' displeasure when the $6 million (US) animated film opened in 20 US cities in late 1978.[7]

Fan response was not nearly as positive as United Artists had hoped. Vincent Canby, reporting for the *New York Times*, addressed a structural problem with the film: 'The major fault of the screenplay ... is that the film attempts to cover too much ground too quickly.'[8] Film critics in the UK agreed with this assessment, and newspapers published scathing reviews. Well-known *Guardian* critic Derek Malcolm wrote that

> Bakshi takes two thirds of the book, encapsulates it in 135 minutes of screen time, and still appears to be gutting it ... Underscored by the ear-bashing Leonard Rosenman score, which sounds as if it is being played by a Marine Band on an off-day, the film has so much to get through that it can rarely take a breath and deal literately with its characters.[9]

Nevertheless, other critics, especially in hindsight, found aspects of the film particularly well done and innovative. 'The sheer amount of material included in the film ... means that the dialogue tends to be brief, but the whole script serves to enhance the character, and the actors make every line count.' Among the hobbits, Frodo was singled out for praise because he 'manages to sound strained without crossing over into whining'. Bakshi's decision to make 'an American cartoon feature' that includes the 'darker, more threatening nature of Middle Earth' was described as a bold choice that takes animation in a new direction, and 'Bakshi's more realistic character designs and rotoscope-aided movement animation also add to the serious feel of the movie.'[10]

In any adaptation, key events and characters are omitted to make the story short or easy enough for casual viewers to understand. In Bakshi's film, the omissions, especially when the more-than-two-hour film ends abruptly and leaves lots of dangling plots, became unbearable for those who either wanted to know how the story ended (but had not read Tolkien's book) or who knew the story well and found the editing egregious. Future filmmaker Peter Jackson later recalled mixed feelings about the movie, especially because

> at the time, I hadn't read the book. As a result, I got pretty confused! I liked the early part…but then, about halfway through, the storytelling became very disjointed and disorientating…However, what it did do was to make me want to read the book – if only to find out what happened![11]

A planned follow-up never materialised, although the Rankin–Bass TV special, the animated *RotK*, provided some closure for fans wanting to see a filmed or animated version of the book.

According to one review, reports of audiences booing at the film's end reached producer Saul Zaentz;[12] perhaps in later ventures he wanted to ensure that *LotR* made audiences happier (and thus made more money), a feat overwhelmingly achieved with the Jackson trilogy. Zaentz and Bakshi might have done well to heed the words of Tolkien's daughter, Priscilla, who knows that Tolkien fans are passionate and knowledgeable. When Bakshi and Zaentz took preliminary character sketches to her, she 'warned them that – whatever they did – at least 20 percent of the audience would say, "That's not the way I think it looks."'[13] Given many vocal *LotR* fans' response, not only immediately after the film's release but in the decades since, Ms Tolkien's estimate was low.

Even decades later, the Bakshi film is often stigmatised by bad reviews, which fuel scholar-fans' further analysis of exactly what is wrong with this adaptation. The obvious flaws are its sudden ending and no real conclusion to the plot threads introduced earlier. However, more seriously, Bakshi did not seem to know when to illustrate the story with broad, sweeping gestures or intimate lines and subtle nuances of character. Tolkien's story has both, and a successful adaptor needs to know when to emphasise something big – such as a larger-than-life (especially to hobbits) battle scene – or something small – such as the important, but far quieter and more personal dialogue between Frodo and Sam. As one reviewer noted in 2000,

> it's far easier to animate large, sweeping gestures than it is to animate smaller, subtle movements. Subtleties, however, are often more appropriate to the story...Bakshi seems to have extreme difficulty filming two people who sit down and have a quiet conversation. This is highly unfortunate, since it is Tolkien's elegantly-crafted dialogue which drives the story.[14]

Furthermore, some characters, such as Sam, are not introduced but simply show up. If the audience already knows the story, there is little or no point to the film (beyond seeing if the story could be filmed). If audiences, by and large, do not know the story, then they can become lost when characters, including Sam, enter it. The same problem occurs with Merry and Pippin, who are suddenly Frodo's travelling companions and are only later 'introduced' by a few lines of dialogue. In the attempt to adapt a long story, Bakshi needed to simplify backstories but still introduce characters (especially hobbits) in relation to Frodo, not assume his audience would automatically identify a hobbit like Sam, Merry or Pippin from the context of a scene.

In ways like these, Bakshi seems to eliminate the beginning and end to the story in order to focus on the dramatic middle, a process that dissatisfies audiences who know the story as well as confuses those who do not. The result is that individual scenes (for example, the use of silhouette against a flame-red background) are striking, and the rotoscoping technology intriguing to film scholars. However, the story – what general audiences want to see and need to understand – seems to have received less attention, and thus may have been sacrificed for the 'art' of filmmaking.

Despite a critical bashing, the hobbits' portrayal is not all bad. One key criticism is that the hobbits all seem very young and, with the exception of Sam, look more human than a distinctly different race. Frodo often acts like the leader of a group of boys off on a camping trip, more Peter Pan than middle-aged Ringbearer. John Boardman's *Dagon* review praised some aspects of Bakshi's animation, calling them a 'mixed bag. The hobbits are fairly good, though Frodo looks a bit young for being the hobbitish equivalent of a human age of 32,' but he fares well compared to Boardman's assessment of Legolas as 'just a blond, lantern-jawed man', Galadriel 'like Disney's Snow White, grown to middle age and wearing a blonde wig', and Aragorn and Boromir 'running around in tunics so short that you wonder where they left their pants'.[15]

In only a few scenes, Bilbo, Merry, Pippin or Frodo appear in live-action segments. The 'live' hobbits typically wear a hooded cape or keep their backs to the camera so that the features of the human actors cannot be seen. They simply seem to be small characters with little needed development in the live-action scenes (for example, Bilbo picking up the Ring in Gollum's cave, Merry and Pippin fighting Orcs). Having 'hobbits' in the live portions of the film does not make them seem more real or even more man-like, so the revelation by *New York Times* critic Tom Buckley that 'a very small actress named Sharon Baird was the model for the hero, the indisputably male Hobbit, Frodo Baggins,'[16] becomes merely an interesting bit of movie trivia.

Although the superficial (for example, costume, physical characteristics) and structural (for example, ending before the *RotK* material) changes often become the focus of criticism, the way the hobbits are individually portrayed sometimes follows Tolkien's story more closely than other adaptations succeed in doing. In fact, some scenes missing from other adaptations (notably the Jackson films) keep Merry and Pippin in closer harmony with Tolkien's depiction of the younger Fellowship hobbits. Bakshi's portrayal of hobbits does provide them some individuality that helps audiences distinguish one hobbit from another. In the first half of the film, the hobbits' story *is* the *LotR* story, but after the Fellowship breaks, the early emphasis on hobbits gradually gives way to the rise of Aragorn and the wartime leadership of Gandalf.

Frodo

Frodo is alternately an innocent 'boy' and a proactive adult Ringbearer in Bakshi's film. Early emphasis on his big brown eyes shining during Bilbo's birthday speech or, 17 years later, his jump for joy at Gandalf's return portray him as a naive, emotional hobbit. He kicks the ground and tosses rocks as he laments that Gollum provided Sauron with information about the Ring's relocation to the Shire. In such a scene, Frodo acts like a young boy.[17]

Youthful Frodo also seems less aware of the dangers facing him as Ringbearer once he and his companions leave the Shire. Inside the Prancing Pony, Butterbur announces the hobbits' presence and then encourages Frodo to sing a Shire song. Put on the spot, Frodo sings about a brown bear and dances on the tables. During this dance, he falls off a table and inadvertently slips on the Ring, which makes him invisible. To avoid further scrutiny, and Butterbur's wrath over the crockery broken in Frodo's fall, the hobbits flee, Strider following them to their room. This song-and-dance scene (also prominent in the *LotR* stage musical) provides audiences with a strong impression of Frodo as a typical hobbit rather than the responsible Ringbearer he later becomes. During the night in Bree, while Nazgûl futilely attempt to find and kill the hobbits, Frodo sleeps soundly. Waking briefly after the thwarted Nazgûl shriek, he even smiles when he sees Strider on guard. He seems content to let Strider look out for him. Such an introduction helps audiences assume that Frodo (or hobbits) are childlike and less capable of dealing with violence. Another flaw with Bakshi's film is the inconsistent approach to dealing with hobbits, at one point making them seem in need of protection but in others giving them the ability to determine not only their fate, but that of others.

Although Bakshi's story often includes character-building details that keep characters like Merry closer in line with the original text, the film also offers contradictory characterisations that can confuse audiences. After Aragorn rebukes Frodo in the early part of their journey, the hobbit looks down and kicks at stones, much as a child would after being reprimanded by a parent. Soon after, however, Frodo puts on the Ring during the Nazgûl attack. When the wraiths see him, he throws off his cape, pulls his sword and attacks. This Frodo acts less fearful and childlike and more proactive and aware of danger. These contradictory images occurring in such short screen time negate any real character development and may leave audiences wondering which is the real Frodo (or questioning whether Bakshi is being inconsistent or merely trying to illustrate Frodo's rapid loss of innocence on the journey).

Even wounded by a Nazgûl's blade, Frodo manages to save himself by riding Asfaloth towards Rivendell. Although Legolas (not the book's Glorfindel) finds Aragorn and the hobbits in the wild, Frodo alone rides the horse, certainly a daunting feat for any hobbit, much less one seriously, possibly mortally, injured. The hobbit takes charge of the horse, too, instead of merely hanging on. Only after crossing the river and watching the wraiths on the opposite shore does Frodo sag in response to the Nazgûls' spell. 'Go back to the land of Mordor and follow me no more!' Frodo commands, even as he weakens. The obliging river rises, apparently because of Frodo's command, a significant change from Tolkien's, or even Jackson's, powerful elves who can command the water bordering Rivendell. In scenes like these, Frodo clearly is the lead character who often takes charge of a situation, even if it seems not only a departure from Tolkien's story but also against all logic.

Especially during his fight with and flight from the Nazgûl, Frodo becomes the master of his own fate, a pattern which continues through the Fellowship's journey into Moria. When Orcs learn of the Fellowship's presence and attempt to attack, Frodo runs to aid Boromir in slowing the Orcs' progress into the room where the Fellowship hides. Yelling 'For the Shire!' he reacts quickly when Boromir is knocked down. He stabs an Orc's foot, which forces the lead Orc's retreat and allows the Fellowship time to escape.

Once Gandalf falls (in this adaptation to a whip-wielding flying Balrog), Frodo despairs that there is no hope for their mission. Even so, the Ringbearer rallies in Lothlórien, where he practices sword fighting with Aragorn, even winning the mock battle. From that point, he never despairs, even when he becomes weary. He steadfastly holds to his course for Mordor.

Unlike other adaptations, notably Jackson's, in which Frodo looks noticeably weaker as his journey progresses, Bakshi's film provides minimal evidence of the toll the quest takes on the Ringbearer. After navigating the Dead Marshes, Frodo staggers and Sam supports him, asking Gollum to slow their pace. When Gollum offers to carry the Ring for Frodo, however, the hobbit rallies once more. He throws off Sam's supportive hand and, thunder rumbling ominously in the background, faces down the obsequious Gollum/Smeagol. The 'camera' pans up to provide Gollum's perspective of a commanding, powerful Frodo. Wise Frodo, his naivete about the Ring long gone, admonishes Gollum: 'Before you would ever touch the precious again, Smeagol, I would put it on and command you to leap off a cliff or into a fire, and you would do it.' In supplication and contrition, Gollum kisses Frodo's foot, but the hobbit disgustedly rubs away the 'kiss'.

Although Sam physically supports Frodo and looks after him by planning meals and conserving supplies, Bakshi's Frodo emotionally supports Sam, instead of vice versa. Sam often seems too simple-minded to understand the gravity of their situation, and Frodo tries to spare him from the knowledge that they likely will not survive the quest. He also does not know how to react to Frodo's praise; after Frodo calls him 'my dearest hobbit, friend of friend', Sam stands, rolls his eyes, whistles, paces and otherwise kills time until Gollum returns to lead them. In the audience's last view of Frodo, he is being supported by Sam and is following Gollum, a rather weak final depiction of an increasingly strong main character.

Frodo seems resilient against the Ring's evil, and highly self-motivated to complete the quest, especially after the Council of Elrond. As with most characters in this film, Frodo's role is not layered or complex but simplified and one-dimensional. In non-battle scenes, or even during small conflicts, Frodo acts as a dominant character of intelligence and perseverance. His sudden transformation from innocent, wide-eyed hobbit into determined Ringbearer indicates his acceptance of his mission and an innate, underlying strength. Only when the film shifts into full-on battle mode does Frodo retire from the film, leaving Aragorn and, ever more obvious, Gandalf to take the flashier role of action hero. Once again, men become the focus of action sequences that conclude an adaptation, thus leaving audiences with a final impression of Aragorn (and man-like wizard Gandalf) as leaders and heroes. Hobbits, whose story falls by the wayside in the Bakshi adaptation as much as in the earlier Rankin–Bass *RotK*, are not the last characters shown on screen and, therefore, their journey is given less overall importance in the story.

Sam

Throughout the 1970s, theatre and film audiences became familiar with the musical *Man of La Mancha*, Cervantes's story of Don Quixote and his faithful companion, Sancho Panza, on their quest. In 1972 the famed Richard Kiley-starring version graced Broadway, and a less successful 1977 film adaptation allowed a wider audience to see the musical.[18] Sancho, like Sam, loyally follows his master on a quest. However, he also provides the comic relief to a serious story. Bakshi's depiction of Sam is similar to that of the Sancho Panza popular at the time. Both characters are paunchy and uneducated, but Sancho seems to have a greater clue about the quest's dangers, and his humour is earthy but witty. Whether Bakshi consciously modelled Sam after Sancho or merely wanted to provide contrast between increasingly self-sufficient, determined Frodo, especially in the middle part of the film, the result is that Sam, more than the other hobbits, least resembles his book self.

He looks different, not only from men but also the other hobbits. He wears a long tunic instead of the shirt and vest over knee-length trousers the other hobbits wear. Shorter and broader than Frodo, Merry or Pippin, Sam reveals his emotions with equally broad gestures or expressions, rolling his eyes or huddling in fear. The excitable, occasionally lisping Sam acts nothing like a hero. His appearance and lack of growth during the course of the film clearly contrast with Frodo's looks and behaviour, making the latter seem even more traditionally heroic. In other adaptations, including Jackson's trilogy and the *LotR* musical, audiences often perceive Sam as one of the heroes, if not *the* hero, in the story; his will and love allow Frodo to reach Mount Doom. Bakshi's Sam does what seems to be his best, but he is consistently hampered by his innocence and lack of understanding about the quest's dangers.

Sam's status as Frodo's servant is never established, yet Sam seems 'inferior' and subservient to the other hobbits in every sense, from his less-than-handsome features to different style of dress to blissful lack of awareness. Sam always looks to Frodo's comfort, but when dangers arise, he runs to hide or cowers in fear. At first his motivation to accompany Frodo comes from a promised visit to the elves, and Sam does appear to be happy in Lothlórien, picking flowers, sniffing them, and tossing them into the air – certainly not the act of a loving gardener (but then, Bakshi's Sam is never identified as one).

On the road to Mordor, gullible Sam acts subservient even to Gollum. When the hobbit asks the long-absent Gollum where he has been, the treacherous guide lies that he has been looking for a secret passage while the hobbits slept and resents the implication that he would be untrustworthy. Sam immediately apologises for offending Gollum and does not consider that he may be lying or leading them into further danger. In this adaptation more than any other to date, Sam serves only as comic relief and a foil for heroic Frodo. Instead of being Frodo's companion and strength, Sam is reduced to a tagalong pack-hobbit.

Merry and Pippin

Gandalf introduces the audience to Merry and Pippin by suggesting that Frodo leave Bag End under the pretense of visiting his Bucklebury cousins. This change not only simplifies the story, including the intricate hobbit genealogies, but further binds Merry and Pippin as two of a kind, not only Frodo's kin but from the same geographic area. Thus, all differentiations between Brandybucks and Tooks are ignored in Bakshi's film.

Although much of the book's early action involving Frodo's preparations to leave the Shire is cut to move the story along, Merry's 'conspiracy unmasked' speech becomes an important piece of exposition in the Bakshi film. Merry explains why he, Pippin and Sam will stick by Frodo, no matter what. He even confides that he once saw Bilbo wear the Ring. Although Merry provides this explanation on the road soon after the hobbits leave the Shire (instead of during a farewell-to-Frodo dinner at Crickhollow, as in the book), this scene builds Merry's credibility and gives audiences more insight into his motivation for accompanying his cousin. After all, Frodo's earlier comment to Sam – 'Merry and Pippin insisted on coming with us as far as Bree' – gives no reason why Frodo's kin would want to come along. The portrayals of Merry and Pippin are wildly uneven in this film, but Merry's speech makes him seem more aware of the Ring and Frodo's mission than earlier scenes in which he and Pippin, happy to be following Frodo, play instruments, sing and dance along the road to Bree.

Bakshi's version of the Prancing Pony scenes also includes details usually omitted from other adaptations. While Frodo, Sam and Pippin enjoy the inn's hospitality, Merry leaves for a breath of air. Once outdoors, he encounters the Nazgûl and falls unconscious after his first confrontation with Evil. Bakshi illustrates the danger through the shadowy wraiths stalking Merry, who succumbs surrounded by an eerie fog. This sequence shows Merry as independent, rather than just part of the group, and also gives him the important role of telling Frodo about the Black Riders' arrival in Bree.

Soon after Strider introduces himself to the hobbits, Merry returns to the inn, Butterbur's servant having found him unconscious in the street. Merry's primary concern is to warn Frodo about the Black Riders; he does not seem as frightened for himself as for Frodo. Pippin, however, comforts both Merry and himself by embracing his cousin, and a frightened Sam soon huddles with them. Again, Bakshi's film provides contradictory images of the hobbits after their rather startling evening at the Prancing Pony. Although Merry is agitated and Pippin and Sam clearly frightened by the Nazgûls' presence, the little group sleeps peacefully under Strider's watchful eye, their earlier fear quickly forgotten. In Tolkien's 'Houses of Healing' chapter, Merry explains that hobbits try to make light of their troubles, but Bakshi's scene instead makes the hobbits seem oblivious to the dangers surrounding them.

Because Frodo's role is crucial to any adaptation of *LotR*, and Sam must be included because of his proximity to Frodo throughout the story, these two hobbits need to be emphasised. Depending upon their artistic preference and the amount of detail they can include in time-constricted stories, adaptors choose to eliminate many details in the development of Merry and Pippin. Usually these hobbits are not developed much or at all as characters, instead being relegated to a hobbit 'type' rather than being treated as individuals. That Merry, in particular, is given as much detail as these scenes from the Bakshi film illustrate is a point in Bakshi's favour, even if the amount of detail in later parts of the film is wildly uneven.

Merry and Pippin's friendship, well documented in Tolkien's book, is often shown in adaptations, including Bakshi's. It is a given rather than a topic explored, a characteristic taken from Tolkien's *LotR* and inserted without explanation. With few exceptions (for example, Merry being accosted by Black Riders in Bree), Merry and Pippin are inseparable during Bakshi's film. They enter the story together; they sit side by side in the moments before the Watcher in the Water grabs Frodo; they nap alongside each other in Lothlórien. They fight together as the Fellowship breaks, are captured by Orcs and escape together, and are last seen in Treebeard's grasp. In physical appearance the two also look similar, more like boys than young adult hobbits. Merry's hair is lighter than Pippin's, but the two dress similarly, and Merry seems no heavier than Pippin, in contrast to Tolkien's descriptions of the two.

Nevertheless, Merry and Pippin benefit from dialogue and actions that help distinguish them, even if their strong friendship is still their most important contribution to the story. Bakshi allows the younger hobbits the following distinctive moments appropriately drawn from

Tolkien's book. Merry explains the 'conspiracy' to Frodo, sees the Nazgûl and is overcome by their presence in Bree, jokes to Pippin about bed and breakfast after regaining consciousness in the Orcs' camp, and, once they escape from the Orcs, knows where they are, in Fangorn Forest, because he studied maps in Rivendell. Pippin has fewer scenes from the book, but he still throws a stone down the well in Moria and, when captured by Orcs, hints to Grishnakh that he knows where the Ring is, a ruse that Merry continues.

Other elements of the story are similar to Tolkien's, but changes were made to simplify the story for film. Aragorn finds Pippin's brooch embedded in the Orcs' trail and knows that the hobbits survived their capture. The brooch simply appears to have been lost; thus, in contrast to Tolkien's story, Pippin loses his status as a clever hobbit who deliberately breaks from the line of Orcs to drop the brooch in hopes Aragorn will find it.

When Pippin and Merry later escape the Orcs by running into Fangorn Forest, Bakshi's Pippin acts like a tired, dispirited child. He complains that they have no food, no idea where they are, and no plan for figuring out which way they should travel. His mood improves as he and Merry climb a small hill into the sunshine, and Pippin exclaims that he almost likes the place. Treebeard, overhearing this comment, appears before the hobbits, who embrace each other in fear. In the following scene, however, Treebeard has apparently won Pippin's friendship, because the hobbit chatters without taking a breath as he explains just what happened to him and Merry. In answer to Merry's question about Treebeard's allegiance, the Ent replies that he does not like Orcs, a fact that makes Pippin immensely happy. He gleefully claps, with Merry joining in.

Although Pippin displays moments of cleverness, he also immediately reverts to childlike behaviour. Bakshi's film tries to portray a youthful, playful hobbit out of his element by creating a boyish character who sings and dances, is comforted by Sam and Merry, grows weary of his 'adventure', but is ever open to accepting friendly new acquaintances, such as Treebeard. What provides a sharp contrast to this childlike portrayal is Tolkien's dialogue and character-building plot points that indicate how much Pippin matures during his journey. By occasionally giving Tolkien's dialogue to Pippin and thus aligning him more closely with Tolkien's depiction, Bakshi merely points out Pippin's jarring lack of character development in his own film.

Merry's portrayal is slightly better, allowing him more moments of maturity appropriate to his age and level of responsibility described in the book. He lightly rebukes Pippin for playing too much in Rivendell, whereas he has spent his time studying maps and gaining information for their journey. He directs Pippin in Fangorn and tries to figure out where they are. In these brief moments, Merry seems like more of a responsible leader (or older relative) than a hobbit in over his head.

Nevertheless, the pair are still shown as ineffectual warriors, most often because of their size. They kill several Orcs during their first real battle, but after Boromir has been shot with several arrows, the stunned hobbits stand behind their friend. After Boromir dies, they run forward and are immediately knocked out by the Orcs, who carry them on such a long run that the audience, as well as the troop, becomes weary of the scene. The hobbits never fight again in this movie; their last scene leaves them quite literally in Treebeard's capable 'hands', as the Ent carries them through the forest.

Although in some scenes Bakshi follows a pattern often established in adaptations of making Pippin and Merry seem especially childlike, the director does give each lines and moments from Tolkien's book that are often overlooked in other adaptations. These brief scenes help the audience distinguish between the two hobbits while understanding their close bond as cousins and friends. The roles of Merry and Pippin in *LotR* are typically and understandably truncated for film or stage, but Bakshi treats these characters fairly well, especially in comparison to the depiction of Sam. Merry and Pippin remind audiences of the importance of close friendships, especially during crises, and, at least in scenes taken more or less directly from Tolkien, illustrate the strength beneath the hobbits' soft exterior.

Bilbo

Although Bilbo quite rightly has a less important role in this *LotR* adaptation, his personality is clearly established through a few scenes, most notably his birthday party at the beginning of the film. Like Tolkien's original, this Bilbo gives the famous birthday speech that both praises and insults his guests. Bilbo makes a strong first impression; the attention-loving hobbit wears a white shirt, brown vest, brown trousers and a long brown coat. Although his attire defies Tolkien's idea that hobbits love colourful clothing, Bilbo's brown colour palette makes him both approachable and rustic. The Ring, rather than Bilbo, receives the greatest makeover. When Bilbo playfully slips on the Ring to become invisible and disappear from his party, Bakshi makes it sparkle and immediately shows Bilbo back in Bag End, laughing over his guests' surprise. The combined change of scene and 'magic' effect make Bilbo seem transported from the party to his home, a feat of true magic that gives the Ring a more playful, rather than menacing, quality.

In Rivendell, Bilbo tells a story to the elves in Elrond's hall. He looks the same as in the birthday scene; his brown hair has refused to grey even though the narrator explains that more than 17 years have passed from the time of the birthday party until Frodo's departure from the Shire. Clearly Bilbo is at home in Rivendell, and his frequent comments about writing a book and his depiction as a storyteller separate him from other hobbits.

Bilbo accompanies Frodo to the Council of Elrond and even volunteers to take the Ring to Mordor. He calls himself the 'silly hobbit' who found the Ring and thus should be the one to destroy it. When Gandalf squelches this plan by telling Bilbo that his role in the saga is over, Frodo next volunteers to carry the Ring.

For all the implied affection between Bilbo and Frodo (for example, Bilbo helps ensure Frodo's safety by giving him his prized possessions, a mithril shirt and Sting), the elder hobbit fails to embrace Frodo as he leaves on his journey. Instead, Bilbo turns away. Perhaps this scene is meant to indicate that he cannot bear to watch Frodo go, but it fails to provide the expected emotional impact of a possible final farewell between surrogate father and son. This is the last time audiences see Bilbo, because Bakshi's film ends with the victory at Helm's Deep and thus deprives audiences of a Bilbo–Frodo reunion.

Because Bilbo is a peripheral character in *LotR*, already having completed his most important task of finding the Ring and leaving it for Frodo, his one-dimensional characterisation in this film is not surprising. Although he becomes angered when Gandalf asks him to leave the Ring for Frodo, Bilbo shows little emotion in other scenes. Instead, he becomes relegated to the role of kindly, eccentric uncle, one who comes and goes as he pleases, a storyteller and likeable traveller who remains apart from hobbit society and lives by his own rules. He seems less connected to Frodo, either by blood or shared interests, than in other adaptations but, because he contrasts with 'typical' hobbits, broadens audiences' perceptions of who and what hobbits can be.

* * *

Unlike other, later adaptations, Bakshi's film incorporates often-edited dialogue or scenes from Tolkien's book that help Frodo, Merry and Pippin at least occasionally to act like their literary counterparts. Sam suffers the most in this adaptation, not only as a weak character within the Bakshi version but in comparison with Tolkien's vision of him. Sam is almost embarrassing in his naiveté. Audiences who only know *LotR* from this adaptation may think of hobbits as childlike beings who often need the protection of humans (or elves or a wizard). The idea of hobbits as uncomplicated 'children' is further strengthened by the film's final emphasis on the battle for Helm's Deep; no hobbit fights in this battle, and the hobbits' individual stories end without resolution.

Bakshi's hobbits represent only one part of his *LotR* story – the quest to destroy the Ring. Aragorn's and Gandalf's epic battle against the Orcs at Helm's Deep concludes the film; they, not Frodo, save Middle-earth by fighting one great battle. The need to destroy the Ring in order to end the threat of Sauron's domination is ignored.

Granted, a planned second film would likely have restored Frodo's importance to the story, but the abrupt ending after a great battle ultimately renders Aragorn and Gandalf more significant characters.

One Adaptation to Rule Them All:
Peter Jackson's *LotR* Trilogy

Although Peter Jackson's cinematic adaptation of *LotR* earned more than $3.6 billion (US) (all three films combined in first-run worldwide release),[19] as well as winning 17 Academy Awards (4 for *FotR*, 2 for *TT*, 11, including Best Picture, for *RotK*) and 9 BAFTAs (3 for *FotR*, 2 for *TT*, 4 for *RotK*), the monetary and critical acclaim are not the trilogy's greatest feat, at least to *LotR* fandom.

Because the trilogy became so popular globally and gained so much press as each film was released, between 2001 and 2003, audiences who only know Jackson's version of the story will likely think of these films, not Tolkien's book, as 'their *LotR*'. In 2005, costumed fans dressing as hobbits created their hobbit finery based on visuals from Jackson's films more than Tolkien's book or other adaptations.[20] Honorary 'hobbits' who love the movies may never read the book, although a surprising number do. Nevertheless, the visuals supplied by Jackson's films provide a clear blueprint for fan-created costumes.

Do Film Fans Still Read *LotR*?

To satisfy my curiosity about film fans' interests compared with those of long-time Tolkien fans, I conducted an online survey in 2007. The majority of the 1171 people who responded to a question about reading *LotR* had read the book at least once. Although 52 percent had read the book more than five times, 85 percent had seen the films five or more times. The films seem to be the more popular way to 'experience' *LotR*, according to these fans' responses. Only 1 percent admitted they had never read *LotR*, 10.7 percent had read the book once, and 36 percent had read it two or three times.

When asked how recently they had read Tolkien's book, 40 percent (of 1159 people answering this question) reported they had read *LotR* within the past year, and another 40 percent had read it more than a year ago but within five years. An interesting finding is that nearly 90 percent of those who had read the book wrote that it was as important to them today as it was when they first read it, and 96 percent expected to read the book again. Those comments certainly indicate that Tolkien fans continue to enjoy the book, even when adaptations like Jackson's are readily available.

More fans, however, watched the films multiple times than read the book more than five times. Fewer than 1 percent of people who responded to the survey saw the films only on their initial release; 57 percent wrote they had watched the trilogy within the past year, with another 34 percent reporting they had seen the movies within the past month. Of the people who had seen the films at least once, 98 percent added that they plan to watch the trilogy yet again.

A majority (80 percent) of fans answering a question about the continuing importance of Jackson's films reported that the trilogy was as important then (when they answered the question in 2007) as when they first saw the movies, 2001–3. If the number of films released each year, or even the number of 'event' or blockbuster films, is considered, *LotR* fans have a long cinematic memory and loyalty to the trilogy.

Although the information from more than a thousand people cannot be truly representative of the thousands of *LotR* fans worldwide, these results indicate that audience interest in the films a few years after their release continued to be high, and people who consider themselves true *LotR* fans typically watch the movies again and again. Nevertheless, Tolkien's book has not been forgotten. An encouraging number of moviegoers also read the book.

A Flawed Gem of an Adaptation

Jackson's *LotR*, especially in hindsight and after multiple viewings on screens large and small, tends to produce similar criticisms among long-time Tolkien fans, in regards to hobbits: problematic ages of the hobbits; creative license taken with characterisations; increased importance of Sam and Pippin, at the expense of Frodo and Merry; change from a hobbitcentric story to a mancentric story; emphasis on battles to overcome Evil.

Jackson, as director, writer and executive producer, needed to move the films along at a brisk enough pace to keep audiences' notoriously short attention spans focused on the story. He also needed to make the 'hero' characters lovable enough that the audience would root for them.

As a filmmaker, Jackson pioneered new techniques, and Wellington, New Zealand-based Weta Workshop would soon be recognised worldwide for its special effects and creative creatures. Its creative geniuses, under the direction of Richard Taylor, found innovative solutions to technical challenges, enabling the *LotR* trilogy to go technically where no films had gone before.

Considering *LotR*'s many cinematic achievements and innovations, critics grousing about character development or the low number of quiet moments in more than ten hours of screen time may seem uncharitable. However, one of Tolkien's strengths in *LotR* is the structured development of characters representing many races of Middle-earth. In particular, the hobbits are described in loving detail and, even in the case of often-mistaken-for-each-other Merry and Pippin, are developed slowly and carefully. Although Jackson and company took great pains with details – and, indeed, their adaptation is richly crafted and carefully designed – some hobbits receive more screen time and attention in the story than others; some visual details or performances bring out different qualities than those emphasised in Tolkien's original. Those differences irritate long-time book fans who know almost everything about Tolkien's characters.

Problematic Ages

The hobbits of the Fellowship in Jackson's films seem to be about the same age, not the range of 28–50 hobbit years specified by Tolkien. Even accounting for differences between men and hobbits,

Frodo, Sam, Merry and Pippin all look to be about the same age. If anything, Frodo, played by then-teenager Elijah Wood, looks even younger than could be reasonably attributed to the Ring's youth-giving powers. In fact, the youngest hobbit, Pippin, is portrayed by the oldest actor, Billy Boyd, who, although in his early thirties at the time, easily could pass for a much younger man.

Frodo's youth gives him a more fragile quality throughout the films; he truly seems to need stout Sam's assistance once the hobbits leave Rivendell. Even when the weary Frodo returns to the Shire, he seems not to have physically aged all that much. His demeanour, rather than his physical appearance, changes most. The Frodo preparing to leave the Shire seems worn down by his 'adventure' and only regains his apple-cheeked vigour once he steps onto the ship leaving for Valinor.

Keeping Merry and Pippin about the same age helps emphasise their forced maturity, especially once they are separated during *The Two Towers* and face battle as the lone hobbits in their respective armies. In Tolkien's book, Merry is a young adult, having come of age five years before the quest begins; only Pippin is underaged. On screen, however, when the time period between Bilbo's birthday party and Frodo's departure with the Ring is a matter of days, not years, only a very young Merry could get away with his antics; a mature hobbit could not reasonably be seen raiding farms or stealing fireworks, unless he was more of a public nuisance or deviant than a prankster.

Sam, although in Tolkien's story much closer in age to Merry than to middle-aged Frodo, needs to be about the same age as Frodo on screen if their close friendship is to seem plausible to modern movie audiences. Instead of a strict master–servant relationship, Frodo treats Sam as a best friend who just happens to be his gardener. Jackson only emphasises Sam's role as gardener a few times in the films: in *FotR*, when Gandalf catches him eavesdropping outside Bag End's open window, and in *TT*, when Faramir asks if Sam is Frodo's bodyguard, and Sam explains that he is the gardener. Audiences accustomed to seeing 'buddy' movies – or those who read a homosexual subtext into the Frodo–Sam dynamic – are likely to enjoy and understand Frodo's and Sam's friendship much more if the two hobbits seem close in age.

Character Differences from the Book

Early in *FotR*, Merry and Pippin act like carefree pranksters, and Tolkien fans might question Merry being defined as 'carefree' in the book. On the screen, the inseparable duo absconds with and then sets off fireworks, as well as steals crops (apparently a common pastime). Pippin's curiosity seems innocent enough, whether in touching the skeleton balanced atop a Moria well or taking a quick peek in the palantir, although at times he seems less curious than overly naive/ sheltered or even silly. Still, Pippin might be seen as more of an innocent young hobbit by his early actions, a characterisation that quickly gives way to the more responsible wartime Pippin in *TT* and *RotK*. By the third film, Pippin has been given much more to do, not only in the trilogy but in addition to key actions taken from the book. He lights the tower beacon in Minas Tirith, actively helps rescue Faramir from a burning pyre, and even saves Gandalf from an Orc determined to stab the wizard. He sings for Denethor – and the audience – a haunting song played over Faramir's charge against the forces in Osgiliath. This song gave Billy Boyd a chance to showcase his talent as a singer and songwriter; he composed the tune used in the film.

In *FotR*, some critics, even fellow hobbit Sean (Sam) Astin, found Merry too 'leprechaunish' instead of 'hobbity'. At times, Merry's crinkling eyes when he smiles and the lilting cadence of his speech do seem more Irish leprechaun than English hobbit. This image is further strengthened at the Council of Elrond when Merry and Pippin pop from their hiding places and frantically scramble to join the newly formed Fellowship,[21] and, in Edoras, when a distraught Merry cries out and leaps away from the rolling palantir's path. Merry's accent and demeanour were sometimes called into question by fans and critics alike; one comic joked about the hobbits' accents, commenting about Frodo's and Sam's obvious regional English accents and Pippin's Scottish accent before laughing about Merry's 'whatever the hell it is accent'.[22] (Merry lacked the Mancunian accent Monaghan would have grown up hearing.) Critics more often wondered why Pippin clearly sounds Scottish;

Jackson determined that the Scottish Boyd need not develop a different accent for Pippin.[23]

Both Merry and Pippin are used as comic relief, as they often are in adaptations, to offset the serious nature of Frodo's journey. Although the increasingly serious tone of the film makes the broader humour of early scenes in *FotR* less appropriate as the story progresses, the balance between Merry and Pippin, developed so carefully in the book, is destroyed in Jackson's trilogy. Pippin receives much more on-screen attention, whether in scenes with Gandalf or Denethor. Although Merry's heroic action of helping Éowyn slay the Witch King is preserved on film, many of the more thoughtful moments – ones which better represent the book character – are relegated to the extended DVD sets.

In one scene reinstated for the extended DVD version, Merry thoughtfully explains to Éowyn why he wants to go to war, something very unhobbitlike.[24] His voice and facial expressions change slightly as he mentions in turn Frodo, Sam and Pippin, creating a wonderfully 'Merry' moment that resonates with the book and reminds audiences that, for all the action sequences about to come, this hobbit only chooses to become a soldier in the hopes that he may somehow help and be reunited with his kin and friends.

In Jackson's trilogy, Tolkien's responsible, thoughtful, more cerebral Merry is supplanted by a hobbit apparently with too much time on his hands in the Shire and makes good out in the larger world. Many of the best scenes from the book involving Merry's maturation – including his friendship with Théoden, healing after the Battle of the Pelennor Fields, and leadership during the scouring of the Shire – have been omitted from the films, but even so, Dominic Monaghan, with a few speeches (for example, at the Ent Moot, with Éowyn before battle), gives Merry more depth in the few quiet moments allowed him.

Poor Sam also has to overcome the comic-relief stigma early in *FotR* before he is allowed to become the ever-loyal, practical, loving caretaker who ensures Frodo arrives at Mount Doom. Not only was Astin's portrayal praised (with fans telling the actor he had been robbed of an Oscar),[25] but the way devoted Sam perseveres against all obstacles makes him a character audiences can root for. Many fans believe that Sam is the true hero of this adaptation, and Astin's emotion-laden performance makes audiences want to identify with Sam throughout the trilogy. His dedication not only to Frodo but to the quest never wavers, despite some additional hardships that Jackson loads in his already-full pack.

For one, Jackson insisted that Astin gain weight to achieve Sam's 'roundness', which not only made the actor feel self-conscious as the pounds piled on, but also made him feel more like silly comic relief. In some scenes, such as when Gandalf catches Sam eavesdropping outside Bag End, the hobbit's common sense, a trait Tolkien emphasised in the book, seems to have been left outside when Gandalf hauls him through the window. Superstitious Sam, who begs Gandalf not to turn him into 'something unnatural',[26] is fortunately left behind in the Shire once the journey begins, but the characterisation of this important hobbit is noticeably sillier early in the trilogy.

Sam also suffers as a character – as does Frodo – by one plot deviation deemed necessary for dramatic conflict. In *TT*, Sam attacks Gollum, who successfully manages to make Sam look like a liar and a thief. Frodo then banishes his friend, who tearfully turns back towards home. Once Sam leaves, of course, Gollum takes Frodo to visit Shelob – and paves the way for Sam to make a grand entrance to save Frodo. The audience never doubts Sam's loyalty to Frodo, but with this newly scripted change to the story, Frodo seems a fool to listen to Gollum rather than his long-time friend. At least Sam is redeemed throughout *RotK*, shining not only as a determined hobbit hero but, by the end of the film, the most responsible hobbit of his generation, one well suited, as his finery in the last scenes reveals, to take his place as a common hobbit elevated to greatness.

Frodo not only seems young – certainly much younger than the middle-aged character of Tolkien's book – but often he is out of his depth. He tries to follow Gandalf's instructions and arrives at the Prancing Pony to meet the wizard, only to learn that he is nowhere to be found. When Pippin inadvertently reveals Frodo's identity and points him out to men surrounding the bar, Frodo rushes to quiet him. In the process, he slips, falls, tosses the Ring in the air, and disappears when the Ring lands on his finger. The image of the Ring slipping onto Frodo's finger, shown as if from above the Ring looking down towards the hobbit, became a wonderful promotional illustration, but it did little to enhance Frodo's stature as a Ringbearer.

A sombre but unlucky Frodo is very different from Tolkien's depiction of a rowdier, more extroverted Frodo-of-the-Shire who diverts attention from Pippin's gaffe by singing and dancing on the table. Other adaptations, including the *LotR* musical, feature a singing, dancing Frodo, full of life and quite entertaining. In Jackson's adaptation, Strider quickly manhandles Frodo away from the astonished patrons and into a room where he severely questions the hobbit's assessment of the seriousness of his mission. The other hobbits, armed with whatever they can grab, burst into the room to defend or free Frodo. Although more serious in this adaptation – at least after Bilbo's party – Frodo clearly needs help in defending himself against threats ranging from Strider to Black Riders to the Watcher in the Water to Gollum. He needs his companions not only to bolster him emotionally but physically.

Frodo's prankishness or youthful foibles are missing from Jackson's adaptation, which is not surprising, given the need to shorten the story, including characters' backstories. Frodo's fear of Farmer Maggot's dogs – a fear generated after the young hobbit got caught raiding the farmer's fields – would only add distracting details to the first film. The antics of young Frodo and his playful nature early in the book's journey (for example, the Prancing Pony song and dance) instead become aspects of Merry's and Pippin's scenes before they leave the Shire. They, not Frodo, raid Farmer Maggot's crops; they display much more lighthearted behaviour throughout *FotR*.

As the film progresses, Frodo changes both through prolonged exposure to the Ring and from his greater understanding of the world, as revealed through his association with Gandalf and Aragorn. Both characters guide Frodo, Gandalf with words of wisdom and Aragorn with stern fatherly care. Film Frodo is a gentle soul forced to endure more than he ever could have anticipated; when the eagles bear him from the lava flow of what was Mount Doom, he assumes a Christ-like pose of supplication. The film fades to white, enhancing the symbolism of Frodo as a sacrificial hero who, although ultimately not the one to dispose of the Ring, carries the burden for all of Middle-earth until the Ring can be destroyed. Wood's Frodo is a hobbit accepting a burden he is incapable of bearing without great pain that never goes away. Without the aid of the entire Fellowship, especially Gandalf, Aragorn and Sam, Frodo would never have completed the journey to Mount Doom.

Jackson's version of Frodo is certainly appealing, not the least for the wide-eyed sincerity provided by Wood. Frodo is attractive (a plus for a film hero), intelligent and sincere; he is a hobbit worth audiences' attention. With the time afforded by the cinematic trilogy, Frodo's gradual decline under the Ring's evil influence is much more believable than that in other adaptations, such as the Bakshi film. Jackson's Frodo gradually grows weaker and more hostile, his appearance more unkempt and his mannerisms more desperate as the trilogy progresses. Although the symbolism of the scene when he is removed from the remnants of Mount Doom may stretch the Frodo-as-martyr metaphor a bit far, audiences can understand the depth of Frodo's sacrifice and his later inability to find complete healing back in the Shire. Unlike other adaptations (in any medium), the Frodo developed throughout this cinematic trilogy well represents hobbits and illustrates, as Tolkien wrote, the Ring's pervasive evil. The transformation of Frodo is one of the strengths of the Jackson adaptation, and Wood's skill as an actor makes Frodo both an endearing and a haunting character.

An even better indication of the Ring's enduring power over the psyche – so much so that it can effect a physical transformation seemingly at will – is found in Ian Holm's portrayal of Bilbo. The jolly, jaunty Bilbo leaving the Shire after his birthday party gradually morphs into a rapidly aging hobbit who regrets placing the burden of the Ring on his beloved heir, Frodo. The Ring has left its mark on Bilbo, its former keeper but not frequent wearer. In Rivendell, when Bilbo outfits Frodo in a mithril shirt, he spies the Ring and asks to hold it once more. Frodo refuses, and Jackson emphasises the Ring's power by transforming Bilbo into a hideous monster, with bulging eyes and demonic mouth. Holm adds a garish snarl to the scene, but the power of the moment comes not with the surprise special effect but Bilbo's reaction to this outburst. Holm's Bilbo recoils and begins to sob in apology for ever finding the Ring, much less gifting it to Frodo. Although Frodo's physical transformation throughout the trilogy clearly illustrates the Ring's gathering strength over the hobbit's body and mind, Holm's transformation in Rivendell even more spectacularly explains the power of the One Ring.

The Rise of Sam and Pippin

In Jackson's adaptation, two hobbits perhaps surprisingly become more elevated in status than in previous television or film adaptations. Sam and Pippin, once they leave behind their comedic antics in *FotR*, develop into more important characters with distinctive personalities, a different approach than that taken by Rankin–Bass or Bakshi.

Sam becomes such a strong lead character that many hobbit fans feel *LotR* becomes Sam's story, rather than Frodo's or Aragorn's. In my *LotR* poll during summer 2007, 10 percent of the 1218 people who chose a favourite character from Jackson's adaptation selected Sam. Considering the huge cast in the trilogy, this percentage is high for a single character. Only 1.6 percent of the 1017 people selecting a least favourite character selected Sam. Those who disliked movie Sam found him too emotional, too tearful when rejected by Frodo, or too emotive when carrying Frodo up Mount Doom – an emotional high point punctuated by crescendoing strings.[27]

Frodo was only slightly more popular with fans as 'favourite character', receiving 11 percent of the votes (to Sam's 10 percent), but he was also less popular with fans who voted in the 'least favourite' category, where Frodo was chosen by 3 percent (to Sam's 1.6 percent). In Jackson's adaptation, the Frodo–Sam dynamic is crucial to the film's dramatic success, but, as in the other hobbit pairing of Merry–Pippin, one hobbit often gains strength at the expense of another.

Frodo physically grows weaker and, realistically, questions whether he will be able to complete the quest. In *TT*, a temporarily crazed Frodo offers the Ring to the Nazgûl attacking Faramir's defences; after Sam tackles Frodo moments before the Nazgûl can clasp his prize, the Ringbearer threatens Sam with his sword. Only upon recovering his senses at Sam's tearful 'Don't you know your Sam?' does Frodo drop Sting in horror, saying, 'I can't do this any more, Sam.' Ever-resilient Sam helps Frodo get back on his feet and provides a sound moral reason why they have to go on, 'because there's good in this world, and it's worth fighting for'.[28] Every time Frodo falls, physically or emotionally, Sam is there to pick him up.

Nowhere is this more evident than in the climactic moment above the fires of Mount Doom when Frodo, bereft of the Ring, hangs by his fingertips on the precipice. Frodo's weary face expresses anguish at his desire to keep the Ring as well as the conflicting relief and remorse at its destruction. Frodo looks as if he would rather just let go. Sam, however, refuses to surrender Frodo to a fiery death. He leans as far as possible to reach Frodo, commanding 'Don't you dare let go! Reach!'[29] Frodo obediently makes the extra effort and clasps Sam's hand.

This scene parallels another life-saving scene between the pair. Towards the end of *FotR*, Sam stubbornly marches after Frodo's departing boat, although he knows he cannot swim. A drowning Sam is saved when Frodo reaches into the water to grab his hand and haul him into the boat. Clasped hands visually symbolise Frodo and Sam's unity and bond, and Jackson emphasises this relationship in both scenes. In *FotR*, blue (water) colours the scene as the camera focuses on the reaching hands that eventually meet and grasp. Frodo literally has the upper hand, and his cooler persona is well represented by the watery blue tint. In *RotK*, red (fire) colours the scene as Sam reaches for Frodo's bloodied, maimed hand. The hotter colour scheme well reflects Sam's emotional, impassioned nature, as well as his fear and anger that Frodo might simply give up. In this scene, Sam's hand is above, Frodo's below; the two have reversed their positions of strength by this point in the film. The 'lesser' – in status, confidence and experience – becomes the 'greater' – or more influential and powerful, by the trilogy's final scenes.

Back in the Shire a few years later, when Sam visits Frodo in his Bag End study, the role reversal seems complete. Sam wears gentrified clothes and returns a book; Frodo has finished writing his part of the story in the Red Book and turns the project over to Sam, who by now seems Frodo's true equal, ready to 'replace' Frodo in the Shire. In Jackson's trilogy, the returned Sam is not shown at work in a garden; because the Shire escaped Saruman's influence and never needed to be 'scoured', Sam is not needed to replant the Shire (with lush vegetation, including a Mallorn tree, or repopulate it with his children). The role of gardener gives way to new-gentry Sam. He is a gentleman, complete with happy home, wife and two children. Jackson's Sam does not get his hands dirty upon returning to the Shire and has become a 'replacement' for his soon-to-depart master, Frodo.

In a similar way, but befitting their reduced roles in the films, Pippin switches places with Merry as the 'stronger' hobbit, although their post-war roles in the Shire once again seem equal (that is, they leave together after Frodo departs the Grey Havens). Merry's role as Pippin's caretaker ends when Gandalf takes palantir-pilfering Pippin to Minas Tirith. There, as previously mentioned, the youngest hobbit is featured in several scenes that build his character and indicate his newfound maturity and responsibility. Pippin's pledge of service to Denethor becomes two major scenes; Merry's to Théoden is cut from the film. Although Merry's role in killing the Witch King is shown, Éowyn's actions are emphasised during the scene, and she has an emotional scene with the dying Théoden (a role given to Merry in the book). Pippin the troll killer is not part of Jackson's *RotK*, but neither is his wounding in battle. Whereas Merry is incapacitated after striking the Witch King and likely would have succumbed on the battlefield had Pippin not found him, Pippin grows stronger from his battlefield experiences and learns to overcome his fear in order to fight on behalf of others.

Astin posits that Jackson respected Boyd's 'admirable and palpable commitment to acting' and wanted him 'to shine in the movie because of it'.[30] Perhaps Pippin's expanded role in the films helped make him, rather than Merry, more of a favourite among hobbit fans. Pippin received 6 percent of 1218 'favourite character' votes in my online survey, whereas Merry received only 2.5 percent. The two were seldom chosen as 'least favourite' characters (fewer than 1 percent each of the total votes in that category). Although the four hobbits of the Fellowship each receive scenes in which they individually shine, Sam and Pippin benefit most from their featured scenes in this adaptation.

The Mancentric Story

Jackson explained to biographer Brian Sibley that 'We knew that we were going to represent the fundamental story – "Hobbit goes on a journey to destroy the ring!"' and the writers' strategy was

> keeping a relationship between Frodo and the Ring, keeping the events totally focused on the forward movement of the journey...Every step of the way, in the movie, Frodo is encountering complications and obstacles but nonetheless it's always a forward movement; it's a story about a hobbit with a ring and the need to destroy it.[31]

Nevertheless, many critics and Tolkien fans felt that, instead of *LotR* as the story of Frodo's journey to destroy the One Ring, emphasising hobbits more than any other race, much of Jackson's story revolves around Strider the ranger, Aragorn the Fellowship's leader and eventual commander of all armies of men, and Elessar, the returned king.

Although Jackson's trilogy appropriately begins and ends in the Shire, many critics and fans feel that too much emphasis is placed on battles between that beginning and end, rendering *LotR* more of a 'war story' than Tolkien intended. Because much of *TT* and *RotK* revolves around battle scenes (Helm's Deep, Pelennor Fields, Black Gate), Aragorn as warrior and commander plays the major role in both films. *RotK*, in effect, ends with the new king's coronation and reunion with true love Arwen; the final 'hobbit' scenes *sans* the leading man feel tacked on, almost as afterthoughts for those who want to know what happened to Frodo and the other hobbits. Because the latter two films' action often centres on battle heroics, the hobbits (even Frodo and Sam) are often off screen for long periods of time.

In addition to his wartime heroism, Aragorn shines as a romantic interest for woman and elf. Éowyn becomes immediately smitten with him. (The number of suitable suitors in Rohan is, admittedly, limited, and finding a hero to take her away from her doddering uncle and his creepy advisor, Wormtongue, seems like a good idea, no matter who turns up at the gate.) Ever the gentleman, however, Aragorn tries to let Éowyn down gently; he is, after all, a one-elf man. In Jackson's adaptation, the romance between Aragorn and Arwen leaps from Tolkien's Appendix C into a full-fledged love story, complete with whispered pledges of devotion and passionate kisses.

Throughout Jackson's trilogy, Aragorn doubts his ability to overcome his flawed heritage (his ancestor, Isildur, decided to keep the Ring, after all) so that he may help destroy the One Ring and defeat Sauron. Arwen frequently reminds him that he is his own man, not merely a lesser copy of his ancestors, and the love relationship between elf and man often motivates Aragorn to keep fighting in spite of self-doubt. In Jackson's adaptation, Arwen's fate is tied to that of the Ring, and as the Ring grows stronger, Arwen grows weaker. To save her, much less to win her as his bride, Aragorn must overcome overwhelming odds to defeat the armies of Mordor.

Although Tolkien also chose Aragorn as *the* hero of *LotR*, Jackson increases the emphasis on Aragorn at the expense of other characters' development. Of course, to make the trilogy more marketable to men and women, young and old, Aragorn must be portrayed as a manly action hero and a sensitive love interest. Combining gory battles with tender love scenes provides something for everyone.

LotR as Action Film

Tolkien's book reminds readers that Evil cannot be vanquished once and for all; it will return at some point. The War of the Ring has vanquished Sauron, but it has not safeguarded Middle-earth for all time. Nevertheless, after the war, life goes on – Middle-earth does not remain in a state of siege, and what was destroyed is largely rebuilt or replanted, a task at which the hobbits of the Shire excel.

Unlike Tolkien's book, in which several chapters remain after the Battle Before the Black Gate, Jackson's story dramatically peaks with the Ring's destruction and the resulting pyrotechnics that signal on screen the demise of Sauron's power. Sauron's fortress falls, the great eye disintegrating in front of the battling armies. A gigantic shockwave halts the battle, and the earth cracks open. Sauron's soldiers flee, and the members of the Fellowship cheer, only to watch in horror as the volcano of Mount Doom explodes. The camera focuses on Merry's and Pippin's shocked and tearful faces as they realise that Frodo and Sam are likely at the heart of that volcano, and the next scenes show how the eagles rescue Frodo and Sam. After that climactic rescue, the 'happy endings' commence, but they merely tie up the loose ends from the three films. War is emphasised most often on screen; the triumph of Good over Evil brings the main action to a close.

Tolkien, however, wrote a very different progression leading to the end of the story. A book can tell the story in whatever length the author chooses; Jackson did not have that luxury and, understandably, cut back the story to its key parts. Although fans have debated the director's wisdom in leaving the Shire unscoured (in Jackson's *RotK* there is no need, because the Shire remains untouched during warfare elsewhere in Middle-earth), having a for-hobbits-only battle after concluding massive battle scenes before Aragorn's coronation would be tantamount to 'restarting' the action, instead of letting the story wind down towards the emotional Grey Havens scene. To his credit, Jackson's final scene in the entire trilogy is Sam's return home to Rosie and babies Elanor and Frodo-lad; the book's final line, 'Well, I'm back,' becomes the final line of the films. Jackson's trilogy begins and ends with the hobbits living peacefully in the Shire.

Tolkien's book emphasises hobbits after the War of the Ring. The long journey back from Gondor, where Aragorn/Elessar and Arwen will rule, involves a series of leave-takings as the non-hobbit members of the Fellowship begin the rest of their lives. Along the way, each hobbit receives accolades. Pippin and Merry serve their kings during the feast to honour Frodo and Sam and have sworn allegiance to Gondor and Rohan, respectively. All are honoured in Minas Tirith, where the hobbits share a house with Gandalf in the days leading to Aragorn's coronation and wedding. Merry receives recognition as Holdwine, the friend of the Rohirrim, as well as gifts from new king Éomer. By the time the hobbits return to the Shire, they have matured as worldly leaders, capable of looking after the Shire themselves instead of relying on others to protect their borders.

What the returning hobbits discover, however, is far from a peaceful homecoming. Friends and kin remain in lockholes built and wardened by men; industrialisation ruins the Shire's lush beauty; hobbits turned out of their homes seek shelter and food where they can. Within a short time, however, Merry and Pippin muster and lead the hobbit militia, Sam explains (as much as necessary) what they have done while away from the Shire and helps prepare his friends for the coming confrontation, and Frodo seeks mercy even for those who persecuted hobbits. War and destruction touch even the once-peaceful Shire, and the returning Travellers must 'scour' all ravages wrought by men – even to the point of, with King Elessar's decree, making the Shire off limits to any but hobbits.

Succeeding chapters detail the hobbits' lives in the months after their return, leading to Sam's marriage to Rosie, Frodo's brief stint as mayor before gradually retiring from hobbit society, Frodo's increasingly serious illnesses, and his and Bilbo's final departure from the Shire. Although other characters make brief appearances in the book's final chapters, Tolkien's emphasis is clearly on the hobbits, as well as the theme that life goes on. The appendices, which document not only the ages leading to the War of the Ring but the following Fourth Age of Men, provide the answer to readers' questions about what happened to the Fellowship long after the Ring has been destroyed.

A film cannot easily cover all that territory, but by shortening the story to emphasise action over quiet moments, battles over the return to peace, and the actions of men over those of hobbits, Jackson's adaptation changes the focus of the story and leaves movie fans who have not read the book with the impression that *LotR* is more heavily weighted as only a War of the Ring story. The shortened story also culminates in a happier conclusion that, because the Evil Eye has been destroyed, all is well. Tolkien more realistically indicates the fluctuations in power between Good and Evil and indicates that hobbits, as well as everyone else in Middle-earth, will likely have to face future struggles. Whereas Tolkien's prose provides a more realistic assessment of Middle-earth's future, that theme would seem too depressing for a blockbuster film's happy (in the case of Aragorn and Arwen) or poignant (in the case of Frodo) endings.

Script Changes Before Filming

Of course, the script eventually shot on film differed greatly from the initial outline and treatment submitted to studios in order to gain their backing, and numerous other rewrites took place even when a basic script was in place. The final filmed version also went through numerous stages along the way that would have resulted in a very different trilogy. At one point, Gandalf catches Merry and Pippin, along with Sam, as they eavesdropped outside Bag End;[32] Farmer Maggot, Glorfindel and Radagast the Brown still appear in the script; Bilbo joins Frodo at the Council of Elrond; and Sam also looks into Galadriel's mirror,[33] all scenes considerably changed before they were filmed.

Some characters revealed considerably different personalities as the scripts were revised. Pippin's lack of self-censorship became an even more important character trait. To make the plot twist of Faramir finding Frodo and Sam in Ithilien not a providential event but the result of Denethor's command to his son to find the hobbits, someone would need to leak information about Frodo's and Sam's mission. In one script, Pippin received this dialogue: 'Gandalf would kill me if I said anything. Look, it's not that I don't trust you... it's just that... it's big stuff! Middle-earth, the Dark Lord, the whole works! And I promised Gandalf that I wouldn't let anything slip; if there's one thing I'm good at it's keeping secrets.'[34] Not only does this dialogue sound far more modern than the tone of dialogue in the resulting film, but the content makes Pippin seem as frivolous as the Rankin–Bass Pippin in the animated *RotK*. This depiction certainly does not match the finished films' portrayal (especially in the later scenes of *TT* or *RotK*) of a mature Pippin who quite capably takes on responsibilities and to whom 'keeping a secret' would not turn out to be a joke.

Instead of early dialogue, the filmed *RotK* scene of Gandalf arriving with Pippin in Minas Tirith provides Gandalf with the opportunity to warn Pippin that it would be better for him simply to listen and not talk during the wizard's discussions with Denethor. A subdued Pippin merely nods his assent and, although still impetuous in offering to serve Denethor, his rash actions emphasise his desire to help (and to repay Denethor for the sacrifice of Boromir). They are not an idle slip of the tongue or an inability to keep a secret. The Minas Tirith scene thus becomes a turning point in Pippin's determination to help fight the good fight, rather than accidentally to threaten the Fellowship's collective mission.

Not only did the hobbits have different activities and dialogue among the script's many drafts, but their very lives were threatened by more than the forces of Middle-earth. Jackson told Sibley that Miramax studio executive Bob Weinstein suggested a script change that would frighten hobbit fans but, thankfully, was never taken seriously by the scriptwriters: "'So there's these four hobbits, right? And... they go on this adventure *and none of the hobbits die?* [original emphasis]...Well, we can't have that," he said, "we've got to kill a hobbit! I don't care which one; you can pick.'"[35] If Jackson had actually heeded Weinstein's advice, the resulting scene would have been dramatic, but it also would have completely changed Tolkien's story and risked the ire of legions of hobbit fans. Given Merry's and Pippin's track records in previous adaptations, one of them would likely have been sacrificed for the sake of cinematic drama.

As it turned out, some of their scenes together barely made it on screen. The emotional scene favoured by Merry–Pippin fans of the cousins' battlefield reunion almost did not survive in the cinema version of *RotK*. The film's already great length, the scene's brevity (remedied with more footage in the extended DVD version of *RotK*) and the likelihood that audiences would assume both hobbits survive the battle because they later fight before the Black Gate were good reasons to cut the scene. It was in, then out, and Jackson later commented that 'The very last thing we did on *The Return of the King* was reinstating a scene reuniting Merry and Pippin on the battlefield of the Pelennor Fields...on the very last day of cutting, we changed our minds and put it back!'[36] This scene provides a few quiet moments in the largely battle-bound *RotK* and emphasises the loving bond between the wounded Merry and Pippin, who continues to search for his cousin long after the battle ends. It further indicates Pippin's maturity and shifts his role to caretaker. Although the reunion bears no similarity to Tolkien's description of the event, it still provides emotional closure to the long Battle of the Pelennor Fields by once more focusing the audience's attention on hobbits, the emotional core of the story.

Critics and Tolkien fans may find fault with Jackson's adaptation, but the final shooting script did provide character-building moments for each hobbit and preserved some of Tolkien's dialogue.

Which Hobbit is Which?
Solving the Problem for Audiences

In creating the look and feel of Middle-earth, and especially the hobbits' Shire, Jackson, Fran Walsh and Philippa Boyens relied on Tolkien's descriptions. Nevertheless, when the characters appeared on screen, the visual impressions needed to be stronger and greater detail taken with minutiae in order to bring the settings and characters to life. The creative team behind the trilogy thus had to base their vision on Tolkien's prose but 'fill up the corners' with their own ideas about hairstyles, makeup, fabric, colour palettes and costumes. The writers, costume and makeup designers, and actors needed to make each hobbit different enough from the others for him to be immediately recognisable on screen; this distinction was especially important for Merry and Pippin, who have fewer scenes and sometimes are lumped together by casual readers or audiences. Also, the four hobbits of the Fellowship most often represented hobbits as a race separate from the men, elves, dwarves, wizards, Orcs, goblins etc. on screen for the majority of the trilogy. Giving each hobbit a distinctive look or personality hook was important for non-book-readers' immediate understanding of each hobbit's persona and social status.

Even ear and foot design required variations suitable to each hobbit's individual 'look'. Special-effects makeup artist Marjory

Hamlin reported that the hobbits' feet and ears were 'designed specifically for them to suit their character ... and these varied quite a bit – it was easy to recognise whose feet and ears were whose at a glance. The hair that was applied to the feet and the ankles ... [blended] with skin tone and hair coloring.'[37]

Costume designer Ngila Dickson agreed that making each character stand out individually was important for the film's success. She explained that designers 'wanted to make each character quite separate; we wanted [audiences] to be able to spot each one from a distance. We wanted to give [audiences] a sense of who each character was.'[38] Key words in this creation process illustrated a hobbit's most basic description: Pippin – eccentric, Merry – braggart, Bilbo – expensive, Frodo – princely, Sam – rustic.

Fabric and colour palette matched a hobbit's personality and social status. Frodo, for example, wears velvet and warm golden browns and maroon 'to set him slightly apart from the others'.[39] Like Frodo, Bilbo's style characterises him as more worldly and wealthy than most hobbits; his and Frodo's colours are richer and warmer, and in Bilbo's case more royal, with deep reds and greens, to elevate the Bagginses from the rural hobbits of the Shire. Sam's country-style clothing was woven just for him, and his clothing features 'very country-mum stitching' with 'patches on the elbows of his jacket'.[40] In contrast, 'braggart' Merry sports a yellow waistcoat with brass buttons because he is 'a sharp little dude'.[41]

This fashion sense, along with cleverness, distinguishes Merry from other hobbits. Although 'cleverness' is insinuated in some scenes, this notable trait from the book became an important hook for Dominic Monaghan's portrayal:

> The thing about Merry that was different from the other Hobbits is that, as well as having the normal Hobbit-y nature of being quite carefree about things and wanting to enjoy the good things in life, Merry is quite sharp. He can read situations well ... he's given a lot of respect because he's well-read.[42]

Merry, for example, well knows the Buckland stories about the Old Forest and trees that can move or talk, as he tells a startled Pippin during their captivity by Orcs near Fangorn Forest. When Pippin wonders what makes the groaning noise in the nearby forest, Merry readily supplies an answer. He also immediately responds when Treebeard explains that he is an Ent; Merry acts pleased with this new piece of information and exclaims that Treebeard therefore is 'a tree-herder, a shepherd of the forest'.[43] This trait provided Monaghan with 'a way in...for Merry'.[44]

In contrast to Pippin's innocent humour, Merry's is more cynical and edgy. Monaghan felt that (as Tolkien so structured their individual stories in the book) Merry and Pippin are equals who understand each other so well that 'a lot of their friendship is unspoken. All they need is to look in each other's direction, and it gives them both hope that they're going to get through this thing.'[45] Unlike Frodo and Sam's more openly emotional relationship, displaying everything from love and devotion to anger and remorse, Merry and Pippin's friendship relies on this subtext.

With so many years dedicated to the development of the script and, in particular, the year-long pre-production cultivation of the Matamata farm that would become the Shire, Jackson could afford to be careful with casting. He took the time to test dozens of would-be hobbits before choosing the actors who would play the pivotal hobbits of the Fellowship. More than a decade after filming ended, the continuing friendship among the actors, especially Boyd, Monaghan and Wood, is a testament to effective casting. Just as the hobbits' friendships grew closer throughout the ordeals of an incredibly long location shoot, so did the real-life friendships among cast members playing hobbits. The results of this closeness, such as Merry and Pippin's ability to communicate with each other without words, enhanced the pair's scenes and added depth to the characters' relationship.

The depth of characterisation could be developed slowly over the course of the films. Merry acts like a silly young hobbit early in the trilogy, but his demeanour becomes much more serious as events warrant. A pivotal point in Merry's development takes place when Gandalf spirits Pippin away from Edoras, and the cousins do not know when or if they will see each other again. By this point in the story, Merry's appearance has drastically changed from that of a carefree, style-conscious young hobbit. He looks much thinner (in part because Monaghan no longer wore the 'fat suit' that added Merry's girth to the actor's lean frame), his collarbones prominent during his farewell to Pippin. His clothing and body are careworn, and Merry quite rightly has outgrown the green coat that looked immaculate and stylish at the beginning of his journey. His anger at his cousin's foolishness at looking into the palantir gives way to uncertainty, and, for the first time, Merry's bravado is gone. Neither Merry nor Pippin quite knows how to react to this change. Such a drastic difference in his confidence and appearance go a long way in illustrating how much Merry has changed during the quest.

Although Merry has fewer scenes than the other hobbits of the Fellowship, outward changes in the way he expresses himself and in his appearance subtly indicate greater inner changes. By the time the four Travellers return to the Shire, decked out in finery and sitting tall on their ponies, Merry again acts confident and almost regal in his return; only among the four, such as a late-trilogy scene in which the hobbits share a drink at the local pub or when a tearful Merry and Pippin leave the Grey Havens together, does Merry again seem less self-assured and more emotional.

Until their separation at Edoras, Pippin relies on Merry's experience and advice to get them through difficult situations. Pippin's geniality and lack of care not only reflect his youthful inexperience but also frequently earn him Gandalf's disapproving label 'fool of a Took'. Reacting emotionally, whether inquisitively or angrily, Pippin often gets into scrapes in the films (for example, knocking a skeleton down the well in Moria, looking into the palantir).

Nevertheless, for all his inadvertent or spontaneous mischief, Pippin also gets on well with the Fellowship and new allies he meets along the way. The young hobbit does not worry about class distinctions or protocol. A slightly inebriated Pippin banters with Gimli when the two are reunited among the ruins of Isengard at the beginning of *TT*; in *RotK*, the hobbit impulsively offers his service to Denethor, Steward of Gondor, seeming unafraid to speak his mind before the imposing ruler. Throughout the trilogy, he and Gandalf establish a child–parent relationship – not bad for an underage hobbit and a venerable Istari.

Perhaps most striking is Pippin's quickly developed relationship with Treebeard. In a matter of a few scenes, the hobbit changes from warning Merry not to speak to the talking tree to finding a rather nonsensical way to force Treebeard to see Saruman's destruction of the natural world, thus prompting the Ents to go to war. Whereas Merry takes a more cerebral approach to problem solving, preferring to pontificate logically about the need for the Ents to fight, Pippin gets to know Treebeard and finds a way to involve him emotionally in the affairs of Middle-earth.

Billy Boyd (Pippin) noted the difference in the two hobbits' personalities and actions, as evidenced during the Treebeard scenes:

> Pippin doesn't understand the whole world as much [as Merry], and he can focus in on this character much more easily. [Because] Merry understands what is happening in the world and with the war and how it is going to affect Frodo and Sam and Aragorn and Legolas, he immediately wants to do something. But Pippin…is more interested in getting to know Treebeard. Through that, he understands more and knows what has to be done [in order] for Treebeard to go in and save them.[46]

This ability to get to know others and then act based on his new knowledge serves him well in Minas Tirith as he becomes a Gondorian guard. He matures to the point that he can look after others, including wounded Merry; he takes care of his friends rather than being the one cared for.

In addition to these personality traits, Pippin's wardrobe is another way to distinguish him from other hobbits. Pippin wears a wool scarf in most scenes; it becomes almost a security blanket.[47] By the end of the film, a stylish paisley ascot befitting an older, more worldly hobbit substitutes for the woollen one. Although the wool scarf was initially designed to make Pippin seem eccentric, costume designer Dickson noted that the scarf 'was really never intended to be used as much as it has been. But [Pippin/Boyd] really, really adopted it.'[48]

In creating makeup, costumes and wigs for the hobbits of the Fellowship, Jackson's talented experts often created a 'look' that blended the actor's physical characteristics with those appropriate for the character. Along the way, however, some descriptive details from

Tolkien's book did not make it onto the screen. As noted in Christopher Tolkien's *The History of Middle-earth*, Sam's son, Pippin Gamgee, named for Pippin Took, recalls that Thain Peregrin had 'hair that's almost golden',[49] an uncommon colour among hobbits. In most adaptations, including Jackson's, Pippin has dark hair. Frodo, according to Gandalf in Tolkien's *LotR*, stands taller than most hobbits and, like Pippin, is fair; he also has a dimpled chin.[50] Although such details are easily pushed aside in importance when a film is cast, even these minor changes can undermine the original text and make adaptations' visual details more memorable than a passage from a book. In future adaptations, and in the minds of audiences or even book readers, Pippin and Frodo may forever be the dark-haired hobbits, with Merry and Sam the fairest of the four.

Director/writer/producer Jackson provided intriguing insights into his ideas for Frodo and Sam in the first issue of the *Lord of the Rings Fan Club Movie Magazine*. In early 2002, Jackson revealed that he thought of Frodo as the character representing the audience, with events seen through his eyes. Jackson considered Frodo 'the absolute heart and soul of the movie'.[51] Although he did not have a particular actor in mind for this important role, a tape that Elijah Wood sent the director sealed the deal; in the homemade *LotR* audition video, Wood became the perfect Frodo for Jackson's adaptation. Sam was more difficult for Jackson to relate to (as Astin also alluded to in his book when recalling his discussions with the director about an appropriate weight for Sam).[52] Jackson admitted that he related more to Frodo and deemed that difference in identification with the book characters was 'a personal thing... Sam's so solid and ultimately doesn't really change as a character. He's the stable, loyal, very brave companion who has to watch as Frodo undergoes this transformation in this tortuous, agonising fight with the Ring.'[53] Still, Jackson conceded, Frodo's transformation can ultimately alienate the audience by the time the Ring is destroyed, allowing Sam to receive more of the audience's sympathy.

Wood called Frodo 'a brilliant character to play, mainly for the arc that the character takes throughout the journey', from an innocent hobbit, 'albeit quite curious and knowledgeable about the outside world, to a Ring-obsessed shadow of his former self'.[54] Balancing

Frodo's increasingly obsessive personality required a calming, steady influence – in short, Sam. Astin considered his character 'the most loyal, obedient puppy dog that you could ever have. But Sam also is a particular fellow. He likes things to be in order...he takes his job of providing for Mr. Frodo very seriously. He's an earnest fellow.'[55] Astin wanted to make sure that Sam in the Jackson adaptation came across as more serious and noble than Sam in Bakshi's film; he wanted to 'make sure that we didn't sacrifice the credibility of the heroism by making [Sam] too roly-poly and comedic, and I think we struck that balance'. Sam as a 'portly yeoman character' was all right, as long as Sam did not become just 'a roly-poly fat boy'.[56]

As with most films, what the audience sees on screen is the result of long discussions and careful planning about every aspect of the film. The audience receives the whole package at once and may not be aware of such careful considerations as individualised foot prosthetics, a character's ideal weight, or variations in clothing, but each detail helps build unique characters. Jackson's creative team maintained a high level of detail in planning everything a hobbit would wear or how he would look, a feat not accomplished in previous adaptations.

Praise for the Trilogy

Despite some fans' and critics' criticism, Jackson deservedly also received accolades for his remarkable achievement in turning what Tolkien perceived as an unfilmable story into a captivating trilogy. The film provided faces and voices for book (or previously animated) characters and gave audiences a further way to identify with the characters, especially the hobbits. That the actors portraying Frodo, Sam, Merry and Pippin are charismatic and captivating, off screen as well as on, endeared them and their characters to legions of fans.

The films also made Middle-earth come alive to audiences, who sometimes had trouble believing that the beauteous New Zealand scenery was not as much the result of CGI as Gollum. To its credit, the lush greenery near Matamata (the Shire), the harsher landscapes of Mount Sunday (Edoras) or Moa Station (Rohan), and the snowy peaks of the Southern Alps (Caradhras) helped interest fans in preserving such beautiful places. If it was good enough for hobbits to die to protect, it became worthwhile for hobbit fans to help preserve.

Jackson's adaptation brought a great number of people to the book or made them want to know more about Tolkien. The trilogy gave one of the most beloved books of all time new life as one of the most accomplished fantasy film series of all time. It also gave fans – and generations to come – a wealth of information about how the film was made, so that *LotR*: the Jackson adaptation has become a classic itself, in addition to (or perhaps in spite of) the book.

A 'Classic' Movie *LotR*

Jackson's trilogy undoubtedly has a powerful influence on popular culture and Tolkien fandom, to the point that, at least for the foreseeable future, his adaptation of *LotR* may be considered the 'classic' version. The imagery in the films helps cement a whole film-going generation's idea of what hobbits are and look like.

In the aftermath of the release of each film in the trilogy came a wealth of *LotR* film merchandise. Although the hobbit toys and action figures may resemble Tolkien's descriptions, the 'look' and 'voice' of the hobbit collectibles have been forever moulded (in plastic, at least) by the actors who portrayed the hobbits in Jackson's films. Action-figure Sam speaks with Sean Astin's accent, and Frodo recites Elijah Wood's lines. The Merry figure wears a miniature version of Dominic Monaghan's costume, and toy Pippin wears Billy Boyd's face in Pippin makeup and wig. The actors' faces were digitally scanned so that official merchandise would look like their on-screen characters, and lines from the movies were reproduced for the toys. Collectible cards, commemorative plates, action figures, movie posters and so on all bear the likenesses of the films' actors-as-characters. This merchandise, which long will survive on eBay as collectibles, continues to influence the way the public thinks of Tolkien's characters. When someone hears a reference to Frodo in popular culture, the image to pop to mind is likely to be Wood-as-Frodo in Jackson's trilogy.

With so much *LotR* merchandise specifically based on the films – far more than the combined products resulting from the Bakshi or Rankin–Bass adaptations – the Jackson trilogy carries far more weight long term in determining how the public thinks hobbits should look, sound and act. Although Jackson and company – including such talented designers as award-winning Ngila Dickson – took great care in making the films as true visually to Tolkien's world as possible, the final vision is still Jackson's.

A Long-Expected *Hobbit*

After much scepticism, anticipation and legal wrangling, New Line Cinema and Peter Jackson settled their legal dispute over the trilogy's profits and paved the way for the *Hobbit* films. Jackson's profile in the film industry rose tremendously in the aftermath of *LotR* and the less successful but still popular *King Kong* (2005). Jackson had a long list of films he wanted to produce, leaving him little time to concentrate on *Hobbit* films for many years. Before his eventual return to the Shire, Jackson produced *District 9* (2009), *The Lovely Bones* (2009), and the Steven Spielberg-directed *The Adventures of Tintin* (2011).

During the years when *The Hobbit* seemed assured as a future film but had no director, several candidates were suggested, in the press and in private, for the job. Well-publicised frontrunners included Sam Raimi, well known for blockbusters like the *Spider-Man* series, but also for his history of filming in New Zealand (for example, *Hercules: The Legendary Journeys; Xena, Warrior Princess*), and Guillermo del Toro (for example, *Pan's Labyrinth*, the *Hellboy* films). In late April 2008, del Toro was announced as the director of what would likely turn out to be two *Hobbit* films.[57]

Almost at once, the joyful news spread throughout fandom. *LotR* film fans clamouring for more Tolkien movies debated the directorial switch from Jackson to del Toro and wondered if Jackson's vision of Middle-earth would be sustained or changed dramatically. Del Toro's reputation for innovative creature design preceded him into

Tolkien fandom, making fans wonder how different the races of Middle-earth would look in future films. Through joint photo ops, an online chat with fans, and press reports, Jackson and del Toro assured fans that executive producer/writer Jackson and director del Toro would work well together. New Zealand film locations and the return of scriptwriters Fran Walsh and Philippa Boyens, in addition to Jackson, further indicated that the *Hobbit* films would build on the New Zealand-as-Middle-earth empire Jackson founded.

With legal delays and continuing uncertainty about a start date for *The Hobbit*, del Toro left the project nearly two years after he was announced as director. He made the announcement on TORN, which showed his and Jackson's respect for fans and this popular website. Although his influence on the films would be felt through the script upon which he had collaborated, del Toro gracefully wished the next director – who, predictably, was Jackson – well and left New Zealand.[58]

In early 2011, years later than anticipated, *The Hobbit* movies began filming in New Zealand. Once again, TORN became a premiere fan site for the release of set pictures and the distribution of news and rumours. Tolkien fans' excitement about new adaptations again began to build with the realisation that the *Hobbit* films were finally back on schedule.

Of course, online casting rumours began years before actual casting took place. As with *LotR* in the late 1990s, fans enjoyed playing 'who'll get the role' in preparation for the *Hobbit* movies. Ian McKellen told *Empire* that he would return as Gandalf the Grey,[59] but in September 2008, Viggo Mortensen, who publicly stated early on his wish to return as Aragorn, reported that he had not been contacted by del Toro.[60] Casting decisions came far more quickly in 2010 and 2011 as filming began, first with the dwarves and the pivotal hobbit, Bilbo.

The actor who took on this role could make or break *The Hobbit*. Fans early on applauded rumours that rising star James McAvoy would become Bilbo, but the actor denied any truth to the rumors.[61] When that rumour was dispelled, another began that soon-to-regenerate Time Lord David Tennant, a popular Doctor in the long-running *Doctor Who* television series, was about to be cast as Bilbo. In hindsight, as TORN staff speculated during the 2011 San Diego Comic-Con, a reporter probably heard rumours that Sylvester McCoy, who played the Doctor earlier in the series, had been cast in a role (which turned out to be Radagast the Brown).[62] Substituting a former Time Lord for a soon-to-be-leaving Tennant may have seemed logical at the time, but the rumour had no basis in fact.

The speculation about casting finally ended in late October 2010 with the announcement that Martin Freeman (best known internationally for films including *Love Actually* and *The Hitchhiker's Guide to the Galaxy* and UK television series *The Office* and *Sherlock*) would play Bilbo Baggins. Jackson sounded pleased with this casting when he described Freeman as 'intelligent, funny, surprising and brave, exactly like Bilbo, and I feel incredibly proud to be able to announce that he is our Hobbit'.[63]

First set photos of Freeman wearing Bilbo's costume met with general approval. In a photo released on 24 June 2011, in the official *Hobbit* blog and the magazine *Entertainment Weekly*, Bilbo is shown in Bag End, a roomful of dwarves in the background. Dressed in a brown-striped shirt and brown trousers, with braces, Bilbo intently reads a long contract while his guests await him. With his sleeves rolled up, younger Bilbo looks very much like a comfortable but not incredibly wealthy hobbit, as befitting his pre-Smaug lifestyle. His pointed ears are visible through light brown hair. The photo's dominant colour scheme is shades of brown, creating a warm but rustic feeling appropriate to Bag End in the days when Bilbo's life was on the precipice of change. Another photo showed Jackson and Freeman in discussion on the Bag End set. Freeman-as-Bilbo was seated at a table, and his large, very furry feet could clearly be seen. Jackson noted that Freeman 'fit the ears, and he's got some very nice feet'.[64]

For his part, Freeman seemed to feel he was a good fit for the role (as well as the feet). He explained in the *Hobbit*'s first press conference in New Zealand that he had watched Ian Holm play Bilbo in *LotR*, a role the actor was reported to reprise in at least one scene with Elijah Wood as Frodo. Freeman elaborated, 'Without trying to blow my own trumpet nor with too much false modesty, I think I'm quite a good match for him. I have to try to echo and give a nod to what he's done, but still be me.'[65] Continuity between *The Hobbit* and *LotR* is crucial in order for the films to seem like part of a very long set. Although Holm and Wood might briefly play their roles in what was called the prequel, Freeman's performance and appearance must make younger Bilbo seem likely to grow into the much older Bilbo of the *LotR* films. If the acting styles or interpretations of character diverged too far, then *LotR* movie fans would likely focus on the differences between Bilbos, rather than enjoying either actor's portrayal of the character at different ages. Freeman wisely made the character his own, but within the acceptable boundaries of what it means to be Bilbo in a Jackson adaptation.

Freeman, although not originally a Tolkien fan, took on the role with enthusiasm, so much so that, after winning a BAFTA as Best Supporting Actor for *Sherlock* in May 2011, he let slip to the press an upcoming *Sherlock* reunion on the *Hobbit* set; Benedict Cumberbatch, who plays Sherlock Holmes in the television series, had also taken a role (later revealed to be two roles: Smaug and the Necromancer).[66] In joking about his gaffe a few days later, Freeman hoped he would not be let go; secrecy surrounding the *Hobbit* films, as was true of *LotR*, was notoriously tight. Nevertheless, Freeman apparently had little to fear that his role would be re-filmed in the near future. Jackson worked around his shooting schedule for *Sherlock* and resumed filming Bilbo's scenes later in 2011. At that point in the *Hobbit* films' production, Bilbo seemed to be in very good hands, and audiences worldwide looked forward to yet another Jackson cinematic adaptation of one of Tolkien's beloved stories.

The Hobbit as Prequel

Although *The Hobbit* is its own contained story, one published considerably earlier than *LotR*, Bilbo is an important character linking the two. The audience, structure and tone of Tolkien's *The Hobbit* are also considerably different from *LotR*'s. Nevertheless, in terms of adaptation, Jackson's three films based on *The Hobbit* have been structured to provide a bridge between the stories and to link Middle-earth events surrounding the earlier *Hobbit* with those in *LotR*. Although Tolkien's many published histories and cosmology of Middle-earth provide a vast context in which readers can place *The Hobbit* or *LotR*, chances are very good that filmgoers will never see *The Silmarillion* as a summer blockbuster. Taking bits and pieces from other works or allusions made in *The Hobbit*, such as the White Council, and turning them into far more important scenes in the filmed adaptation is one way to incorporate more of Tolkien's characters and events important to the complete history (and audience understanding) of Middle-earth.

As soon as the official film titles were released in May 2011, Jackson began answering questions, both through interviews and official sites, including his Facebook page. One early question involved the White Council, a meeting only briefly mentioned in *The Hobbit* as an explanation for Gandalf's departure from Bilbo's story. The book follows Bilbo on his adventure, but Gandalf goes away for a while, only to return at a most opportune time in Bilbo's story. Jackson's *Hobbit* explains, through scenes written only for this adaptation, what takes place at a meeting involving Gandalf, Saruman, Elrond and Galadriel. Characters not in Tolkien's *Hobbit* nonetheless can logically appear in Jackson's *Hobbit* films.

Jackson confirmed rumours that changes such as these would help expand what is a rather short book into three feature films. Because the new scenes have only a passing reference in Tolkien's *The Hobbit*, as well as Jackson's *LotR*, the filmmaker can turn them into whatever he sees fit. In visualising the White Council, artists John Howe and Alan Lee, whose art graced the cinematic trilogy, again took the lead. Jackson explained that 'both the White Council and Dol Guldur will feature in the movies. And not just in one scene either. Just how to visualise it has been a challenge, but fortunately Alan Lee and John Howe went crazy with ideas, and it should look pretty cool.'[67]

Although Jackson does take liberties in adapting Tolkien's works, he does so from an understanding both of Tolkien's words and the necessities of making an entertaining film. Although, as noted previously in this chapter, Jackson's trilogy still earned criticism as well as praise from film critics as well as Tolkien fans, this filmmaker, more than others who have adapted Tolkien's stories, seems to have the support of the fan community. Because Jackson and his co-scriptwriters have read Tolkien's words – and respect and understand them – and they have a successful track record in making films people want to see, the *Hobbit* films have been anticipated more than most adaptations.

Through Facebook pages, websites and impromptu appearances at the 2011 Comic-Con, for example, Jackson reminds hobbit lovers that he is a fan too, and he reaches out to fans to share news. When a filmmaker like Jackson does so, the motivation seems far less 'pay to see my movie' than 'here's something you'll think is cool, and I want to share'. Because of Jackson's approach to adapting Tolkien's books, fans are more likely to think of the *Hobbit* films as a special cinematic experience, one shared between those who make this adaptation and those who stand in line to see it on a big screen.

6

THOSE MUSICAL HOBBITS

Most people think in terms of visuals when they hear the word 'adaptation', but Tolkien's world has been adapted for music as well as more visual media: musical themes scored for a film, as in Howard Shore's award-winning soundtrack to Jackson's films; songs sung by animated characters like Sam in the Rankin–Bass *Lord of the Rings*; orchestral themes such as Johan de Meij's original compositions inspired by *LotR*; a musical parody like *Fellowship!*; a fully fledged *LotR* stage musical; a children's opera of *The Hobbit*. These adaptations emphasise specific, often emotional elements of Tolkien's hobbits' story. Music can evoke their homeland Shire, loving relationships or battles against foes ranging from Smaug to Sauron, and Tolkien fans can learn a lot about the hobbits' characterisation from music or lyrics.

The Lord of the Rings Musical

Tolkien probably never envisioned singing, dancing hobbits on stage, but in 2006–7, only a few years after Jackson's blockbuster films, a musical Middle-earth attracted theatre patrons first in Canada and, nearly a year later, in the UK. Although *The Lord of the Rings* musical[1] failed to win many critics' favour, two versions of the theatrical production entertained audiences in Toronto and London, where the show closed on 19 July 2008, after playing to more than 700,000 people. Producer Ken Wallace promised audiences that the musical would continue around the world, although that assessment later seemed premature, and by 2012 no touring company had yet produced the musical.[2]

London-based theatrical producer Wallace and Saul Zaentz, who owns the rights to stage and film productions (and produced the 1978 *LotR* film), partnered to originate the musical in Toronto, where they joined with Canadian theatre impresario David Mirvish and concert promoter Michael Cohl. Their $30 million (Canadian) production featured innovative revolving, elevating sets and technical wizardry to rival anything Gandalf might conjure, were he so inclined.

A plus for hobbit lovers is the story's grounding in the Shire at both the beginning and end of the production. This adaptation comes full circle with emphasis on a lush, happy Shire before the War of the Ring and Bill Ferny's and Saruman's treachery even after the Ring has been destroyed. Quite predictably, the musical concludes with Gandalf guiding a weary Frodo into the West and away from a newly reunited Sam and Rosie. Although much of the rest of the musical was criticised for straying too far from Tolkien, or even Jackson's adaptation, with which many theatregoers were undoubtedly familiar, the sheer spectacle of the staging made this adaptation an innovative experiment, one that received a wide variety of reviews.

As a first introduction to Tolkien's hobbits, however, some theatregoers were won over by the story, which surpassed their expectations for what musical theatre could be. Even years after the play closed, some fans fondly recall seeing the musical and introducing their friends to Frodo. A young woman posting a message in July 2011 on the musical's Facebook fan page enthusiastically wrote that 'it was spectacular!! I took 2 friends who hadn't even seen the movie and went with a very negative attitude, i.e., that theatre is boring, and they came out amazed and wowed!!!'[3] Other Facebook posts indicate a waiting audience for the musical's revival or streamlining to a size manageable for touring companies. Although praise like this is undoubtedly heartening to the production's cast and crew, the show itself often suffered from technical glitches, budget woes and, ultimately, criticism from hardcore Tolkien fans and reviewers.

As with all adaptations involving Tolkien's hobbits, the reception is often a 'love 'em or leave 'em' affair. The playwright and composer continued to tweak the production during the Toronto run and the show's transition to London's West End. As a result of these changes, Frodo and Sam become more important to the musical, but Merry and Pippin often remain in the wings. The characterisations of the four hobbits of the Fellowship, as well as Bilbo and other hobbits in the Shire, differ greatly from both Tolkien's and Jackson's visions of what hobbits look like and how each character should best be realised. Although many differences can be attributed to the specific needs of a book, movie or play, the musical adaptation retains much of the 'feel' of Tolkien's Shire while presenting a very modern view of Frodo.

The Toronto Production

In June 2006 I attended two performances in Toronto. By then, the musical had undergone practical changes to ensure that the vast stage, with its many moving sections, worked smoothly.[4] In addition to the technological changes, the story had also been streamlined from a running time of about three-and-a-half hours to a more watchable three.

The audience around me during those June matinee and evening performances indicated the majority came to see the musical because it promised to be an extravaganza. They seemed peripherally familiar with the story – some had seen the Jackson films – but few were devoted Tolkien fans.[5] Their response was overwhelmingly positive. The musical's key numbers, two which feature Frodo, gave them few hummable tunes to take home, but the sheer wizardry of transforming the Princess of Wales Theatre into Middle-earth received the most applause.

Shortly before the performance began, the stage turned into the Shire, vines twining up the sides to the boxes and lighting creating a soft, lush scene. Cheerful hobbits chased butterflies around the stage and through the first few rows, their joy contagious among the guests seated near the stage.

This early glimpse of the Shire preceded a brief narration of Bilbo's backstory with the Ring, which led to the first song-and-dance number: Bilbo's birthday party. In this adaptation, Bilbo seems a benevolent sort, bespectacled and dressed in finery. The hobbits of the Shire join him in the revelry. With the exception of Frodo, who even early in the story is much thinner and quieter than his compatriots, all hobbits are well rounded, fun-loving characters. This setup allowed audiences to understand just what Frodo, Sam, Merry and Pippin would eventually fight for and brought them into the story as fellow 'hobbits' attending Bilbo's celebration. The tone and 'magic' of the Shire well reflected both Tolkien's and Jackson's works.

Once the quest begins, Frodo and Sam rightly lead the other hobbits through the tale. The best 'hobbit' musical scene comes early in the show, when all four hobbits anticipate their upcoming journey. 'The road goes on' is perhaps the most memorable song from the entire production, in either the Toronto or London versions, and is clearly based on Tolkien's work.[6] The chorus, 'The road goes on, ever ever on', is an obvious variation of the first line of Bilbo's famous travelling song, 'The road goes ever on'.[7] Later lyrics mention Sun and Moon, as well as being lured from home to travel ever farther away, common themes for adventuresome Bilbo. As emphasised in book or films, Frodo's 'adventure' turns out very differently from Bilbo's, but the thrill of the open road captures the hobbits' imagination during the 'Road goes on' production number, in which elves and rangers, as well as hobbits, sing of upcoming journeys.

Sam and Frodo begin the song, but Merry and Pippin also take a turn leading a verse. The younger characters are quickly summarised as typically 'hobbity', concerned primarily with good food and comfort. Pippin looks forward to the next mealtime, dreaming of succulent pears; Merry plans a menu of fresh trout and newly churned cream. Whereas Merry and Pippin become stereotyped as youngsters thinking only as far ahead as their next meal, Frodo and Sam seek adventure and have at least a rudimentary understanding of how far they might be swept once they step outside the Shire.

In a plotline straight from Tolkien, Frodo distracts the Prancing Pony crowd with his tall tale of a too-fond-of-brown-beer cat jumping over the moon. As befitting a musical, a song at the Prancing Pony provides Frodo with an opportunity to divert attention from Pippin's inadvertent slip about a Baggins in the crowd's midst, disrupting Frodo's attempt to keep his presence low-key or secret. To change the subject, Frodo entertains the patrons with a rowdy rendition of 'The cat and the moon'.[8]

This adaptation's Frodo captures the audience's attention by jumping on a table, singing and dancing with great gusto during a musical interlude. In most scenes, however, musical Frodo seems more tentative and older than his cinematic counterpart with whom audiences are probably most familiar. A huge point in his favour, however, is a closer resemblance to Tolkien's Frodo. James Loye, Frodo in both the Toronto and London productions, showed audiences more of the type of hobbit Tolkien's pre-war Frodo could be – an earthy, funny storyteller. His vivacity highlights the striking contrast between pre- and post-quest Frodo, and as a musical number, this 'hoe-down' works better than most production numbers. Theatregoers might not have remembered the lyrics after the performance, but the dance sequence again brings the story to life and engages the audience.

As might be expected, Merry and Pippin suffer in this musical adaptation. Although as members of the Fellowship they are hard to displace entirely, they seldom act decisively or take centre stage. They join in the chorus of the rousing Bree song-and-dance number but are soon carried away by Orcs (in the Toronto version, off stage; after Boromir's death scene, Aragorn explains to Legolas, Gimli and the audience what has happened to the hobbits). True to the original story, Merry and Pippin meet the (stilt-walking) Ents, who truly tower over the actors and increase the illusion of the hobbits' smallness in the great world. They then disappear for a while as the story focuses on two fronts: Aragorn's journey towards becoming king, and Frodo's and Sam's journey to Mordor.

During the lone (but enormous in scope and sound) battle scene, Merry briefly returns to the stage to 'assist' *Xena, Warrior Princess*-like Éowyn in dispatching the menacing Witch King, but his role is not nearly as prominent as in book or films, especially Jackson's. This Merry wanders the stage, occasionally fighting, but mostly seeming ineffectual. Pippin also fights a few Orcs here and there, and when he and Merry are reunited after the battle – both slightly scruffy but basically unscathed from their encounter – they boast of their accomplishments with dialogue along the lines of 'I'm a knight of Gondor!' and 'I've been made a rider of Rohan!'

Perhaps even more startling than their abbreviated part in the story is their physical appearance. Merry and Pippin, like Sam and other 'typical' hobbits in this production, are very well rounded, to the point that the youngest hobbits could be compared to Tweedle Dee and Tweedle Dum. Their costumes, again coming closer to Tolkien's descriptions than any cinematic version of Shirewear, look less homespun than Sam's but are still appropriately woolly. Merry wears a red/yellow/orange striped vest over a white shirt; Pippin's similarly styled vest is woven in earth tones of green, brown and black. Both wear brown trousers and are appropriately barefoot, with a band of thick fur across the centre of each foot. As in the film but not in the book, Merry's honeyed hair is lighter than Pippin's brown locks (a reversal of Tolkien's description of Pippin having uncommonly light hair).[9]

As the story unfolds, Frodo becomes increasingly frail, his costume grimier and more tattered. Frodo's features are more delicate than those of other hobbits, and his dark curls contrast ever-paler skin tones. Frodo's class status is clearly superior to Sam's, as indicated by a finer weave of cloth and brass buttons on his original brown vest and finely patterned brown plaid trousers. Sam's clothing is plainer – brown vest over white shirt, green trousers. Next to fair Frodo, Sam seems less refined, a true 'common hobbit'. This physical and stylistic contrast serves them well in their many scenes together.

Another musical highlight of the Toronto production was Sam's and Frodo's duet, 'Tell me a story', another tune that would survive the trip to London.[10] This quiet song highlights Frodo's and Sam's close friendship and their understanding of Shire customs and culture, but it also indicates personal differences between the friends. As Frodo and Sam (Loye and Peter Howe, who originated the role in Toronto and brought it to London) sit by the campfire, they wistfully think back to the Shire and the hobbits from whom they descend. Sam praises the Harfoots and Stoors who steadfastly till the land and tell stories of their brave ancestors – even if these steady, sturdy hobbits also want to ensure nothing changes from year to year. Keeping the status quo is a virtue in this song, which makes Frodo's and Sam's 'adventure' seem even more atypical of hobbits.

Sam sees Frodo as someone apart from the Shire – an adventurer or a saviour to be revered in song and story for generations to come. He sings of Frodo being 'brave and bold', to which the self-effacing Frodo instead rhymes 'tired and cold'. Frodo praises Sam as a valiant companion and promises that his role in the quest will become the stuff of new songs and stories to endure beyond their lifetime. This Frodo seems much more aware that his heroism (and sacrifice) are more a matter of circumstance than design or desire.

With this song, audiences learn that Frodo and Sam will never fit completely into hobbit society; as 'heroes' and 'adventurers', their experiences might be praised but not understood by Shirefolk. In addition to this number providing a respite to the increasingly fast-paced action leading to the play's climax, the interaction between Sam and Frodo brings a typically 'hobbity' moment to life while intimating how Frodo and Sam, as friends and heroes, can never truly return to everyday Shire life.

This scene is even more touching than a similar one in Jackson's *Two Towers*; both are quiet reminders of the friends' closeness and mutual admiration. In neither version is Sam's class status mentioned, and the relationship between Frodo and Sam seems a more modern friendship rather than a devoted master–servant bond. In the musical, Frodo and Sam recall stories passed from generation to generation; their common bond as hobbits unites them against 'outsiders', whether friend or foe.

Although such musical highlights delighted the Toronto audiences, the show closed prematurely, on 3 September 2006. The multimillion dollar production played at the Princess of Wales Theatre fewer than six months, certainly much less time than expected. Nevertheless, upon its closing, the show was promised to be retooled for a London run beginning in 2007; a *Toronto Sun* article reported that the musical was being 'partially rewritten for the U.K., with significant changes to the second and third acts and a greater emphasis on the songs and music, which some critics dismissed as forgettable'.[11]

According to producer Wallace, Toronto was perhaps not the best place for a *LotR* musical because of its British roots, noting that *LotR*'s 'spiritual home...is in London'.[12] However, Jackson's international success with the *LotR* trilogy and the fact that Tolkien's book continues to be reprinted around the world certainly indicate that the story's themes and characters should appeal to audiences outside the UK.

Perhaps the greatest challenge was not the Canadian public's lack of cultural familiarity with hobbits but the massive cost of the highly creative and technologically sophisticated production. The musical provided audiences with previously unseen special effects, including spiralling sections of stage, stilt walkers and huge 'puppets' creeping spiderlike across the stage or propelling Balrog-ised bits of paper 'ash' into the audience. The reworked version needed to bring more hobbitry to the heart of the production, a feat that London audiences largely feel was accomplished, if word-of-mouth reviews and box-office receipts are effective indicators of the London version's superiority over the original Toronto production.

The London Production

As a group, the hobbits in the reworked London musical of *LotR* become a greater presence on stage. The revised story, which underwent a 'major rewrite',[13] emphasises Frodo, unlike the Toronto production, which primarily dealt with Aragorn's journey to become king and to win his true love, Arwen. Costumes, key musical numbers featuring the hobbits and some casting survived the trip across the pond, but the show's length, story emphasis and other production numbers became streamlined or refocused. Of the 'hobbits' in the original production, Loye (Frodo), Howe (Sam) and Owen Sharpe (Pippin) reprised their roles; Richard Henders succeeded Dylan Roberts as Merry. Instead of the 65 cast members boasted at the start of the Toronto run, London featured a cast of 50.

Like the Toronto production, previews were halted because of technical problems; during one performance, an actor's leg was injured by the moving set.[14] In part, the musical's staging faced massive changes because Drury Lane's stage is considerably smaller than that in Toronto's much newer Princess of Wales Theatre. Whereas the building could be physically adapted to fit the production in Toronto, the historic London theatre could not. Part of the streamlining involved solving the problem of less space without sacrificing the innovative staging or set design.[15]

Despite changes to story or staging, the musical retains its immediacy with the audience, particularly in the initial Shire scenes. Making the audience feel a part of Tolkien's world, especially of its beloved Shire, is crucial to the story, especially on stage. Empathising with hobbits is a precursor for the audience later identifying with Frodo and Sam on their journey.

Although Frodo, of all hobbits, is the obvious audience focal point – and Loye's performance in the role was very strong – Sam easily gains audience empathy and wins their devotion in this adaptation. He might be more fearful (for example, of Gandalf) early in the play, but his character gradually becomes strengthened during his journey to Mordor. Sam continually looks after Frodo, draping a cloak about him, lightening the mood by playing and then singing a fireside song of home, physically supporting his ever-weakening friend as they pace the stage. In this version, Frodo seems physically much weaker than in other adaptations; his departure for Valinor is hardly a surprise, even for audiences new to the story. Sam, in contrast, truly comes into his own. When the returned Sam stands face to face to join hands with Rosie Cotton, he is confident and determined. He is clearly a survivor who, just like the hardy forebears of which he sings, can ensure the Shire stays strong long after Frodo fades into the West.

Making the Musical Different from the Jackson Films

In such a massive undertaking as bringing *LotR* to the stage, some parts of the story had to be significantly revised or removed. Shaun McKenna and Matthew Warchus struggled through many script drafts in workshops and performances, trying to capture the essence of the Frodo–Sam dynamic within the larger themes inherent in the story. Hobbits, especially Frodo and Sam, needed to be easily recognised and understood by audiences, but they also had to suit this particular musical and the demands of theatre. Audiences had to be able to accept that the way a hobbit acts and looks on stage may differ from the same character's actions and appearance on film.

Although the public might have been more interested in the musical because they had either seen or heard about the recent *LotR* movies, the stage production needed to lure interested audiences into the theatre while distinguishing itself from the filmed story. Creating a different 'look' for the hobbits helped differentiate the musical from the recent Jackson cinematic adaptation. Another way to separate the two was to emphasise key elements of the play's plot and to provide a backstory so that theatregoers could quickly get up to speed in identifying individual hobbits and understanding their motivations for journeying outside the Shire. Not only the play, but the printed programme, helped achieve these objectives.

For the Toronto programme's plot synopsis, Tolkien Creative Consultant Laurie Battle detailed Bilbo's history with the Ring; this background was also provided through the opening narration. Bilbo's role was emphasised in the programme and on stage more in the early production than the revised London show. The first two paragraphs of the Act I setup explain how Bilbo won the Ring from Gollum during a riddle contest.

The three-page synopsis in the Toronto programme also tells how Frodo becomes the Ringbearer. In this version, he seems to have little choice, at least until the council in Rivendell; Gandalf refuses to take the Ring, and no one else is available to carry it from the Shire. Battle summarises that 'only little folk like the Hobbits, who lead simple lives far from the great events of Men in distant lands, can risk possessing the Ring without being corrupted. Frodo must take the Ring to Rivendell.'[16] Only in Rivendell does Frodo 'volunteer' to continue this task.[17] Late in the play, in contrast to his earlier more passive persona, Frodo takes on a crucial role in the scouring of the Shire scenes. He confronts Saruman, which leads to the final altercation in the Shire.[18]

This version of the story comes closer to Tolkien's, although in the book Frodo pleads for mercy and an end to violence; his cousins directly confront the ruffians and eventually lead the hobbits into battle against them. Tolkien has Frodo confront Saruman/Sharkey at Bag End, but Wormtongue (not Bill Ferny, as performed on stage) kills Saruman. Battle's London synopsis merely indicates that 'the hobbits return home to a drastically changed Shire',[19] and the story's emphasis shifts to Sam's reunion with Rosie, a relationship well established in the opening scenes, similar to Tolkien's backstory for Sam.

Whether on stage or in programme notes, the hobbits' story is shortened to make the details palatable for an audience needing only the basics in order to enjoy an evening at the theatre. What to Tolkien enthusiasts might be glaring omissions become, to writers and producers, details to be cut for a streamlined stage production. As scriptwriter McKenna admitted, when faced with the enormous task of making the story accessible for stage, 'one of the advantages of not being a complete Tolkien aficionado [is that] I could cut material without having any emotional attachment to it. I could just say that it doesn't work in the context of our production and so we're not glued to it.'[20] Although a certain distance from the material may help when trimming it for an adaptation, comments like this in the press tended to alienate fans of Tolkien's book and, therefore, likely lost the theatrical adaptation some goodwill. (In contrast, Jackson has gone out of his way to make Tolkien fans understand that, although he is a filmmaker, he is also a fan who respects Tolkien's work and will not cut it willy nilly. McKenna's comment seems less fan-friendly.)

McKenna thought the stage version could become more moving and personal than a filmed adaptation. The most important parts of the book involve 'the very human story about faith and friendship and desire and addiction and triumphing over yourself, all of which seemed to me things that the theatre could do so well'.[21]

Whereas Jackson's adaptation, especially the battle-heavy *Return of the King*, was often criticised as being too much of an action or, worse yet, war film, audiences (and scriptwriters) understand that a very visual medium like film needs to present action sequences, sometimes at the expense of quiet moments between characters. Similarly, McKenna's assessment that theatre is a more personal medium for storytelling necessitated the cutting of action sequences and group scenes in favour of a more intimate theatre experience, one that encourages quiet moments, life-affirming songs or excessively trimmed plot points referring to battles and great, sweeping story developments. Adaptations for different media require different ways of restructuring the story, and in the *LotR* musical Frodo and Sam often seemed truer to their book selves.

Unfortunately, as in most adaptations, Merry and Pippin serve as catalysts to set up a scene or simply represent hobbits among the other races of Middle-earth. Only Jackson's recent films give Merry and Pippin more to do, often in changed, expanded or new scenes going beyond the bounds of Tolkien's prose (for example, Pippin lighting the beacons in Minas Tirith, Pippin pushing Faramir from the pyre). On stage, Merry and Pippin become interchangeable 'other hobbits'. Perhaps this is the greatest loss to these two hobbits Tolkien described in such carefully structured detail. In an adaptation into another medium, the book's nuances of character are easily pared to save time on stage or screen. Whereas Frodo and Sam must remain the heart of the hobbit story, others, most notably Merry, Pippin and Bilbo, are likely to become part of the background as 'typical hobbits'. Only slight variations in costume, lyrics or dialogue distinguish them from each other or hobbitry at large, which is a significant change from Tolkien's careful character development.

Outside influences, such as the factor of movie celebrity, can also influence public perception of characters and their preference for one interpretation over another. The *LotR* musical's characters may be better remembered on their own merit than for the celebrity of the actors portraying them; the theatrical story is more powerful than the fame of the actors, acquired through their roles in this musical. Although it may not be fair, theatre actors (unless they also are television or film stars) seldom gain the attention or fame of actors who make it big in films or on television. Theatre audiences usually remember a story's characters, not individual actors, which served Tolkien's story well during the musical's run.

On stage, the hobbits' appearance differs greatly from that of men or elves. Without the benefits of CGI or tricky camera angles, hobbits must look distinctly different on stage from (and less 'human' than) other characters. In the *LotR* musical, hobbits (with the exception of Frodo) are rounder (aided by lots of padding) and plainer than other characters. They look much less like the actors portraying them and more like a true race distinctly different from humans.

Theatregoers sitting in the balcony or back row may not see each actor's face clearly, or, because so much happens on stage at one time, may focus on more than a character or two at a time. Theatre audiences are much more likely to be caught up in the story than to scrutinise (or idolise) one actor or performance. Fans would likely walk by a 'hobbit' without recognising him if they saw him on the street. James Loye, for example, will be much less likely than Elijah Wood to be called Frodo in public in the years following his performance. The 'hobbit' illusion is better maintained in a theatrical performance, even in a multimillion-dollar production that garners worldwide attention.

A possible problem with the relative anonymity afforded the actors playing hobbits on stage is the lack of easily recognised stars in the lead roles, which can affect box-office receipts and the length of a play's run. Although the actors playing the hobbits might be well known in theatrical circles and have their own fan base among theatregoers who have seen them in other plays, they were not 'name' actors at the time of their *LotR* casting. In the 2000s, the most successful plays in Toronto, London or New York often were those featuring film or television stars who, for a limited time, took a role in a play. Theatre, perhaps more than film, has begun to rely more heavily on actors whose names, rather than the title of a play or the popularity of a story, will draw large audiences. *LotR* relied primarily on story and creative theatricality in order to pull in crowds.

Gary Russell, author of *The Lord of the Rings: The Official Stage Companion*, summarised the issue of 'celebrity hobbits' when he described first hearing of Dominic Monaghan's role on the television series *Lost*; the media identified the actor not with his upcoming role as Charlie Pace but with his famous former role as a hobbit. With Monaghan's/Merry's face plastered on huge movie screens, sometimes in close-up, in addition to the films' international media blitz, film fans easily (and probably forever) identified Monaghan with his *LotR* role. Russell wondered whether Dylan Roberts, playing Merry in Toronto, would share Monaghan's fate as being forever recognised as a 'hobbit'. The author concluded 'probably not – the mass audiences who gravitate towards movies and television are rarely replicated on the stage', and most audiences, even of a well-known musical or play, 'would be hard pressed to remember anyone other than the headlining stars' names, and certainly not their faces'.[22]

In years to come, the actors associated with cinematic adaptations are far more likely to be remembered for their roles as hobbits than are the actors who starred in a theatrical adaptation. Actors who succeed the original cast of the *LotR* musical have far fewer audience expectations to live up to, and producers can more easily change their interpretation of hobbits without an outcry from fans who associate specific actors with clearly remembered characters.

For better or worse, the *LotR* musical kept hobbits in the news and public awareness in the years after Jackson's films; the play also gave audiences another concept of what hobbits look like and which parts of their story should be immortalised. In some ways the musical remained true to Tolkien's work, but in others it necessarily (or just creatively) differed greatly. What stand out in this adaptation are Frodo's and Sam's mutual respect and love in a friendship that transcends adversity and separation. Sometimes that depiction of the hobbits' life-affirming relationship was not enough for the critics or diehard fans of Tolkien's works.

A (Sometimes Very) Critical Reception to the Musical

From the very beginning, the *LotR* musical was plagued with complaints. Although the Toronto production benefited from lots of tweaking (of the show as well as the technology) during previews held between 4 February and the world premiere on 23 March 2006, it still suffered critics' lukewarm reception. The *New York Times* called it 'incomprehensible' and compared the exotic Finnish–Indian music as 'Enya meets ashram'; Britain's *Sunday Telegraph* reported the show 'weary', with none of the magical fascination created by *The Lion King* or other family-oriented musicals; the *Toronto Star*, while praising the special effects and innovative staging, complained that the story made the characters 'pawns in a giant rapid-fire chess game'.[23]

Perhaps this production was doomed to disappoint critics, Tolkien fans who know the book by heart, or movie fans accustomed to the Jackson adaptation. As *Time* reviewer Richard Corliss noted in March 2006, the creative team, including playwright Shaun McKenna, had to adapt Tolkien's complex story while figuring out

> how to blend narrative, drama and music in a three-act production – and do it all without retakes or post-production computer effects. Most daunting was the task of satisfying all those Tolkienites whose image of Middle-earth has been shaped by many readings of the sacred text and latterly by Peter Jackson's Oscar-laden film version.[24]

Director Matthew Warchus told *Entertainment Weekly* just before the musical's premiere that the way to blend these elements successfully is to create a workable story with the requisite heroes but not just go through *LotR* by

> trying to check all the boxes … So the center of the story is Frodo, Sam, and Gollum, but we do spend time in the story telling the Arwen and Aragorn romance as well, and Merry and Pippin are very much there … [Y]ou don't have to have seen the film or read the book to follow what's happening.[25]

By making the play self-contained, the production team perhaps wanted to avoid the pitfalls of other adaptors, such as Bakshi, whose film ended up being incomprehensible to audiences unfamiliar with Tolkien's book.

Hardcore Tolkien fans, especially of the book more than any adaptation, can easily find fault with this version of the *LotR* story. Whole sections and characters are missing in the effort to make the story short and sweet for theatregoers. Key characters in the book have been omitted during the process of constantly paring the story to Frodo's journey to destroy the Ring and Aragorn's rise as the returning king. The many stirring battles described in detail in the book are converted to one great battle, primarily as a proving ground for battle leader Aragorn and a dramatic climax for the forces of Good (men, elves, a dwarf, Éowyn, Merry and Pippin) and Evil (Orcs).

Other critics, as well as theatregoers mesmerised by the play's spectacular effects and revamped plot, nonetheless found quite a bit to like about the *LotR* musical. In Toronto, it received nominations for the Dora Mayor Moore Awards for theatrical excellence. *LotR* was nominated for 15 awards and won in these categories: Outstanding New Musical, Outstanding Production of a Musical, Outstanding Direction of a Musical, Outstanding Performance by a Male in a Principal Role – Musical, Outstanding Costume Design, Outstanding Lighting Design and Outstanding Choreography in a Play or Musical.[26] Michael Therriault (Gollum) consistently won critics' praise for his performance, which propelled him to a Dora Award over fellow castmates Brent Carver (considered by many fans and critics to be a tepid Gandalf) and Peter Howe (another critical darling for his performance as Sam).

In London, *LotR* received nominations in seven categories at the Whatsonstage Theatregoer's Choice Awards, the only awards decided by the public; in 2008 a record five thousand fans nominated their favourites, and twenty-five thousand voted online. In addition to the musical, several actors, many who starred in the Toronto as well as the London production, garnered nominations: the See Tickets Best Actor in a Musical (James Loye as Frodo), Best Supporting Actress in a Musical (Laura Michelle Kelly as Galadriel), Best Supporting Actor in a Musical (Michael Therriault as Gollum), Best Director (Matthew Warchus), Best Set Designer (Rob Howell), Best Choreographer (Peter Darling) and Superbreak Best New Musical.[27] London's *LotR* won for Best Set Designer but often lost in other categories to

Hairspray. Loye's Frodo came in third in the best actor category, with 12.3 percent of the votes; the musical itself, receiving 24.7 percent of the votes, was placed second to *Hairspray*.[28]

As a musical play, *LotR* initially benefited from Jackson's popular trilogy only a few years before, which attracted audiences still hungry for more of Tolkien's stories but who may not have wanted to take time to read his books. Riding on the trilogy's coattails into Toronto may have been the play's undoing, however. It never lived up to the expectations of many theatregoers but still made its mark as an innovative theatrical adaptation, one that successfully kept hobbits in the news in the years between Jackson's cinematic adaptations.

Fellowship!

In 2004, another musical capitalised on the popularity of Jackson's trilogy. Comedic actors got together in Los Angeles to forge a *Fellowship!* as a hilarious homage to *The Fellowship of the Ring*. The musical played in Southern California to rave reviews,[29] but not only for its music. This parody neatly skewered primarily Jackson's film, but, as *Comedy LA* reviewer Mike Valdez noted, 'The success of this play hinges on its tone which doesn't mock the source material so much as uses it as a framework to make fun of everything else, including the production itself.'[30]

As cast member Brian D. Bradley explained, Tolkien wrote 'possibly the strongest hero structure, with all the elements you need for a serious story; it's just the twist you give it so that it'll sell as comedy'.[31] He recalled that after their reception at San Diego Comic-Con, he knew *Fellowship!* would do extremely well.

Tolkien fans loved scenes like 'One Ring', the musical number in which Gandalf explains the significance of the Ring to Frodo. References to Sauron being reduced to a big red eyeball (as portrayed in Jackson's trilogy) and the Ring's inscription, which is far too long to fit inside, provided some of the song's humour. Bradley recalled that when fans watched this number, 'they just screamed. They had never thought of the scene that way before. All the "in" jokes worked so well because it was *their* thing.'[32] Even while parodying *FotR*, however, the cast was mindful of the important character relationships at the heart of Tolkien's story. Bradley added that '*Fellowship!* is about the relationships that characters have, their bond, loyalty, very "human" things.'[33]

This fellowship modernised the story while poking fun at its seriousness. Aragorn's and Arwen's duet, for example, becomes a power rock ballad that dissolves into 'elvish' gibberish. As the actors always pointed out during interviews, they are *LotR* fans themselves who think Tolkien's and Jackson's oh-so-serious treatment of the story could use a loving tweak. Although the musical initially played only in the Los Angeles area, its website and performances at places like San Diego's Comic-Con in July 2004 and ORC (One Ring Celebration) in January 2005 helped expand its popularity with *LotR* fans around the world.

The costumes and props set the scene while clearly representing a low-budget production. Director/writer Joel McCrary noted that

> one of the moments that represented who we are is the part where the Fellowship travels in canoes. Basically, what we did was have the actors leave Galadriel, who reminds them to 'Drink lots of water!' and stay hydrated [laughs]. Then the lights go down. When they come up, there are two little one-foot-long canoes with action figures of each of the characters mounted on remote-control cars. They travel across the stage while epic music is playing. All of a sudden, Allen [Simpson, who played keyboards during performances] and Chris [Kirschbaum, who played drums] get up and stand with their hands out like the Argonath. It's one of those moments that's so silly, but the nature of this is that the movies were so beautifully done with such great CGI effects. With a little shoestring-budget theatre piece, how can you pull that off? The fact is we kind of do, while showing the puppet strings.[34]

Although the budget may have been much lower than that of most adaptations, the creativity behind *Fellowship!* certainly matched that of larger productions.

In this low-budget adaptation, the style as well as the quality of costumes and props adds to the humour. Typical of a take-off of the

LotR film 'look', the hobbits wear easily identifiable Shirewear: vest, long-sleeved shirt, trousers cut just below the knee. Instead of having hairy feet, the barefoot actors' costumes include a ridiculously furry anklet. 'Gay Sam' wears a hot pink shirt in contrast to the other hobbits' more subdued attire; Bilbo, building on his Borscht-belt comic persona, is attired in a ruffled shirt, silky smoking jacket and bow tie. The actors don curly or wavy long wigs, just as in the movies; the best hirsute look is Gandalf's obviously fake (and drooping) white beard. YouTube clips of performances and photographs from the *Fellowship!* website show the ways these costumes and makeup approximate the look found in Jackson's films' high-end creations. Although audiences clearly recognise *Fellowship!*'s budget constraints, they can nevertheless easily distinguish the hobbits from men, elves, dwarves, or wizards, despite the fact that they all are about the same height and, indeed, the same actor might be a hobbit in one scene and a Nazgûl in the next.

Cast members played several characters, with women sometimes acting the roles of male hobbits or dwarves, and Bradley memorably doubling as Galadriel and Gandalf. Lisa Fredrickson played Gimli such that 'no one could've have done it better'.[35] Kelly Holden-Bashar received reviewers' accolades as Pippin, 'who here is portrayed as a popular class clown, with a catch phrase repeated by the cast – "Oh, Pippin" – which gets funnier as the show goes on'.[36] Her performance gave new meaning to being a well-rounded hobbit; 'Pippin' was pregnant. When asked about the casting, Holden joked that she could have played either Gimli or Pippin in order to wear an appropriately sized costume, and her personality better suited that of the youngest hobbit.[37]

As with any parody, the humour only works if the audience knows the source well. This parody really has two sources: Tolkien's book and Jackson's *FotR*, but playing with the film's version of characters made the humour timely for a wider audience, given the then-recent popularity of the films. This parody played well to two audiences: *LotR* fans (who sometimes came costumed to the musical) and comedy fans seeking good entertainment, not necessarily *LotR*-themed humour. *Fellowship!* handily provided the laughs for both groups; a rudimentary understanding of Jackson's adaptation of *FotR* was all that was necessary to get the jokes or cultural references.

Sam's and Frodo's on-screen relationship, for example, sometimes invites questions about the depth of their closeness. Modern audiences looking for possible homoerotic overtones in Sam's loving looks at Frodo in the film had a field day at *Fellowship!* when Sam openly lusts after an oblivious Frodo. When the hobbits sing about what they will miss most about the Shire, Merry (Ryan Smith) comments, 'Hey Sam, I bet you'll miss Rosie.' Sam wrinkles his nose. 'Eh, not so much.' He reprises the chorus after the object of his affection exits the stage, poignantly singing 'As long as you're here, right by my side, home's never too far away'[38] while gazing longingly off stage. By the end of the show, Frodo admits that fate has brought Sam and him together on this journey, and Sam sings, 'We're more than just friends.' Both then harmonise, 'I'd walk through the fire, as long as I'm walking with you.'[39] Although Frodo may never realise in just what way Sam loves him, the audience understands the joke and its reference to some fans' interpretation of the film.

The other hobbit pair, Merry and Pippin, often seem interchangeable to casual audiences, and *Fellowship!* also plays on this theme. Holden elaborated on the development of the Merry–Pippin dynamic for this parody:

> The joke with people who aren't savvy about Tolkien but would go to the movie is that they'd ask, 'Which one's Pippin, and which one's Merry?' We decided to have fun with that a little bit … Why don't we just have, no matter what happens, people think Pippin is blameless? Everything that's problematic or scampish throughout the story – they're being too loud or something – why don't we make everyone blame Merry, no matter what? It became such a large part of the Merry–Pippin story and had a really sweet resolution [in the duo's part in the closing song]: 'You are the one person who really knows me, knows who I am, and we're going to go on our path.' That was a choice we made in terms of the parody.[40]

As a result, Merry is frequently overlooked in this production; even the other characters often forget his name. Pippin, however, comes across as a true friend. At the end of *Fellowship!* Merry is pleased that

Pippin knows exactly who he is. 'You know my name. I'm with you 'til the end,' he sings. Holden noted that

> Pippin and Merry are always overshadowed by Frodo and Sam, but they sacrifice so much. At first they seem the least capable but come through being so wonderfully capable. One thing we wanted to show was the beauty of their loyalty. Even though they at some point may cause more problems than they solve, they're such a vital part of the whole mission. Their optimism and enthusiasm keep everyone else going as much as anyone else's bravery or intelligence... Those two little hobbits' heart is just as vital to the journey's success.[41]

Although the parody mines humour from the Merry–Pippin connection, it also shows that these two friends truly do know each other, a fitting tribute to one of the strongest friendships in Middle-earth.

Each song varies in style to accommodate the humorous mood being set, and even a song that begins thoughtfully ('The lament of the ring') soon turns into a musical pun that invests a serious scene from the movie (in this case Boromir's attempt to take the Ring from Frodo) with character-appropriate humour. Much of the show's musical humour came from rehearsals, such as when 'Frodo' had a higher range than 'Boromir'. As the song moved into progressively higher keys, the result turned into the perfect way for Frodo to evade Boromir in the scene; he simply sings higher and higher until Boromir can no longer follow.[42]

Co-producer and lyricist Allen Simpson arrived later in the project but quickly got up to speed. He praised the 'unique nature of this show' that allowed so much collaboration among everyone involved. Although the lyrics were written by everybody working together, Simpson composed the music, which mixed musical styles to create specific high points in the show. 'Rather than parody a style of Broadway, we considered what would be a funny juxtaposition of that character to sing... Whatever the moment is – we found a genre that turned that number into an emotional 10.'[43] With so many Tolkien and movie fans working together, *Fellowship!* provided insights into Tolkien's characters while interjecting humour.

Parodies typically exaggerate a few prominent traits of each character, and *Fellowship!* emphasises the traits most obviously shown on screen in Jackson's film. Frodo is quietly confident and becomes the one to whom the other hobbits turn for answers. In 'The lament of the ring',[44] Frodo questions why the Ring is his burden; he grows tired of carrying it. In the 'sing-off' with Boromir, Frodo finds a unique way to escape with the Ring. Even in this parody, clever Frodo manages to succeed where others fail.

Pippin's obvious trait, other than being class clown, is his obsession with food. In Jackson's *FotR*, Pippin becomes concerned by Aragorn's lack of appreciation of second breakfast. When Aragorn nixes the hobbits' planned meal break and instead tosses Pippin an apple to eat as they hike, the fruit bounces off his head, leaving Pippin to lift a confused face to the sky.[45] In *Fellowship!* Pippin takes a firmer approach in educating Aragorn about the ways of hobbits. Holden commented that whereas general audiences may be familiar with the concept of wizards, elves or dwarves, hobbits are different to other types of characters. Although 'It's a hobbit thing', unlike other songs, may not move the story forward, it is an important slice of life that introduces the audience to hobbits. Holden explained that they wanted to 'paint a picture of life in the Shire. What do they talk about? Eating and smoking hobbit weed!'[46]

Pippin's song is all about eating the many meals of the day, the pace increasing as the list progresses. Every time Aragorn attempts to interrupt, the youngest hobbit sets him straight about still more meals to follow. The chorus, 'We are thankful for this bounty, all of our family, food, and friends. For these blessings, oh how we sing – it's a hobbit thing,' neatly summarises the hobbits being overly fond of good food, drink, pipeweed and fellowship. Led by Pippin, the hobbits blissfully sing, 'We hope mealtime never ends.'[47]

Merry, on the other hand, is obsessed with pipeweed. He eagerly anticipates new experiences on the quest: 'Maybe I'll find new things to smoke and get myself invited to a dwarven rave.'[48] His major concern about what to bring with him is the amount of pipeweed needed for four hobbits. Even in the last number, when he and Pippin must rely on each other after the breaking of the Fellowship, he answers Pippin's line ('Although I'm afraid, I'm with my best friend. Merry, you're all that I need.') with 'I'm with you to the end. Just don't bogart my last bag of weed.'[49] This line plays off the *RotK* scene when Merry gives the departing Pippin the last of the Longbottom leaf, as well as an earlier scene in *FotR* in which Saruman admonishes Gandalf that he has grown foolish after smoking too much of the halflings' weed – scenes and lines that can be re-interpreted if 'weed' is substituted for 'pipeweed'.

Fellowship! remained popular long after its initial production, in large part because of fans' positive word-of-mouth reviews and sales of the musical's soundtrack. In October 2010 *Fellowship!* once again graced the stage, this time playing at the New York Musical Theatre Festival. There it won the award for Outstanding Ensemble Performance.[50] In 2012, it returned to a warm reception in Los Angeles. Nearly a decade after Jackson's trilogy debuted on screen and several years after its initial Los Angeles run, the cast of *Fellowship!* continued to find hobbit fans to laugh along with them.

Even in a parody, truths emerge about what audiences know and love about hobbits. What is positive about obsessive personalities Pippin and Merry is their close friendship, a relationship highlighted in Tolkien's book and Jackson's trilogy. The same is true of Sam and Frodo; although the parody presents an openly gay Sam whose unrequited love for Frodo provides much of the humour, the musical, like the book, emphasises the pair's devotion to and reliance on each other. The parody reveals kernels of truth that tickle audiences with inside jokes and popular-culture references.

De Meij's *The Lord of the Rings* Symphony

Stage musicals, whether serious or parodies, are hardly the sum of 'hobbit music'. Symphonic and opera music also has a role in popularising Tolkien's characters, and composers' adaptations provide unique insights into yet another way to consider the Professor's prose.

Between March 1984 and December 1987, Dutch composer Johan de Meij wrote his Symphony Number 1, best known as *The Lord of the Rings* symphony. It consists of five movements, the final one dedicated to the hobbits. Key characters and scenes from Tolkien's book inspire each movement; the first presents Gandalf, followed by Lothlórien, Gollum and the Journey in the Dark section (Mines of Moria and the fateful Bridge of Khazad-Dûm). After the symphony's premiere in Brussels on 15 March 1988, it received acclaim and has been played internationally many times. In 1989 it received first prize at the Sudler International Wind Band Composition Competition in Chicago, and in 1990 garnered an award by the Dutch Composers Fund. In 2001 the London Symphony Orchestra recorded the best-known orchestral version.[51]

Perhaps creating music based on *LotR* events and characters is the most difficult type of adaptation because it is not supported by visuals, as are film or stage productions in which music primarily supports what is being watched. A composer must create characters and events from nuances of instruments and layers of harmony or dissonance. On screen or stage, the choices of instruments and styles suggesting the Shire, for example, have been remarkably similar; flutes or clarinets typically indicate a simple, rural lifestyle through melodies that can be varied numerous ways as the story progresses. With a five-movement symphony, de Meij must highlight personalities and synthesise whole concepts and events without visual aids and within a relatively short piece of music.

The Hobbit section of the *LotR* symphony provides two contrasting themes: a 'happy folk dance' to signify the hobbits' 'carefree and optimistic character', followed by a softer, more solemn hymn that shows 'the determination and noblesse of the hobbit folk'.[52] For listeners not familiar with European folk dances, the first section may sound more like a march, carrying with it possible military overtones. Instruments harsher than those heard in 'Shire' music created for stage and film build an exuberant melody; snare drums and horns herald this different interpretation of hobbit life. In contrast, the quiet hymn is softer, with strings carrying the melody. This piece leads to Frodo's departure from the Grey Havens and gently, gradually fades to silence.

One of the benefits of original orchestral music is that listeners are freed from other artists' (directors', actors', costumers') interpretations of character or scene. The audience can envision whoever or whatever seems appropriate in response to the music. My interpretation of the first section of the hobbit piece recalls Merry and Pippin riding happily through a triumphant Shire in the days after its scouring of the ruffians. Tolkien wrote of the captains resplendent in their outworldly uniforms, mail shining in the sunlight. The drums and horns easily emphasise the young captains' joy at being home in the Shire while still recognising their responsibility to guide the Shire in war or peace. A bouncy folk tune seems appropriate for the scene Tolkien described of these two famous hobbits who, ever mindful of the quest and its cost, help rebuild a stronger, but still quite rustic homeland. Quite the opposite, the hymn brings to mind Frodo as Ringbearer and hero unable to return to his life; the quiet Grey Havens theme hints that Frodo, like the melody, fades into Shire legend.

However listeners interpret de Meij's symphony, it continues to be enjoyed wherever there are *LotR* fans. In early 2008, the Knoxville Wind Symphony proudly announced its 'Storm of Sauron' concert,[53] featuring the *LotR* symphony. News of the event quickly spread among fans online through local news affiliates as well as fansites like TORN.

Dr Marshall Forrester, Director of Bands at Carson-Newman College and conductor of the Knoxville Wind Symphony, found an excellent fit between de Meij's symphony and Knoxville's musicians. Forrester noted that shortly after its debut, the *LotR* symphony 'took the band world by storm'. At 40 minutes long, this composition is one of the longest for bands, and Forrester reported that the Knoxville performance received a standing ovation and warm comments, although some audience members were surprised to learn that the symphony predates Jackson's films.[54]

Although symphonic adaptations reach a fraction of the audience of large-scale theatrical productions, films or Howard Shore's much-hyped *LotR* symphonic performances based on the soundtracks from Jackson's trilogy (discussed later in this chapter), they are important as yet another creative endeavour that reflects the power of Tolkien's story and characters and helps ensure their ongoing appeal.

The Hobbit Children's Opera

Music inspired by Tolkien's books and characters continues to proliferate. In May 2004 composer Dean Burry, the man behind other successful children's operas in his native Canada, debuted *The Hobbit* as an opera suitable for a children's production company but enjoyable to audiences of all ages. The Toronto production, commissioned by the Canadian Children's Opera Chorus, later toured Prince Edward Island, New Brunswick and Nova Scotia. In May 2008, a revised opera premiered in Sarasota, Florida.[55]

Although familiarity with Tolkien's story undoubtedly enriches the audience's enjoyment of the opera, Burry explained that reading the book before seeing the opera is not necessary. In addition, audiences who have seen *LotR*, perhaps the Jackson adaptation, might be encouraged to come to an opera based on another of Tolkien's works. Burry noted that 'there's been such a buzz over the *Lord of the Rings* trilogy because of the movies, and so I think parents will have an easier time bringing a lot of kids, boys particularly, to something like [the opera] because they can relate to it. People know that it's an exciting story.'[56]

The opera blends Burry's response to two creative and pragmatic needs for a children's opera. The work has to involve a large number of singing roles to allow as many children as possible to become involved; many other children's productions require only a few main roles and, perhaps, a background cast of walk-ons. The ideal children's production gives some adults and many children a chance to shine on stage. The theme of the work also has to appeal to children but interest adults (as well as the composer). Happily, *The Hobbit* as a story offers such appeal. As Burry enthused, '"It is a tale that truly sings."'[57] It also provides the requisite large cast for a children's production.

> The sheer size of cast makes adaptations of *The Hobbit* difficult for most professional organizations to do ... but most children's choruses are larger and can take advantage of the fact that there are many roles and a lot for everyone to do. Also, in the Middle-earth mythology, *The Hobbit* is one of the more straight-forward stories without the

hardcore knowledge required to fully understand *LotR*, so it was a story that, with some trimming, could be reduced to a manageable dramatic plot that anyone can enjoy.[58]

Burry's interest in setting *The Hobbit* to music began at a surprisingly young age. After he read the book during Grade Six, the budding composer 'always imagined setting those song lyrics someday'. He also wanted to bring something different to *The Hobbit*; in this adaptation, Burry 'tries to link elements [of *The Hobbit*] to the greater history of Middle-earth'.[59] He does not worry about his adaptation being compared with any others, including *Hobbit* films. His opera is

> several levels of distance from a realistic version of *The Hobbit*...
> The opera takes you into another world altogether...It's that elvish story. That is another layer of distance from what *The Hobbit* would be like if it were really taking place [such as a live-action film]. Then you have the fact that mine is in a theatre. Then you have the fact that mine is a musical. Then you have the fact that it's a story within a story. That [layering] was deliberate to make this opera work as *The Hobbit* but be unique as well.[60]

The two-act opera begins in Rivendell with the aging Bilbo reminiscing about his life. Burry believes this introduction is important to provide a framework for the story to follow. By letting the audience hear the story from Old Bilbo, they are immediately brought into the plot and made privy to the hobbit's memories of an extraordinary adventure. Burry explained that

> I need to set up the convention that this is Elvish theatre and we are in Rivendell – the 'Opera-within-an-opera.' Tolkien himself suggests that *The Hobbit* is Bilbo's own memoir (*There and Back Again*), so why wouldn't [Bilbo] adapt his own work in the time spent in Rivendell? By having Bilbo played by an adult, it creates a reality so we accept the children as elvish players.[61]

After this prologue, the next five scenes take the audience from Bilbo's first meeting with Gandalf in Hobbiton to Rivendell to the Misty Mountains and finally, just before the intermission, to Bilbo's encounter with Gollum. The second act begins with Bilbo's and the dwarves' nearly disastrous run-in with wargs and goblins before their rescue by the eagles. The company becomes captured by the Mirkwood elves before escaping on barrels headed towards Lake Town. A highlight of this production is a seductive Smaug, who has his own song. As in the book, Bilbo's adventure ends with the Battle of Five Armies and his eventual return to Rivendell. Burry's 12-scene adaptation is remarkably faithful to Tolkien's plot, and Bilbo, quite naturally, is the star of the show.

> Musically, the opera provides different voices for the elves, dwarves, and hobbits. Burry envisioned a different musical style for each of the races and was inspired by real-world styles. Hobbits are Celtic (that is pretty much the case in all adaptations), Elves are French Renaissance (madrigals like 'Oh Where Are You Going' and 'Sing All Ye Joyful', the finale), Dwarves are Slavic ('Far Over the Misty Mountains'), Goblins [are] German Expressionist ('Snap! Clap! The Black Crack!'). The Lakemen are high Anglican English. Smaug certainly has a seductive side, hence the charming, yet sinister tango when he tries to trick Bilbo.[62]

Just as Tolkien provides different linguistic backgrounds for different races in Middle-earth, Burry does the same with the musical style, and each race has at least one distinctive song to help audiences get to know them. The music not only summarises key elements of the story but provides an emotional depth as audiences understand not only what is happening in the story but how and why each race acts and reacts as it does to the action unfolding on stage.

In the two Sarasota performances in 2008, as in many theatrical adaptations, Bilbo was played by a young woman (Maria Sulimirski and Brooke Saba each taking a turn for one performance). The contrast from an older male actor playing Bilbo in the prologue to the youthful, higher-voiced Bilbo undertaking the adventure helps audiences distinguish the shift in time; they also see Bilbo mature from the inexperienced hobbit before his life-changing adventure and the older hobbit very much at home with the elves in Rivendell. The costuming provides no new insights into hobbits, but the opera appropriately presents a vision of Bag End and the hobbits of the Shire that is familiar to anyone who has read *The Hobbit*.

Bilbo begins as a typical stay-at-home hobbit. Throughout the opera his often-repeated refrain expresses his wish of being back in his comfortable home instead of traipsing about Middle-earth, often in the cold or damp, and with far fewer meals than he usually enjoys. This refrain captures Bilbo's early reluctance to leave the Shire and his hobbity love of comfort. The Bilbo portrayed in Burry's opera is very much

> a bit of an Everyman (Everyhobbit), and for most of us, life is a balance (and sometimes battle) between the known/comfortable and the unknown/exciting/scary. Most of us want to push to be something more than we are, even though it is usually hard... That's the way to understand [not only] hobbits but humanity as well.[63]

Bilbo's story provides exciting entertainment for children but allows some depth of interpretation for older audiences. Adults can understand Bilbo's reluctance to leave the familiar for the unknown; they may also better appreciate the way that such an adventure outside the hobbit's comfort zone (as well as geographically outside the Shire) can expand his worldview and help him become the worldly hobbit seen at the beginning and end of the opera.

Film and TV Soundtracks from the 1970s to the 2000s

'Hobbit' music plays an important role in television and cinematic adaptations, and fans gain insights into characters and differences between the adapted characterisations and Tolkien's original by hearing these soundtracks. Although the music is part of the television specials and films discussed in Chapters 4 and 5, soundtrack CDs or audio downloads are often played alone, and fans may be content to listen to a soundtrack as entertainment separate from watching television or a film. Therefore, the following soundtracks should be considered both as part of the television specials or films but also separately as standalone music that adapts characters aurally instead of visually.

The Rankin–Bass TV specials often bridge scenes with songs, and characters like Sam sometimes receive their own musical numbers within the animated story. The animated television specials added two ballads to 'hobbit music': 'The greatest adventure: the ballad of the hobbit', from 1977's *The Hobbit*, and 'Frodo of the nine fingers', from 1980's *The Return of the King*. Renowned American folk singer Glenn Yarbrough sang both, and his style was more appropriate to the mid- to late 1970s musical genre that refused to give up its 1960s' roots to the emergence of disco than to later periods. By 1980, the Yarbrough folk sound was less mainstream, but by keeping the same singer and style of music for both *The Hobbit* and *RotK*, Rankin–Bass unified the animated stories.

'The greatest adventure' (music by Maury Laws, lyrics by Jules Bass) matches a children's story theme with Bilbo as a strange role model-protagonist. Although Bilbo is the only hobbit shown in the story (Bag End and an apparently abandoned Hobbiton indicate the hobbit community), he is identified by Gandalf and the dwarves as a burglar, by Gollum as a thief, and by Smaug as a liar and a thief. In this way Bilbo is a questionable 'role model', but in one respect he admirably serves as a guide for young people who watch the animated story: Bilbo is an adventurer who keeps reminding himself to keep going and to be brave when his friends need help. 'The greatest adventure' sets the story early, as Yarbrough sings all verses while the opening credits roll. The most memorable lines, 'The greatest adventure is what lies ahead ... The changes ... are all yours to make; the mould of your life is in your hands to break.'[64]

When Bilbo questions whether he can bravely continue, for example, to keep going farther in Smaug's cave, his interior monologue provides the voiceover for his timid actions. Just as Bilbo seems about to turn back, Yarbrough's song returns with a few encouraging lines, and Bilbo immediately decides to continue his adventure. This pattern of self-doubt followed by uplifting lyrics encourages children to follow Bilbo's example. The lyrics, as well as folk genre, appropriately echo the 'can do' and 'be yourself' attitudes of the mid-1960s to the mid-1970s, when popular music shifted away from light rock and folk heralding the Age of Aquarius or even the sensibilities of a 'Make your own kind of music' (as sung first by Cass Elliot but covered by many artists in the early to mid-1970s). Children and parents who matured in the hippie era would likely find the musical message in Rankin–Bass's *The Hobbit* empowering.[65]

Nostalgia for the song, a staple of many fans' childhood memories of Tolkien on TV, gave it new life through the documentary *Ringers: Lord of the Fans*. Popular Southern California indie band Arlo recorded a new rock version specifically for the documentary, allowing fans not familiar with the Rankin–Bass classic to hear an updated version and ensuring that the tune remains an active part of Tolkien fans' canon.[66]

Yarbrough's other Rankin–Bass ballad, 'Frodo of the nine fingers' (also composed by Laws with lyrics by Bass), helps audiences unfamiliar with the earlier sections of *The Lord of the Rings* (*FotR* and *TT*) to understand what has happened to Frodo and why he would want to leave Middle-earth with Elrond, Gandalf and Bilbo. During a strange scene created for the Rankin–Bass animated *RotK*, a minstrel at Bilbo's birthday party, here a quiet affair with the four hobbits of the Fellowship, Bilbo, Elrond and Gandalf, reminds the aged Bilbo why Frodo has only nine fingers.[67] Unlike the *Hobbit* ballad, this song failed to become a 'classic' in part because of its specific tie to the story and because it has little else to recommend it. Nevertheless, a 2006 YouTube fan video dedicated to 'Tolkien lovers everywhere' immortalised the song for audiences more familiar with Jackson's films; the 'Frodo' ballad plays over key scenes of the Ring story featuring Elijah Wood as Frodo.[68] By 2011, several fan-created music videos as well as the original Rankin–Bass version could be found on YouTube, each receiving thousands of hits.[69]

Audiences who read the credits to both Rankin–Bass programmes might think that Yarbrough's music deserves special attention, based on the type size of credits. In an interview many years after recording the soundtrack to these specials, Yarbrough laughingly confessed that the credit's emphasis came about purely by coincidence and Rankin's disgust with voice actors' demands. When Rankin asked him how he would like to be credited, the singer replied that he did not care so much about the credit as long as he was paid for the work. Rankin's rancorous attitude softened, and he admitted that he was frustrated from 'dealing with all these big stars that want everything, and they want top billing, it's just driving me nuts. Finally, I decided to list everybody in alphabetical order in little, tiny letters.' When Yarbrough finally saw the finished product months later, he was surprised to find his name in large letters, but Rankin proved true to his word by listing the actors' names just as he had promised.[70]

The Rankin–Bass animated versions have plenty of detractors, but the ballads, in particular 'The greatest adventure', illustrate how hobbits have often been used as role models, particularly for children. Although the music, as well as the style of animation, dates the programmes for audiences now used to live-action spectacles, *The Hobbit* and *The Return of the King* remain important adaptations that show how hobbits, especially through music written about them, kept Tolkien's characters in the public eye in the late 1970s and early 1980s and gained a foothold in classic children's music.

Just as the Rankin–Bass soundtracks provide insights into hobbits, Howard Shore's soundtrack to Jackson's *LotR* adaptation often emphasises hobbits through music, most notably with Pippin's song for Denethor (in *RotK*), which provides the emotional punch needed to contrast the willful Steward of Gondor with his about-to-be-sacrificed-in-battle gentle son. Even in serious scenes, hobbits lighten the mood with song more than any other characters, and the music or lyrics emphasise the Shire as an ideal and hobbits as the most lovable of Middle-earth inhabitants.

Shore, whose complex score for Jackson's trilogy gracefully supported everything from quiet interpersonal moments to chaotic battles, accomplished what no one else has done: he created individual themes for multiple characters followed throughout 12 hours of film. This feat took him five years,[71] but from the numerous awards and fan acclaim he received after the films' release, the time was well spent.

Among the many accolades for his score, Shore won an Oscar in 2003 for Best Score and as a co-creator (with Fran Walsh and Annie Lennox) of Best Song, 'Into the west'. The *RotK* score won a Saturn award for Best Music. For his work with *RotK* alone, Shore received awards from the Broadcast Critics Film Association as Best

Composer; the Golden Globes, Online Film Critics, and Las Vegas Film Critics Society, all for Best Original Score, and Grammys for the soundtrack and 'Into the west'. Furthermore, the American Society of Composers, Authors, and Publishers (ASCAP) recognised Shore's contributions with a Lifetime Achievement award.[72] Although *RotK* won more awards across the board than the first two instalments of the trilogy, Shore's work for *FotR* and *TT* received plenty of recognition. For *FotR* he won a Grammy for Best Score for a Soundtrack,[73] and *TT* brought him an ASCAP Film and Television Music award for the score for Top Box Office Film and another Grammy.[74]

The soundtracks reflect the many races, characters and events within the grand scope of Tolkien's story and Jackson's adaptations. Within the many hours of music, however, hobbits receive a great deal of individual attention. The Shire theme is a prominent part of the score, with the familiar notes played alone or in combination with other themes to recall where Frodo, Sam, Merry and Pippin began their journey, and to show how far they have come, geographically and spiritually; 'the first three notes of the Shire theme rise stepwise up a major scale to forever call the hobbits back to their verdant homeland.'[75] To reflect Tolkien's important themes of friendship, responsibility and love, as well as emphasise the hobbits' love of life in all its sensual pleasures, the 'hobbit music' embraces 'basic and unadorned musical elements'.[76]

Four variations on this theme follow the hobbits on their journey and record their loss of innocence. A lone whistle or clarinet often plays the Pensive Setting; a folk dance with a Celtic feel is provided in the Rural Setting, which features the bodhran, guitar, dulcimer, harp and fiddle; the more solemn Hymn Setting requires a full orchestra; and the Hobbit's Understanding provides a bridge across other themes and complicates the melody, just as the hobbit's new understanding of the outside world and its dangers complicates their formerly simple lives.[77] Through these rich variations, Shore's soundtrack emotionally underpins the hobbits' psychological growth as they travel farther than any hobbits have ever gone.

Because hobbits enjoy music as much as any other sensual aspect of life, the soundtrack quite naturally illustrates lighter moments, as when, in particular, Merry and Pippin sing drinking songs. Bilbo's birthday party provides an excellent opportunity to show Frodo's lighthearted enjoyment of dance in what becomes his last carefree night before the Ring enters his life. Shy Sam fears to dance with Rosie Cotton, but Frodo takes the choice away from his friend by thrusting him into the dance, perhaps symbolising how Frodo would inadvertently force Sam to become involved not only in the hobbit community but with Rosie in the ongoing dance of life.[78]

Soon after, in a scene from the extended *FotR*, tipsy Pippin, encouraged by Merry, sings 'Hey ho, to the bottle I go' while standing atop a table at the Green Dragon. This scene is mirrored in the aftermath of the Battle of Helm's Deep, when the hobbits show the warriors of Rohan and reunited members of the Fellowship (minus, of course, Sam and Frodo) how hobbits celebrate. Pippin and Merry again dance atop a table as they drink and sing their ode to the Green Dragon.[79] Whether the hobbits sing in tune or dance well, the brief musical interludes illustrate how the most typical of hobbits, Pippin, expresses emotion through song; Merry, as Pippin's erstwhile companion, enthusiastically celebrates with his cousin and encourages him to sing more.

These brief songs emphasise the contrast in Pippin's demeanour and emotion when he sings at Denethor's request. Asked to choose a hobbit song appropriate for the Steward's halls, Pippin forgoes the jolly drinking songs in favour of a wistful song about an uncertain future for a traveller far from home. The haunting beauty of Pippin's clear voice contrasts with Denethor's savagery, not only in the meal he eats during the song but in his choice to send Faramir on a suicide mission; as the hobbit's voice fades at the end of the song, a single tear rolls down his cheek.[80] Not only is Pippin horrified by Denethor's command to his son, but he is also the lone hobbit in Minas Tirith, the first time in his life he has been long parted from his kin. Pippin's separation from his beloved Shire and all it represents is echoed through the lyrics and simple eloquence of the performance. To reflect the most emotional of beings in Middle-earth, Jackson's choice of Pippin as the 'musical' hobbit nicely contrasts the harsh reality of Middle-earth with the sheltered innocence of the Shire.

With the release of each film's complete recordings, *LotR* fans enjoyed the soundtracks on their own merits. Beginning in 2003, Shore toured the world to conduct his six-movement *LotR* symphony; in 2008 the tour continued, but other *LotR* events, such as the performance of the complete score to *FotR*, were added to his calendar. The concerts were still continuing at the time of writing.[81] Although Shore has composed soundtracks for numerous other films, his work with Jackson's *LotR* has endeared him to fans and gained him global recognition for translating Middle-earth into inspirational music and providing harmonious interpretations of Tolkien's hobbits.

Fans were thrilled in early 2011 when they learned that Shore would score the *Hobbit* films. TORN announced Shore's first consultation with Peter Jackson and speculated on the type of music that would be included in the new soundtracks.[82] The composer's preparation included reading *The Hobbit* to get the rhythm of Tolkien's words and his sense of storytelling. During an interview in March 2011, Shore explained that the prose 'translates to me into a musical language. You're creating something in a mirror image of the author's work, except you're composing in music.'[83] Although connections needed to be made between the earlier *LotR* compositions and those new for *The Hobbit*, Shore emphasised that the tone of *The Hobbit* differs from that of *LotR*, leading fans to speculate that the soundtracks for the later films would be lighter-hearted and emphasise hobbits even more.

Music Inspired by Hobbits

Many other composers and musicians have been inspired to write Celtic-themed music as a result of Tolkien's works, especially *LotR* or *The Hobbit*. Popular band Emerald Rose, for example, gained a wider fan base after performing at Oscar cast celebrations in 2003 and 2004, where 'we had a lot of hobbits dancing by the end of the party'.[84] The band has played numerous US fan conventions such as ORC, ELF (East Coast *LotR* Fan Convention) and Dragon Con. The fan documentary *Ringers: Lord of the Fans* also features the band.

Emerald Rose created a CD featuring Celtic-styled music specifically for 29 February 2004 *RotK* Oscars party, and VIPs who attended the bash received copies. *Songs for the Night Sky* was released in limited edition in March 2004, and several songs were remixed and enhanced for the 2005 CD *Archives of Ages to Come*.[85] Not surprisingly, these musicians are Tolkien fans well versed in the Professor's stories as well as recent adaptations of them.

Band member Clyde Gilbert doubts that the band will ever leave behind Tolkien as a source of inspiration, even as they branch out into other types of music. Fellow musician Larry Morris concurs, adding that 'We reach into mythology and fantasy, as well as science and humor, quite a bit in our song writing. I'd like to hope that our future songs spark the imagination and create that sense of wonder that Tolkien was able to create in his books.'[86]

In addition to more recent influences and styles, the Celtic-style songs which made them famous at the Oscar parties will always be part of their repertoire. Gilbert explained that

> Many of the songs of the Shire seem to reflect the rustic charm and contentment of its residents, and I can see the same influence in our music whenever we sing those traditional Irish folk songs. The songs that Aragorn and the 'Lords of the West' are mostly concerned with are obscure or occult knowledge, which again I believe is reflected in many of our more 'serious' songs – the remembrance or chronicling of things nearly-forgotten; their allies the Rohirrim have an equally-inspiring musical tradition, but they reflect the wilder landscape in which they live. We go there too, as we all live in the Southern Appalachians by choice; we all four left the City and moved to the countryside to be closer to the elements.[87]

Like many musicians and artists, Gilbert, who also creates jewellery inspired by Tolkien's themes and characters, was first introduced to Tolkien's stories as a child. The first influence was the Rankin–Bass *Hobbit*, but he quickly began reading the Professor's books, beginning with *LotR* and graduating to *The Silmarillion*. In short, Gilbert credits Tolkien's 'profound influence on my creative and philosophical development, one which definitely inspired me to pay attention to the course of my life in a very deep and positive way'.[88]

Another fan-favoured band (albeit one now disbanded), Brobdingnagian Bards, may have taken their name from *Gulliver's Travels*, but their sound is distinctly Tolkienesque. They too played one of the Oscar parties (dubbed 'Into the West') and were featured at several Tolkien events; one of their final performances before the group disbanded to pursue individual projects was A Long-Expected Party in September 2008. In 2004 they produced a CD of Celtic-flavoured *LotR*-inspired songs, *Memories of Middle-earth*.[89]

Hobbits specifically influenced Bard Marc Gunn and in fact helped get him started on his professional musical career. As a youngster, Gunn 'first fell in love with Tolkien [by] watching *The Hobbit* cartoon. I loved it. Shortly after that I read the book for the first time... My favorite characters were halflings, aka hobbits. Something about seeing the world from a smaller perspective appealed to me.'[90]

Fellow Bard Andrew McKee explained that 'it is easy to get inspired by Tolkien. I can't read his stories and not feel strong emotions.' Reading Tolkien's works are like

> going back to the root of fantasy. Seeing something in its purest form before it has been changed, diluted, or turned cliche by overuse. Because of that, the characters seem simple yet complex at the same time. They have depth but are easy to understand... like a simple melody you can't get out of your head but you appreciate the genius it took to create such a wondrous simplicity.[91]

As a child, McKee enjoyed the animated adaptations of *The Hobbit* and *LotR* and admits that they still inspire him today. 'I think all the music I do owes a little to Tolkien.' After all, he enthused, 'how can I not include something Tolkien? That would be like talking about the history of physics and ignoring Einstein or civil rights in the U.S. and ignoring Martin Luther King, Jr. It can't be done!'[92]

In 2000 Tolkien even helped the Brobdingnagian Bards develop their bestselling song, aptly entitled 'Tolkien', which 'shot up to the top of the Celtic charts [on MP3.com], where it remained until the site closed. It was by far our most popular tune, with over half a million downloads.'[93] During a Renaissance festival, the duo improvised music while they strolled the grounds, Gunn strumming the autoharp and McKee improvising a melody. They hit upon a pleasing combination and asked a friend what the resulting song reminded her of; 'Tolkien,' she replied, and the title stuck.

In 2001 the Bards' performance at the Kansas City Renaissance Festival prompted yet another such Tolkien-inspired collaboration. As they again improvised music, Gunn remembers, 'a melody struck. By the time we were finished, my autoharp was out of tune and we were both stunned into mesmerised silence. We named it "Fellowship of the Ring", and decided then that we needed a CD of "Lord of the Rings" music.' That CD eventually became *Music of Middle-earth*.

Many of the Bards' songs of Middle-earth revolve around hobbits. A crowd-pleaser at gatherings like A Long-Expected Party is the rowdy 'Don't go drinking with hobbits'. Gunn would like to have an entire album of hobbit drinking songs that would be 'not just "about" hobbits. I always found it more interesting to write songs that they might sing in Hobbiton.' Not all of Gunn's songs recall the antics of Merry and Pippin in an inn, however; some songs, such as 'Ring of hope,' are quieter and inspired by one specific hobbit: Sam. Gunn thinks of Sam as 'the steadfast, loyal friend who, despite his small stature, had a big heart and helped Frodo go through his ordeal. I realised not too long ago that most of the songs I've written were inspired by him.'[94]

The hobbits as portrayed by these bands are often rowdy, fun-loving characters who enjoy dancing or drinking. Especially during fan events, crowds of costumed 'hobbits' enjoy kicking up their heels, singing and dancing to the music and generally role playing as real citizens of the Shire. These bands' songs encourage that interpretation of hobbits and mesh with the images of Merry and Pippin singing a drinking song in Rohan or Frodo pushing Sam into dancing with Rosie during Bilbo's birthday party, scenes immortalised in Jackson's adaptation. Not only the music, but the experience of listening to it played live in a fan-friendly setting, encourages everyone who listens to become an honorary hobbit, at least through the band's next set.

As long as *LotR* continues to reach new generations, composers, musicians and singers will follow Tolkien's lead in giving his characters unique voices, whether the music reminds listeners of a long-ago Shire or brings Tolkien's themes into a very modern musical context. True adaptations of Tolkien's stories, such as television or film versions of *LotR* or *The Hobbit*, certainly provide opportunities for musical interludes that illustrate a specific view of Bilbo, Frodo, Sam, Merry or Pippin, but these stories also provide plenty of inspiration for original compositions that go beyond the specifics of Tolkien's words or his characters' scripted personalities.

7

HOBBITS AS ART

Visual artists have long been inspired by Tolkien's stories and specific characters. A scene such as Bilbo's birthday party, for example, might motivate artists to illustrate the event as they perceive the hobbits, especially Bilbo, would look during such an auspicious event. In short, they are adapting Tolkien's prose into a new medium, a still-life work of art. Some artists create a montage of paintings or drawings to capture key moments in a large event, such as a battle, that seems too big to portray on a single canvas. Other painters or illustrators may adapt Tolkien's prose descriptions of characters into portraits, deciding on a representative expression and pose for posterity.

More recently, artists' sources of inspiration have gone beyond Tolkien's texts. Film or television adaptations in particular may become the vision on which artists base their understanding of a character's or place's 'look'. In the late 1970s, Bakshi's film or the Rankin–Bass animated television specials carried more weight in determining for many artists how hobbits 'should' look. Even more influential in the 2000s are Jackson's *LotR* and *Hobbit* films. Although the artists discussed in this chapter may first have become aware of hobbits on film or television, they have also become familiar with

Tolkien's descriptions. The resulting art, an adaptation itself, may thus be a personalised vision blended from Tolkien's works and earlier adaptations.

Whatever inspires artists to portray hobbits in works of art – including but certainly not limited to paintings, illustrations, calendar art and lithographs – the sheer amount of such art must be considered an important form of adaptation.[1] Tolkien-themed art has been both practical in its uses – to illustrate books, sell calendars or enhance a film (for example, create backdrops, provide transitions between scenes, make end credits more visually appealing) – as well as valuable as art for its own sake. Evocative Tolkien-themed art helps fans gain insights into a character (and the artist) while enhancing their appreciation of the work. The beauty of a work of art, and the pleasure of those who interact with it, is as important a 'purpose' as works created for commercial, pragmatic uses in, for example, a book or film.

Tolkien's *Hobbit* and *LotR* inspired other writers and artists to envision their own fantasy worlds, full of mythic creatures, such as dragons, and evoking a lost, roughly medieval time, sometimes on another world far removed from Earth (or Middle-earth). Since *LotR*'s publication in the mid-1950s and a surge in fantasy art and novels in the 1960s and 1970s, several artists have gained popularity by blending elements from recognisable history with the fantasy elements of specific literature, including fairy tales and historic legends. The result has been a wealth of fantasy art in the past half century, and a few artists representing different styles of specifically 'hobbit art' or more generally Tolkien-themed fantasy art are introduced in this chapter.

As Tolkien artist Steve Hickman once noted, Tolkien's memorable characters include elves, dwarves, goblins and kings living in such now-typical fantasy settings as a forest or a castle. The persistence of these images in fantasy art and literature, however, might unduly influence later artists, who might feel pressured to make their creative expression conform to 'stereotypical' images of what are now considered 'standard' fantasy subjects. If someone draws a hobbit, for example, the character is expected to be short. Confusing 'short' with 'childlike' is often a common problem with modern hobbit art. Hickman elaborated that hobbits may be stereotyped as little people, but they 'are not children, nor are they short adults – they are hobbits, and any painting that depicts hobbits should ring a bell in the mind of the viewer, which lets them know, "Yes, that is what they would look like!"[2] Through his art, Hickman and other Tolkien artists who remain true to the Professor's prose and artistic depictions of hobbits and Middle-earth strive to maintain the integrity of Tolkien's characters and world.

The range of Tolkien-themed art is as diverse as the style of artists who create it. Whether parody or almost devotional, whether based on Tolkien's stories or Jackson's (or others') adaptations, decades of Tolkien-inspired artworks portray hobbits in a variety of poses and attitudes. Although their small stature compared to that of other characters, from men to Ents, often makes them seem younger or more innocent than other characters, their characterisation also evokes intense emotional responses from those who view the illustration. On canvas or in a print, hobbits frequently become a focal point for the eye because of the emotion they lend to the scene being depicted. Audiences often empathise or sympathise with hobbits, who provide an entry point for those who view art to enter the illustrated scene and vicariously experience Middle-earth.

Through the Eyes of Tolkien

Artists inspired by Tolkien may create their own art that, in turn, inspires other fans' creativity. All Tolkien-themed art, however, reflects its roots in Tolkien's works. The Professor embodied the complete creative master. His precise technical skills with language became blended with artistic expression through music (in the form of lyrics his characters sing) and poetry or chants (which his characters recite), as well as the illustrations gracing the stories he wrote. Tolkien's art has been called 'inseparable from his fiction, a felicitous marriage of text and art that combines to form a pleasing whole'.[3] It is no wonder that Tolkien's many-faceted talent inspires further artistic explorations of Middle-earth.

Some fans who know Tolkien primarily through adaptations of his stories may be surprised to learn that he created maps of Middle-earth and illustrations depicting hobbits and the Shire, although he was much more confident painting a story with words. In the 1930s, Tolkien wrote to publisher Houghton Mifflin that his own illustrations might not be the best choice for *The Hobbit*, that, in fact, 'if you need drawings of hobbits in various attitudes, I must leave it in the hands of someone who can draw. My own pictures are an unsafe guide.'[4] Even if he felt unsure of his ability to draw hobbits adequately, Tolkien had a very specific mental vision of what they should look like. He wrote to his publisher this description of hobbits: 'Fattish in the stomach, shortish in the leg. A round, jovial face; ears only slightly pointed and "elvish"; hair short and curling (brown). The feet from ankles down, covered with brown hairy fur.'[5]

Despite the author's self-criticism of his art, several of his illustrations and maps appeared in his books and, much later, his drawings were reproduced in the first Tolkien calendars in the 1960s. Even more recently, Tolkien's art, much of it previously unpublished, has become the subject of whole books, including *J.R.R. Tolkien: Artist and Illustrator* (1995) and *The Art of* The Hobbit *by J.R.R. Tolkien* (2011).[6] For the first, authors/editors and Tolkien scholars Wayne Hammond and Christina Scull published more than two hundred of the Professor's illustrations, whereas the latest volume includes a hundred more, this time related solely to *The Hobbit*, quite impressive numbers of illustrations from someone who considered himself far less than a professional artist. The publication of books devoted to Tolkien's art indicates popular recognition of the Professor's importance as an artist.

In a 2011 interview, Hammond and Scull explained Tolkien's illustration process:

> Tolkien had mental pictures of his characters and scenery ... His skill at painting and drawing allowed him sometimes to put his visions into pictorial as well as verbal form, and sometimes he used pictures – particularly maps – to help him work out points of story ... Some of his *Hobbit* illustrations, however, influenced the writing of *The Lord of the Rings*, as he had established certain features of Hobbiton and Rivendell (for instance) in pictures which were not described in the text of *The Hobbit*, but which then entered into its sequel.[7]

As the seventy-fifth anniversary of the 1937 publication of *The Hobbit* neared, fans became more interested in all aspects of Tolkien's work, including, as Scull and Hammond noted, his 'own enduring visions of Bilbo Baggins, Smaug, Bag-End, the Misty Mountains, and other characters and places known to readers around the world'.[8] The posthumous recognition for Tolkien's art surpasses the praise received during his lifetime. Although his greatest fame will always be as author, Tolkien is more frequently being revered as a complete storyteller: scholar, author, artist. That he retained so much control over his stories, especially during a time when the writing–publishing process still largely relied on manual, rather than machine, labour, is further testament to his dedication to these characters.

To understand Tolkien's Middle-earth, hobbits in particular, readers must gain an appreciation of the places and characters as he saw them. In Tolkien's illustrations of the Shire, as seen in *The Hill: Hobbiton Across the Water*,[9] for example, the hobbits' homeland is indeed tranquilly beautiful and well worth protecting from outsiders. Greens, yellows and blues are dominant colours, creating a bright landscape. The viewer's eye skims over the bridge across the river, shown at the bottom of the illustration, then up the golden road past homes and fields to the top of the hill, where a single leafy tree stands at the centre top of the drawing. Around it, puffy clouds sail across a brilliantly blue sky.

A much more sombre scene awaits Bilbo as he floats atop a barrel in Tolkien's *Bilbo Comes to the Huts of the Raft Elves*.[10] The hobbit seems small indeed in the illustration featuring massive trees along the riverbanks. Bilbo's journey will eventually take him towards a more open, brighter waterscape, but at the point captured in this picture he has just emerged from a darker setting (and a dark time in his adventure). Because of the enormity of the trees and river, Bilbo looks very small as he sits astride the barrel, facing forward, with his jacket carefully laid across the slats behind him. Although Bilbo is the smallest living creature in this illustration, Tolkien nevertheless portrays him as competent and calm, despite his escape during the latest phase of his adventure. According to the scale used in Tolkien's illustrations, hobbits may be shorter than other characters or dwarfed by a setting, but their spirits and determination are much greater than their size indicates.

A Hobbit-themed Picture Paints (at least some of Tolkien's) Thousands of Words

As artist Steve Hickman noted earlier in this chapter, the best way for later artists to honour Tolkien is to keep their vision of his characters true to Tolkien's descriptions and characterisations. Jef Murray and Ted Nasmith have taken that approach when they create works of 'hobbit art'.

As in Tolkien's art, Murray's hobbits are dwarfed in size by the larger world portrayed in paintings, but the size of their heart, or character, is never minimised. The hobbit-focused paintings clearly illustrate deep emotion, typical of what hobbits would feel in the situation being depicted on canvas. Like Tolkien, Murray is a devout Catholic whose faith supports his approach to art. Part of the joy of painting is the spiritual act of subcreation, and Murray believes in combining prayer with his art. His trust in the Thomistic ideals of 'truth, goodness and beauty' forms his subject matter; he does not like to dwell on the darker sides of Tolkien's world. Although Murray appreciates that well-known artist John Howe – whose designs have been featured in Peter Jackson's *LotR* and *Hobbit* films – deals with darker themes very well, he explains that 'I'm not John Howe.' For Murray, emphasising the positive aspects of Tolkien's world – the virtues of goodness and light – is essential to his art.[11]

To Murray, Tolkien is

> a bringer of hope. The world he created is our own world, but in a pre-modern time... The dangers were, in some ways, more palpable; the horrors more visceral and immediate. And yet, his characters either prevailed or were defeated depending on how well they understood and lived the deepest truths of Tolkien's own Catholic beliefs. Thus, faith, hope, and charity were rewarded, whereas nihilism, despair, and greed led to ruin... Like Tolkien, I don't wish to dwell on the deep and malevolent nature of evil. Rather, I'd prefer to explore what it means to be a good person struggling against evil.[12]

Murray's depictions of hobbits[13] emphasise their goodness, in paintings such as *The Road Goes Ever On* (Bilbo), *Woody End* (Frodo), *Ithilien* (Frodo and Sam), *The Watchers of Cirith Ungol* (Sam), *At the Grey Havens* (Sam), *Sam and Rosie*, *Entwash* (Merry and Pippin), *Treebeard* (either Merry or Pippin). In *Ithilien*, for example, Frodo and Sam sit together and take comfort from each other's presence. Their backs turned to the viewer, Merry and Pippin kick their feet in the *Entwash* and enjoy their first carefree moment in a long time. *Sam and Rosie* captures a courtship moment, when shy Sam holds out a flower to Rosie, whose hands are clasped behind her back, although her adoring eyes clearly show her affection for Sam. The emotion behind these pivotal personal moments in close relationships makes Murray's hobbits accessible to viewers, who respond to the scenes and read into the paintings their own interpretations. In this way, Murray's art becomes personal to individual viewers.

The hobbits in Murray's paintings and sketches look very different from other artists' depictions, largely because Murray does not try to define a specific look for a character. One of my favourite paintings is *Treebeard*. In this painting, Treebeard the Ent talks with a hobbit, who, according to Tolkien's *LotR*, has to be either Merry or Pippin. By standing atop boulders at the edge of the forest, the young hobbit can better converse with the Ent, who seems engrossed in their discussion. Murray lets those who view the painting decide for themselves whether Pippin or Merry is the featured hobbit. The determined set of the hobbit's chin and his intense gaze, shown in profile in this painting, seem, to me, to be an effective portrayal of serious-minded Merry. However, other fans may interpret the hobbit as ever-social Pippin. Interpreting Murray's paintings is very much an interactive process that makes the viewer part of the 'creation' of the painting's meaning.

Murray approves of this interpretive process, because 'Bilbo, Frodo, Sam, Merry, and Pippin (and even Nob, Fatty Bolger, the Sackville-Bagginses, etc.) are all so intimately a part of the very souls of Tolkien readers, that I fear lest I disturb the magic of the words through the ineptitude of the artist!' Although Murray's fans would certainly disagree with the latter part of this statement, they would agree that a strength of Murray's art is its reflection of his view that Middle-earth itself 'is most important, not strictly just the characters that inhabit it. I know you need both, but... Middle-earth itself is an ongoing and important "character".'[14] Thus hobbits are often shown interacting with the natural world or characters from outside the Shire.

The artist nevertheless views the hobbits as unique characters whose individuality tends to come out in sketches more than in paintings. To Murray, Frodo is a seeker of Truth, Goodness and Beauty who understands the cost of his commitment. Bilbo most closely represents Tolkien. Common man Sam is the proverbial salt of the earth. The 'soldier hobbits' Merry and Pippin 'represent those who learn the difficult lessons of what it means to be vigilant and to protect others, even at great cost to themselves'. Along the journeys described in *The Hobbit* and *LotR*, these hobbits are transformed from their initial carefree selves into 'other', those who can never completely fit in with Shire hobbits because of their growth and maturity. Although Murray clearly understands hobbits, he finds that 'these qualities are hard to capture in paint without doing a detailed portrait', but sketches allow him to evoke them.[15]

When asked if Jackson's *LotR* films influence his art, Murray exclaimed, 'I certainly hope that [they] haven't influenced my work!' Although quick to praise the artistic gifts of those who worked on the films, he disagrees with 'the more horror-film-like qualities [that] came from Jackson himself, and these are aspects I have the most difficulty with'. As might be expected, Murray's artistic inspiration comes most often from the books: 'As an artist, one could hardly do better than Tolkien for written inspiration for painting and sketching; he is deeply poetic in his words, and his poetry readily lifts itself off the page and onto one's canvas if one will allow it.'[16]

Tolkien's Christian faith and, secondarily, his understanding of legendary literature inspire Murray and influence his art. To this artist, Tolkien's works call readers to a distinctive way of living:

> The roots of these myths strike at the very nature of mankind, reminding us how long our journey has been, and encouraging us to continue resolutely on our path to Goodness, Truth, and Beauty (which are, after all, God). We are all called to be watchful

and resolute in our sharing of faith, hope, and charity. We are all called to be as forbearing as Frodo, as wise as Gandalf, and as noble as Aragorn.

The Professor's stories help readers understand that, despite personal hardships or global chaos, all will be well if this charitable and hopeful approach to life is taken. This, Murray claims, is 'Tolkien's legacy to us all'.[17]

Perhaps one reflection of Murray's emphasis on the positive is his colour palette. Unlike many other artists inspired by Tolkien, Murray paints in vivid primary colours; his canvases and prints enliven Tolkien's pre-modern world. He admits that he frequently uses blue, his favourite colour, but every painting also incorporates deep reds and shades of yellow. He seldom uses black because he does not want to deaden a colour. The blended greens, golds, oranges and purples bring a richness to each painting's subject matter; Murray's colour palette imbues the scenes with vivacity and regal splendour. In fact, Murray prefers to paint with oils, which he describes as 'liquid jewels'; he enjoys working with the viscous nature of oil paint, which allows him almost to sculpt with paint.[18] Murray's act of painting seems as life-affirming and powerful as the colours he chooses.

The link between painting and sculpting goes beyond his ability to push and pull the paint into pleasing forms. Like a sculptor, Murray lets the subject emerge as he works. Sculptors often explain that the medium, such as stone, decides what it wants to become; the form of the medium itself determines what the work of art will ultimately be. Murray similarly explains that 'sometimes I don't know what my paintings are until very late in the process. Sometimes I never know what they are.' During a 2008 presentation before Tolkien fans attending A Long-Expected Party, Murray happily noted that in one painting the hobbit sitting beneath a tree could be Frodo or Bilbo; comments from those who have seen the painting have been divided on exactly which character sits beneath the Party Tree. At this 2008 gathering of Tolkien fans, however, Murray heard a new interpretation: the hobbit represents the person viewing the painting, bringing him or her into the scene. Although this interpretation clearly was not part of the artist's intention in painting the work, he liked this 'reading' of his art and found the insight not only creative but personally rewarding. After all, 'the creative process is part of discovering who you are'.[19]

The palette may rely on softer hues, but Ted Nasmith, like Murray, frequently makes hobbits his subjects. His colourful pastels often render the Shire as an inviting place to visit, much as Gandalf does in one of Nasmith's most often displayed works of the wizard arriving at Bag End, a painting entitled *One Morning Long Ago*.[20] Gandalf, walking swiftly towards the round green door, is adorned in blue-grey robes and a very large pointy hat, just as readers might imagine. Bag End's door is only slightly deeper green than the lush hill into which the hole is built, and the late summer sky is a perfect sky blue with a few little white clouds floating along. The scene of tranquility and simple riches reflects Tolkien's descriptions well. Like Gandalf, those who view this artwork may envision themselves trotting beside the wizard as they look forward to Bilbo's hospitality.

Nasmith similarly felt welcomed into Tolkien's linguistic landscape. As a teenager, he discovered Middle-earth, and *LotR* became a favoured book. In the 1970s he submitted his work to be considered for the Tolkien calendars, only to receive polite rejections. Shortly before Tolkien's death, he even sent some pictures to the author, who replied that the portrayal of Bilbo was too childlike.[21] Heavily influenced by Greg and Tim Hildebrandt's Tolkien calendars of the late 1970s, Nasmith used their insights and his own interpretation of Tolkien's characters and themes to develop a more distinctive style, one that 'echoes the luminist landscapes and Victorian neo-classical styles'.[22] This style gained popularity and, beginning in 1987, Nasmith's work was selected for Tolkien calendars for 1988, 1990, 2002–4 and 2009, and the artist's Tolkien-themed paintings have won him critical and popular recognition, such as Hugo awards as best artist.

Nasmith values the intricacy of the world Tolkien described but would like to expand upon the author's vision. Middle-earth is 'full of vast, lost, misty expanses and its unique mixture of the familiar and strange. [Tolkien's] emphasis on light and shadow in particular, whether metaphorical or literal, justifies any artist's interest.'[23] Nasmith's understanding of and affinity for the stories helps him to conceptualise them with integrity. The precision of his art is 'almost photographic', according to Jef Murray. 'The sweeping vistas of his landscapes and the sheer scope of his architectural renderings take one's breath away.'[24]

As a Tolkien scholar who has had close contact with the Professor's family, not only through the previously mentioned letter from J.R.R. Tolkien but through assistance from his son Christopher, Nasmith might be in a position to criticise Jackson's adaptation, even though he was asked to work on the *LotR* films' design. The artist appreciates Jackson's work on such a mammoth project but explained in one interview that 'I've really enjoyed what Jackson has accomplished – with some reservations about his changes, or the "Hollywood factor",' adding that the 'films will only be properly assessed over time.' One aspect of the successful adaptation troubles Nasmith, as it does many fans of the book: 'I feel apprehensive about issues of the confusion two separate Lord of the Rings may create – the original book and now the movie. We'll have to see if that becomes a significant problem over time.'[25] The prevalence and continuing popularity of images or 'looks' from the Jackson films, especially with *The Hobbit* being added to the cinematic story in 2012–13, may have a permanent influence on the way the public thinks of hobbits and may, in years to come, render Tolkien's art or descriptions far less memorable to a growing percentage of *LotR* or *Hobbit* fans who have only seen Jackson's films.

Nasmith, however, is well versed in Tolkien's texts, and his interpretations reflect the original texts far more than a cinematic adaptation. The hobbits in Nasmith's paintings often seem innocent or naive, with a purity that accounts for the Ringbearers' ability to be near the Ring for so long before it begins to corrupt them.

In *Treebeard*, Merry and Pippin perch like two tree-climbing boys as the Ent carries them. Although the large face of Treebeard, taking up about a third of his trunk 'body', clearly dominates the painting, Merry and Pippin still exude an innocent enthusiasm. Nasmith distinguishes between the two small figures by their hair colour, one with light hair and one with brown, and by their attire.

In *Green Hill Country*, three hobbits on a hike look remarkably similar, wearing white shirts and light brown breeches, packs slung across their backs. They look sturdy but not plump, but their very curly hair helps physically define them as hobbits. The darker-haired, ruddy-cheeked hobbit whose face is visible is Frodo, whose profile indicates a serious nature or maturity, although he, like the other hobbits, looks young. The lush pastoral setting, again with a bright blue sky over fields and forest beginning to hint of autumn's arrival, presents an idyllic picture appropriate to the hobbits' pre-war Shire. The irony of this scene is the hobbits' lack of understanding just how far they will one day journey or how much their world will change before they return to the Shire after the War of the Ring.

Leaving the Shire paints a very different atmosphere. A very mature and much older-looking Frodo idly looks to the side of the road as he rides away from home. In contrast with his paintings of an earlier, happier Shire, this work has deeper hues, the shadowed greens of the grass and trees hinting at the darker world into which the hobbits ride. Broad-faced Sam, cloaked in a green hood, clearly looks worried as he rides next to Frodo. Merry and Pippin ride behind, the latter probably the flaxen-haired hobbit waving goodbye to Fredegar Bolger, who sits on a pony poised to return to Crickhollow. The blond wears a stocking cap and seems more intent on the departure than the brown-haired hobbit just behind him, looking ahead. A mound of supplies on a pack-pony indicates Merry's careful planning of what they might need for the journey. The background, although again blue, illustrates a misty Shire tree row blending into the blue-grey haze. Unlike many artists, who make Frodo seem childlike or the same age as the other hobbits when he leaves the Shire, Nasmith portrays him as appropriately older. Nasmith's style not only helps create a romantic fantasy of scenes from *LotR*, but his degree of detail related to the book shows just how familiar he is with this beloved story.

As is the case with many artists whose paintings reflect Tolkien's themes, Murray's and Nasmith's works have been reproduced as calendar art, a primary way that many Tolkien, *LotR* or *Hobbit* fans initially became interested in the wide range of art illustrating Middle-earth.

A Brief History of Well-loved Tolkien-themed Art:
The Famous Calendars

Highly collectible, widely diverse, and insightful into the world of hobbits – Tolkien calendars have long been an important part of 'hobbit art', as well as a gateway for fans to enter the visual realm of Middle-earth. Before films or television specials, the calendars introduced Tolkien's readers to visual adaptations of *LotR* or *The Hobbit* and expanded their vision of what the Professor described. Calendar art reflected the best of Tolkien-themed paintings and drawings and supplemented the official artwork published with the stories. Having one's art selected for a Tolkien calendar has long been prestigious, and some artists, such as the Hildebrandts, became well known in particular because their art appeared in these calendars.

Hobbits generally fare well in these calendars. Although they are never the sole focus of an entire calendar (even Tolkien's *The Hobbit* includes illustrations of characters other than Bilbo), hobbits are often featured characters within a scene. When Tolkien-themed calendars evolved to include depictions of characters from popular adaptations, the hobbits were again shown in familiar poses representing key moments in their television or film stories. Especially in calendars using images from Jackson's films, hobbits frequently appear as 'character of the month'. Merry and Pippin are most often paired in a shot instead of featured individually, but most often Sam and Frodo each warrant a full page or an individual photograph from the films.

The artistic styles used to portray hobbits, however, varies with time, place and artist. Michael Herring's *The Scouring of the Shire*, December's art in the 1980 J.R.R. Tolkien calendar, emphasises the effective if unorthodox hobbit militia. Two ruffians stand in a ditch; hobbits standing on the embankment thus look taller than the men they are surrounding. The hobbits carry rocks, a bow, a club or an axe and seem prepared to fight. The men look like modern models; the hobbits seem boy-sized but have much older faces.[26] In the 1982 J.R.R. Tolkien calendar illustrated by Darrell K. Sweet, July's *The West-Door of Moria* shows three hobbits, a man and a dwarf watching Gandalf try to open the door. A blond hobbit sitting behind Gandalf seems to offer advice; chin in palm, his other hand points out something to the wizard. The hobbits' hair is very light and straight, and the hobbits look like small men, albeit with hairy feet.[27] The 1994 J.R.R. Tolkien calendar, illustrated by Michael Kaluta, has a comic book/novella look and prominently features hobbits. December's *Meriadoc the Magnificent and the Children of Samwise Hamfast* shows a gigantic Merry in relation to the children's size; the shield of Rohan lies on the floor before him, a doll leaning against it. One child sits on Merry's crossed knee as the Master tells a group of children a story. In this illustration, Merry has curly reddish hair and light grey-blue eyes; he looks like a muscular young man, except for his very hairy legs and feet.[28] HarperCollins Glasgow published an Italian version of the J.R.R. Tolkien Calendario 1996. April's selection, *Due Hobbit nella tama di Shelob*, by Andrea Sfiligoi, portrays a grimacing Sam carrying a sword; he wears a green tunic, full-length red trousers and a brown cape. His straight brown hair, parted in the middle, takes on a reddish cast, and he sports long sideburns. Whereas Sam has a large nose and looks more ordinary, the unconscious Frodo, blood on his chest from Shelob's attack, is still a handsome hobbit, although he looks very young.[29] Even when the depictions vary in artistic adaptation, the characters and scenes they represent are familiar to Tolkien fans; the style often says more about the artist and culture than Tolkien's characters. In these representative calendar illustrations, the hobbits, despite variations in dress or hair colour, are noble characters who play a dominant role in the scene being depicted.

The official Tolkien calendars, however, are the ones Tolkien's readers consider to be the definitive calendar art. Since 1973, official Tolkien calendars have been produced annually. Although many fans or individual artists created unofficial calendars even earlier (and still do so today), having art included in the calendars published by Ballantine and, beginning the following year, by George Allen & Unwin often meant that a Tolkien artist had arrived.[30] Over the years the calendars highlighted the works of the Hildebrandt brothers, Ted Nasmith, Alan Lee, John Howe and Tim Kirk, among others, who interpreted Tolkien's *Hobbit, LotR, Silmarillion* or *Children of Hurin* as themes for a year's worth of art. Tolkien's own art, however, served as the focal point for the first calendars. In 1973 only his and long-time HarperCollins illustrator Pauline Baynes's drawings were included in the calendar; the 1974 calendar featured the same art under a new (lavender) cover.

Beginning in 1974, other publishers got in on the act, some with their own designs. That year at least five Tolkien-themed calendars were published. Ballantine or Allen & Unwin licensed publishers in other countries to modify their calendars for use in other languages; in 1974, Het Spectrum sold a Dutch Tolkien calendar. Although the Ballantine and Allen & Unwin calendars used only Tolkien's and Baynes's art, Faun Fantasy Press issued a limited run of its own calendar, featuring nine artists (including Tim Kirk).[31] As Tolkien-themed calendars gained popularity, more calendars by more publishers turned up each year.

In 1975, in honour of the late author, the American Tolkien Society published a calendar through Pant-Hoot Publications. In 1976 Ballantine published the first of three calendars (1976–78) illustrated by Greg and Tim Hildebrandt, although Allen & Unwin's calendars, whether produced for the UK, Canada or New Zealand, still featured Tolkien's art from *The Hobbit* or *LotR*. Related topics, such as a calendar quoting the Inklings, also varied the number and types of Tolkien-themed calendars being sold in the late 1970s.

Of all these artists whose work was reproduced in official calendars, Greg and Tim Hildebrandt are likely the best known purely on the basis of their calendar art. Although their artistic careers began in 1959, their work in the 1970s surrounding fan favourites *Star Wars* and *LotR* cemented their reputation and gained them a much larger fan base. Their artistry provided illustrations for the 1976–78 Tolkien *LotR* calendars, and their images of hobbits within the calendars became iconic images for book readers.

Ian Summers, the art director for Ballantine books, commissioned 14 paintings from the brothers after seeing samples of Tolkien-themed art from the often-outrageous twins. In an interview, Summers once recalled that, during a luncheon celebration of the first calendar's proofs, the Hildebrandts dressed in 'capes and top hats with feathers' as they handed out copies of the proofs to people passing on the street.

The artists and publisher shared a laugh, and Summers later wrote that 'laughter and outrageousness characterized our relationship'.[32] Because the Hildebrandts' first Tolkien calendar (the 1976 issue) became the world's bestselling calendar, the artists were quickly commissioned to create two more. The resulting calendars not only became highly revered among Tolkien fans, but they inspired other artists to create their own Tolkien-themed art.

An important early influence on the brothers' lifelong passion for art was Walt Disney, especially his animated features *Snow White and the Seven Dwarfs* and *Fantasia*. On their official website, Tim Hildebrandt called them 'wonders of the world' and emphasised how much they inspired his creativity.[33] Although the brothers studied animation, they never worked for Disney. Instead they made documentary films and, in the late 1960s, switched artistic paths to illustrate children's books. After their phenomenal success with the Tolkien calendars in the mid-1970s, they illustrated fantasy books and films, including the original *Star Wars* movie posters. Much of their philosophy of art is revealed in the conclusion to their official biography:

> The art of the Brothers Hildebrandt has brought the fantasies and dreams of children of all ages to life. Their work is a pathway leading to the written word and a journey into the imagination. Their legacy will continue to ignite the desire for children and adults alike to embrace literature in all its visual glory.[34]

Certainly this legacy includes a huge contribution to Tolkien art. Gregory Hildebrandt, Jr., recollected his father's and his uncle's fascination with *LotR*. After receiving a 1975 Tolkien calendar, Tim Hildebrandt 'almost instantly...immersed himself in rereading the trilogy', insisting that his brother do the same. 'For the next three years, my father would put aside his desire for a gallery show and immerse himself in a world of hobbits, wizards, dwarves, and elves.'[35]

The Hildebrandts' process differed from that of other Tolkien artists; they based their paintings on scenes first photographed with family members, or even themselves, enacting the roles. Later, the brothers would photograph other faces to use in place of theirs in the final art, but acting as a hobbit or a ranger was very much part of the family business in the 1970s. Greg Hildebrandt's son wrote in a retrospective of the Hildebrandts' career, *Greg and Tim Hildebrandt: The Tolkien Years*, that he was tapped to be Frodo in the photographs leading to *At the Prancing Pony*. The young Hildebrandt can also be seen as the inspiration behind Frodo in other paintings, such as the famous *The Fellowship*. The brothers' father, George, became the face of Bilbo Baggins for *Bilbo at Rivendell*.[36]

Because photographs of real people were used to pose a scene that would later become a painting, the resulting images of hobbits in particular differ widely from the depictions created by other artists. Frodo's body may be dressed like (and have the hairy feet of) Tolkien's hobbits, but his face clearly looks like a human boy's – specifically like that of young Gregory Hildebrandt, Jr. Although the men and elves look remarkably realistic and lifelike as a result of this process, the effect makes hobbits look far more human than a separate race. In effect, the hobbits are miniature men because the inspiration behind each painting was a photograph of a costumed child.

In perhaps the Hildebrandts' most famous artwork, *The Fellowship*, Gandalf and Frodo are at the centre and thus, in perspective, larger than the other characters. Light shines most prominently on Frodo's face as he looks not only forward but towards the journey; Gandalf shields his eyes as he peers into the distance, and most likely into the future as well. Greg Hildebrandt explained that the closer to Frodo and Gandalf a character is in the picture, the more important he is to the story.[37] Therefore, Sam, walking on Frodo's right, is clearly one of the most important characters. His double chin and rounder face help identify him as a chubbier hobbit, which is appropriate to the book, but otherwise his appearance, including attire, looks like that of the other hobbits. Merry and Pippin are widely separated in this work, one at the front of the company, one at the rear; they, like Frodo, look like young boys. Not surprisingly, both of Frodo's cousins look remarkably like him; all three hobbits were 'played' by Gregory Hildebrandt, Jr.

As an adult writing about his father's and uncle's artistic process, he recalled his reaction to seeing early sketches of what would become *Captured by the Orcs*, a painting in which Merry, with a bandaged head, and Pippin stare in fright at the huge, horned-helmeted Orcs holding them captive. The firelight emphasises the hobbits' expressions. Gregory Hildebrandt wrote that the Orcs were 'something from a nightmare', and his jaw dropped in amazement when he saw who was being held captive by them. 'It was me! I was the one who was tied up as a sacrifice to the dark creatures. In fact, there were two victims, and they were both me! Well, actually, they were going to be Merry and Pippin, the hobbits.'[38] Young Hildebrandt discovered first hand what it might feel like to be a hobbit of the Fellowship.

When Tim Hildebrandt died in 2006, CBR (Comic Book Resource) News posted the sad notice that 'the world lost one of its most popular and beloved artists'.[39] Ain't It Cool News reminded science fiction/fantasy fans that 'before Alan Lee and John Howe, Tim and Greg Hildebrandt were the go-to guys for Tolkien artwork. Their fantasy work was very childlike and innocent, which fit with many of Tolkien's themes.'[40]

Just as the calendars introduced many Tolkien fans to the Hildebrandts' work, so too did they make larger audiences aware of Tim Kirk, whose art has been praised for 'his unique vision and powerful imagination that combines to evoke a sense of wonder'.[41] Initially lending his talents first to Hallmark greeting cards and later to Disney's Imagineering, Kirk became popular among Tolkien fans beginning with the 1975 official calendar, and some of his best-known works portray hobbits.

In the oil painting *The Riddle Game*, published in this calendar, Bilbo leans backward, Sting in his right hand, as an accusatory Gollum points a finger at him. The hobbit's profile shows a broad face crowned with dark (but straight) hair and a prominently pointed ear. Whereas Gollum seems agitated, Bilbo looks serious but confident. Once again, Bilbo represents hobbits' ability to take care of themselves rather well in difficult situations, something that no doubt surprises other characters, including Gollum.

Many of Kirk's paintings reflect the Disney animation style, such as his portrait *Galadriel*, in which she wears flowing white robes as she presents the light of Elendil to Frodo. Blonde and graceful, this Galadriel could be related to Disney's Sleeping Beauty. Frodo's profile is to the viewer, but his outstretched hand and upturned face indicate his willingness to accept the gift, and his nearby pack indicates his readiness for the next phase in his journey. Although Kirk's hobbits may look deceptively innocent, they are still willing to step up to a challenge and do their part to protect Middle-earth.

In these and other Kirk paintings of hobbits, they seem competent, sturdy characters. Their faces may often be turned away from the viewer, as Frodo's, Pippin's and Sam's are when the three pack-laden hobbits take the road leading to *Maggot's Farm*, but the impression they leave with the viewer is one of readiness and hardiness. The gentle Disney-styled characterisations also make the hobbits seem innocent and pure, as if they are untainted by the outside world's influence. This is especially true in *The Mirrormire*; a gruff Gimli points to the reflective waters as two very wide-eyed hobbits peer at their reflections. In all these *LotR*-based paintings, the hobbits are typically dressed for travel, packs on their backs and occasionally carrying a walking stick.

Kirk was an early *LotR* reader, first encountering the book in 1964, and in the early 1970s choosing it as the focus of his master's thesis project in illustration. The artist became fascinated with Tolkien's books as a source of inspiration for art because the author's 'uniqueness and vivid imagery…make *LotR* such a challenge – and ultimately a joy – to illustrate. The results are bound to be intensely personal and heartfelt – and controversial!'[42] Certainly Kirk would appreciate controversy among fans and critics about some adaptations' depiction of Tolkien's stories and understand the merits of debating the many and varied depictions of hobbits.

By the 1980s, the most intense interest in Tolkien's work had died down, and the number of television and film adaptations created in the late 1970s signalled that peak interest had passed, at least for a while. Nevertheless, several publishing companies (for example, Unwin Paperbacks, Ballantine/Random House) continued to produce official calendars. Fan-based groups took up the slack, developing their own Tolkien calendars for members. The American Tolkien Society and American Mensa Tolkien Special Interest Group (publisher of *Beyond Bree*) published several calendars that decade.

The wide range of publishers and topics continued into the 1990s, with satirical calendars also entering the market.

The Mythopoeic Society's 'NOT Tolkien Calendar' in 1990 gave fans a laugh with its irreverent illustrations of beloved characters. As the calendar's creator, Lynn Maudlin, explained, the calendar was designed to be a not-so-serious take on *LotR*. December, as the end of the year, became the 'butt' of several artistic jokes:

> Tim Callahan's illo … is truly classic – he was going for that Frank Frazetta fantasy look (which is hard to render in black & white, but Tim managed it), all muscular and rounded, lots of buttocks. I especially love Théoden's throne with the back-ends of horses making the front sides … and Éowyn's buttocks being reflected in a shield (shield maiden of Rohan indeed!) … ah, good fun.[43]

By the 1990s, Tolkien fans (not just those groups of which it would be expected, like Harvard Lampoon, who published *Bored of the Rings* in 1969 during the initial heyday of *LotR* popularity on college campuses) were able to parody the stories they loved, and the range of material for independent calendars reflects irreverent humour as often as book-referenced detail.

Although the range of Tolkien-themed calendars discussed so far have emphasised English-language versions, popular calendars featuring hobbits and other Tolkien characters have been a staple worldwide. Since the 1960s, Tolkien calendars in English, but often with different designs by region, have been sold in the UK, North America (Canada and the US), Europe (Czechoslovakia, Finland, France, Germany, Italy, the Netherlands, Spain) and Australasia (Australia, New Zealand). Internationally, several countries have published calendars featuring national artists and, of course, using the native language. In 1994, for example, the calendar produced by the Finnish Tolkien Society involved the work of Mikko Raunonpoika Juhola, Jukka-Petteri Halme and Petri Hiltunen; the Polish Tolkien Society's included the pen-and-ink drawings of Helena Strokowska, Ryszard Derdzinski, Maciej Wygnanski, Karolina Stopa and Malgorzata Pudlik.[44] In addition to the long-running series by Ballantine/Random House and Unwin & Allen/Grafton Books/HarperCollins/HarperPrism/HarperEntertainment, smaller publishers provided Tolkien fans with a wide range of artistic choices for their wall and desk calendars. Those who wanted daily reminders of Tolkien's characters could find a style and theme appropriate to their interests.

It has not been only the works of professional artists or talented fans that have kept Tolkien's hobbits in public view from the late 1970s to the present. As television and film adaptations became popular, more calendars arrived to celebrate Tolkien's works, even if the character illustrations reproduced the look featured in a specific adaptation. In 1979, the Rankin–Bass calendar cover presented a smiling Bilbo standing outside the door to Bag End, as if welcoming *Hobbit* aficionados to step inside. Also that year, a calendar cover showed the animated cast of Bakshi's *LotR*, with hobbits prominently featured. It was a good year for Tolkien calendars, with at least seven being marketed to fans by different companies. The themes ranged from adaptations (Rankin–Bass and Bakshi) to Tolkien's art to the Inklings to scenes from *The Silmarillion*.

The increased number of calendars featuring still images from live-action films, for example, illustrates the more recent pervasive power of adaptations in popular culture. Even years after a film's release, audiences who saw the film – especially a blockbuster – can easily identify characters from it. The continuing popularity of Jackson's *LotR* adaptation, for example, made film-based calendars a lucrative business throughout the 2000s. Although calendar designs varied by country, Tolkien-themed calendars in the US between 2001 and 2012 featured scenes and characters taken directly from Jackson's movies, just as merchandise of all types displayed images of the actors portraying characters in the films.[45]

When their popularity finally began to wane as material for calendars, at the end of the decade, the calendar-marketing strategy took a different direction. Images from the more recently published *Children of Hurin* and previously published official Tolkien calendars (not spin-offs from adaptations) again became more important. In the early 2010s, the *Hobbit* films, like their *LotR* counterparts from the preceding decade, likewise provide plenty of images to be used in Tolkien-themed calendars.

Because Tolkien calendars are a tradition, one that still has the potential to make a great deal of money, especially with film tie-ins, this form of Tolkien-themed art will continue to have a powerful visual impact on consumers and help form new fans' impressions of the way hobbits are meant to look. Adaptations may come and go – and generate multiple calendar designs produced by different companies at the height of their popularity – but the long-running series of Tolkien calendars produced by the offshoots of Unwin & Allen or Ballantine remain the gold standard not only of Tolkien-related calendars but any dealing with fantasy.

Still Art from Moving Images

In the 1970s, in conjunction with television specials of *The Hobbit* and *RotK*, merchandise featuring the images of animated characters naturally made its way into the marketplace around the time of the initial broadcasts. Perhaps most famously, depictions of Bilbo from the Rankin–Bass specials graced the covers of children's books summarising the TV special's plot, but the hobbit also beckoned potential buyers from the covers of albums (and, later, CDs and DVDs).

The practical use of art to entice consumers to buy products with tie-ins to television specials or movies is just a small part of the way still art pertains to filmed images. To help create the atmosphere important to making Middle-earth look real on film, Jackson brought together an incredible number of artists to design everything from elaborate sets to costumes to armour to weapons. However, the best-known Tolkien artists to work with Jackson on cinematic design are Alan Lee and John Howe.

Lee's[46] reputation is so well known, both within and outside Tolkien circles, that one fan guide effusively notes that 'In the collective mind of the public, if there is one artist who is most strongly identified with Tolkien, that would be Alan Lee, who is one of three artists featured on the official website of Tolkien's British publisher.'[47] Lee, along with Howe, was a concept artist for Jackson's trilogy, a job he seemed to enjoy greatly. Whereas Howe worked primarily with creature designs in *LotR*, including that of the Balrog, as well as designs for weapons and armour, Lee focused on Helm's Deep and Rivendell. The two collaborated on other settings, with one artist taking more responsibility for some aspects more than another. Lee, for example, designed Hobbiton and Bree, but Howe specifically tackled Bag End, both interior and exterior, and the Green Dragon.[48]

During presentations at the Tolkien 2005 conference, Lee confessed that he often liked to visit the Golden Hall of Meduseld when filming was not taking place, simply to admire what seemed to be a very real fortress surrounded by mountains. The carvings and finely wrought designs, even in those corners that would never be seen on film, made the set come alive.[49] As a designer, Lee not only envisioned ways to bring Tolkien's world to life on screen but appreciated the care and artistry in the completed product. His work on *RotK* earned him a well-deserved Academy Award for Best Art Direction. When initially signed as director of the *Hobbit* films, Guillermo del Toro announced his plan to invite Lee and Howe to provide designs,[50] and, after del Toro departed the long-delayed project, new director Jackson indeed brought the artists back on board for the *Hobbit* films.[51] Their expertise, especially in illustrating hobbits, made them an invaluable source, even if the shift from still art to moving images would prove to be more of a challenge than Lee, in particular, might have anticipated.

As illustrator of *The Hobbit* book, Lee has had a great deal of experience sketching hobbits. Six posters are often reproduced from illustrations in *The Hobbit*, among them *Bilbo*, showing a rustic hobbit leaving Bag End. That such a distinguished artist well versed in Tolkien's world might have difficulty conceptualising movie hobbits may come as a surprise. In his *The Lord of the Rings Sketchbook*, Lee explained that his early drawings of Frodo portrayed him as young, in part because the artist was unsure just how fast hobbits would mature in comparison with humans. A young-looking Frodo also presents an interesting contrast with the centuries-old Gandalf. Lee noted that he 'kept Frodo in a state of indeterminate youth, alongside Gandalf's indeterminate old age'.[52] Hobbits are difficult even for experienced artists to draw because, as Lee writes, 'Trying to design a generic hobbit that fitted the author's description, while avoiding the traps of looking too childlike, comical, or grotesque, was more difficult than I'd imagined.'[53] What eventually helped Lee was his friendship with 'Frodo' scale double in the *LotR* films, actor Kiran Shah; at 4 feet, 2 inches tall, Shah helped Lee gain a true 'hobbit' view of the world as he sees it. Even an experienced artist sometimes needs to look at his subject from a different perspective.

Like Lee, Howe is well known for his fantasy artworks and long association with Tolkien's stories. He, however, admits to being influenced by the actors' portrayals ever since he worked as a conceptual artist for Jackson's films. Before the films, he relied on his mental visualisation of characters, based on Tolkien's descriptions. After seeing, for example, Elijah Wood as Frodo, Howe has 'had a really hard time erasing him from [his] imagination when [he's] trying to draw the character',[54] although he still returns to Tolkien's words for inspiration.

Artist Jef Murray praised Howe's 'fine details, such as subtle Celtic knot work on armour, that one might miss at first glance', but also noted that Howe realistically captures the more difficult beasts in Tolkien's works. 'His "fell beasts" are slick and dank, his gargoyles and trolls menacing. While viewing his heroes and battle scenes, one can almost hear the clink of metal on metal and feel the brush of feathered shafts flying.'[55]

When Jane Johnson of HarperCollins was asked in an interview about Howe to describe his art, she cautioned against considering Howe as 'the painter of monsters and Alan [Lee] as the painter of landscapes'. Nevertheless, her favourite Howe painting, which she commissioned in the 1980s, is fondly referred to as 'the Hobbit-barbecue picture' because it shows a terrifying group of Uruks around a campfire on a mountain's ledge. Johnson and director Jackson appreciated Howe's ability to emphasise such dramatic moments, including Merry's and Pippin's capture by the Uruk-hai.[56]

As Howe's work on the Jackson adaptation of *LotR* progressed, he moved from initial sketches to the construction of detailed sets. An unusual part of the job involved discussions about such details as 'the relative merits of ceramic hobbit pipes or doorknobs'.[57] Of course,

Howe's long experience as a Tolkien artist gave him clear insights into hobbitry.

In his painting *The Black Rider*, the hobbits hide beneath a tree, obscured by its roots, as the head of a massive black horse and its hooded rider edge over the bank. Although limited to a corner of the canvas, the hobbits are clearly emphasised. They huddle together so closely that only their faces are easily seen. Three of the four stare wide-eyed out of their hiding place, but the fourth hides his face in his hands, creating a sense of vulnerability. Two hobbits brandish swords to protect their Ringbearer, and the feeling of anticipation created by this scene makes those who see it hold their breath much as the hobbits must be doing.

Although both Lee's and Howe's Tolkien-themed art goes far beyond 'hobbit art', their influence on the way hobbits are portrayed both in books and on film has a significant bearing on the way readers and audiences years from now will perceive hobbits. Because their bodies of work encompass more than one medium and reflect both the original source and adaptations, Howe and Lee will remain two of the most influential Tolkien artists of all time.

Mapping Middle-earth

Yet another type of cinematic art helps audiences understand more about hobbits, specifically where they lived and travelled in relation to the rest of Middle-earth. Because maps were integral to Tolkien's books, especially *LotR*, they became an important element of Jackson's adaptations. Maps were frequently used as transitions from one scene to another, and a skilled artist/calligrapher/mapmaker needed to make these images realistic according to details provided in Tolkien's texts but also aesthetically pleasing, fitting with the 'look' of Jackson's films.

Appropriate to Tolkien's world and the author's affinity for maps, Jackson's films – and official books, prints, games and other products derived from them – feature a plethora of maps drawn by New Zealand artist, calligrapher and cartographer Daniel Reeve.[58]

He drew the maps seen in the films' transitions between scenes, such as the important visual transition in space and time between Aragorn's coronation and the hobbits' return to the Shire. He also created the Red Book, in which Bilbo and Frodo detail their adventures, and helped the actors develop the hobbits' readable but distinctive handwriting.

Close-ups of Reeve's maps sometimes indicate subtle, but very Kiwi-themed changes from Tolkien's maps. A deviation in one, for example, changes the coastline of Middle-earth's Forlindon and bay of Lune into the artist's homeland coastline just north of Wellington.[59] Reeve's maps look similar in style to Tolkien's but bring elements of his own style (and the New Zealand landscape) to the films.

Reeve knew early on that he wanted to work on Jackson's trilogy:

> I had written all these bits and bobs over the years and played with my calligraphy pens…but I learned that Peter Jackson was to make *The Lord of the Rings* in Wellington, and I already knew how to do this stuff, so I prepared this sample and sent it in, just posted it to Wingnut Studios with a letter explaining that if you don't already have elvish calligraphers, this is the sort of stuff I could do. They realised immediately that they didn't have any calligraphers – I think they had one lady in the art department – and this landed in their lap. So they phoned up straightaway.

From that day in late 1999, Reeve began working on the films. In addition to maps and the Red Book of Westmarch, Reeve was called upon to create other props, including scrolls, ancient books, Bag End's party signs, and Bilbo's birthday banners. The production's pace required a fast turnaround of projects, but Reeve quickly caught on to the proportions needed to work with two scales: one for hobbits and one for humans. Frequently he needed to create props identical in all but size. 'Once you got into the rhythm, you could do it pretty quick. They had an exact mathematical formula, and everyone knew the maths [for scale drawings].'[60]

The beautiful calligraphy seen in the films forms the menus and titles for the movie DVDs; the artist also developed a series of fonts based on characters and places. Each hobbit, for example, has his own font. Perhaps his most famous work for the films is in elvish;

Reeve gracefully wrote the Ring inscription used both in the movies and for merchandise.

Whereas Lee and Howe had to return to New Zealand to work on the *Hobbit* films, Reeve simply had to drive a few miles from home. In November 2010 he announced on his website that he too had begun work on Jackson's *Hobbit* films,[61] undoubtedly to apply once again his talents in illustration, cartography and calligraphy to the first of Bilbo's adventures. The details provided in everything from the design of on-screen banners, signs and documents to the maps highlighting the hobbits' journeys help create an appropriate Shire atmosphere representing hobbit culture as distinctive in Middle-earth.

Adaptations of Adaptations: 'Unofficial' Art Based on Jackson's Films

Of course, artists not working on the films themselves are also inspired by what they see on screen. As a result, they often translate a film scene into a still work of art, such as a lithograph, that is not officially tied to the production. Whereas some artists turn primarily to Tolkien's words for inspiration, long-time Tolkien fan Jerry Vanderstelt frequently tackles *LotR* themes as shown in the Jackson trilogy.

While he works, he often listens to audiobooks of Tolkien's tales and especially appreciates the power of Tolkien's story, as well as its 'sense of longing when Tolkien's obvious Christian influence comes through by the way he builds his story'. The artist tries to re-create visually 'the same sense of wonder Tolkien had in his books and tap into the vast realm of Middle-earth history'.[62] Vanderstelt's 'love of the books sparked [his] interest in creating *LotR* artwork based on the films'.[63]

Jackson's films took his art in yet another direction. 'I love creating move tie-in art, especially *LotR*, because the PJ version of *LotR* really made the books come to life for me, and I wanted to be part of that visually. Of course, you always have your own visions when you read a book, but I believe PJ nailed it down very well. It's hard to go back and read the books without seeing Ian McKellen as Gandalf or Cate Blanchett as Galadriel.'[64] In addition to lithographic art, Vanderstelt has worked on a wide range of movie tie-in projects: the *LotR* pinball machine, works for the Bradford Exchange, and pieces directly for New Line Cinema licensing. Beginning in 2007, he has completed one lithograph a year for each of Jackson's *LotR* films.

Because Tolkien's themes benefit from in-depth analysis (and visual interpretation), Vanderstelt finds a montage of related paintings easier to create than a single portrait of one character. This process is particularly helpful with lithographic art. Vanderstelt tries 'to make interesting and overlapping themes...and tie them all together for hopefully a conducive overall theme'.[65]

The actors' performances seem to have heavily influenced Vanderstelt's art. In one painting, Pippin looks up with an expression similar to that when he first holds the palantir in the film. The artist's 'goal visually is to try to bring out each character's personality in one shot'. Pippin's personality presents some interesting challenges to capture visually because 'he actually *looks* for trouble!...Without Merry to steer him, Pippin would be in even more trouble than usual. Gandalf always seems to be scolding him for his foolishness, but Gandalf really loves him, because he knows Pippin is just being himself!' When Vanderstelt uses this analysis to paint Pippin, he prefers to portray this hobbit 'in a more serious mood where maybe his expression shows his need to take things seriously for once, and try not to get hurt!'[66]

Vanderstelt obviously thinks carefully about the characters before he begins a painting. He summarises other hobbit personalities this way:

> Frodo is the calm yet wise one of the four. He seems to carefully think about whatever he is doing...Sam is the faithful, unwavering helper. He does not care about being the bravest or strongest, nor does he hold back from admitting his own weaknesses. He has pride, ...but he doesn't put it first. Merry is probably just a typical hobbit for his age, sensible to a point, yet [he] likes to have as much fun as the next in the Shire![67]

These interpretations, blending book and film portrayals, form the basis of Vanderstelt's recent art, whether film merchandise or a series of lithographs and prints.

The *FotR* lithograph/print, for example, depicts the members of the Fellowship in appropriate action poses (for instance, Gimli swinging an axe, Legolas drawing his bow) or expressions of concern (for example, Frodo, Aragorn). The artwork also includes Saruman, Arwen and an imposing Witch King. Scenes from the first film, including the arrival of the Black Riders and the entrance to the Mines of Moria, help summarise the key players and events in *FotR.* As might be expected, the Ring is front and centre, with the parchment-styled background nicely offsetting the deceptively innocent-looking gold Ring. This approach to adapting images from film into a unique combination of characters in action poses has helped film fans bridge the gap between moving images and still life and see how adaptations can further inspire artistic interpretation leading to the creation of yet more works of art. No doubt the *Hobbit* films will similarly provide creative inspiration. Vanderstelt calls *The Hobbit* 'a great book', and certainly 'the desire is there' to continue his art based on Tolkien's work and Jackson's adaptations.[68]

Perhaps an unexpected artform, but one that nonetheless derives its inspiration from Jackson's adaptations, is cartoon art. Comic strips or cartoons may be a far cry from paintings, maps or lithographs, but they are another interesting film-themed adaptation. Dozens appeared in the early 2000s when *LotR* popularity most recently peaked. Comic strip websites poked fun at fans eagerly awaiting the films or made insightful jokes about *LotR* characters as they are depicted on film. TORN often published cartoons or posted links to them, which allowed fans to laugh at 'inside' jokes (and themselves). *The Dork Tower*, for one, frequently spoofed *LotR* fans' enthusiasm for the films in the early 2000s.[69] Even later in the decade, *LotR* continued as an occasional theme, particularly in comic strips featuring child characters and their play. *Sheldon* also began a series of comics about 'playing Sauron's army' in mid-2008.[70]

Not surprisingly, Jackson's trilogy inspired *Mad Magazine* to parody the films. The *RotK* cartoons featured 'Dodo Gaggins', 'Spam', 'Baggybuns' and 'Pimple' as caricatures of Frodo, Sam, Merry and Pippin. In one chaotic battle scene, after Baggybuns exclaims that, although small, he would be a useful warrior, Théoden promises to take him into battle: 'Hey, I'm no fool. As long as I've got you sitting up front, you block 80% of the arrows coming at me!' In the same panel, Pimple explains that he's a 'midget who finds a magic ball in the water next to a talking tree, which lets the giant evil eyeball fry my brain'.[71] Although no *LotR* character escapes *Mad*'s parody unscathed, blunt insights into the cinematic hobbits' psyches are particularly on target.

Cartoons were even highlighted in the first issue of the official *LotR* fan club's magazine. Bill Amend, creator of the comic strip *Fox Trot*, became a Tolkien aficionado upon reading *The Hobbit*. His character Jason, a science-fiction and computer geek, naturally grew up playing Dungeons and Dragons. For Amend, having Jason migrate to Middle-earth was a natural move, noting that 'Jason's interests are amplified representations of my own, so as my excitement about the films grew, his grew even more so.'[72]

Amend knows film fans well, and understands their obsession with detail. In one comic, a devoted book fan worries about Jackson's attention to realistic detail: 'Already I fear they didn't use real undead ringwraiths to shoot this one scene.'[73] The absurdity of the statement is only matched by the real-world 'obsession' of fans spending hours peering pixel by pixel at a screen capture from the movie. Some cartoons more actively involve hobbits, including a series in which Jason and Marcus act out roles as Frodo and Sam. When Peter Jackson comes looking for his actors, who are taking a lunch break, Jason notes, 'You might have informed us that root beer stains mithril.'[74] *Fox Trot* cartoons from the *LotR* series were initially published online and in more than a thousand newspapers around the world.[75] In December 2007 Jason turned the family Christmas tree into an Ent.[76]

The level of interest in such comics, whether a continuing series or a standalone joke, reflects media frenzy about long-anticipated movies and the people who obsess over them. As such, they indicate as much about the power of popular culture over Western societies as they illustrate the ongoing popularity of Tolkien's stories.

Whether comedic or meditative, practical or aesthetic, Tolkien-themed art uniquely inspires or unites readers and audiences and helps make *LotR* and *The Hobbit* shared cultural experiences. The focal point of much of this art is the hobbits, who are the characters most likely to provide an entry point into Tolkien's stories and make those who view the art identify with them. The adage 'seeing is believing' is especially true with these visual adaptations of Tolkien's prose, and whichever images of hobbits audiences find most appealing or personally meaningful are the ones they will likely think of as 'real'.

8

MAKING MEANING OF HOBBITS: THE ROAD TAKES SOME STRANGE TURNS

Adaptations of Tolkien's works are made for, and largely by, fans, old and new (and those making these adaptations hope to attract a wide audience that will make new fans for them and their stories). Throughout the previous chapters, professional adaptations – on radio or television, in film, on stage, in music and as art – have retold the Professor's stories in different media. They reflect trends in entertainment and technology, as well as issues and interests important at the time the adaptation was made. Some adaptations gain greater public acceptance than others, but these variations on Tolkien's themes, like the original texts, are likely to rise and fall in popularity in years to come.

What sustains the best adaptations and keeps Tolkien's original works firmly in the public imagination is fandom. Although formal criticism, historicism and other scholarly analyses document and commemorate texts or performances, fans keep the stories and characters alive. They maintain interest in hobbits, create the market for hobbit-themed entertainment and merchandise, and return to the original books and favourite adaptations. They promote Tolkien's characters in popular culture and introduce succeeding generations to the Professor's words.

Fans read into the story whatever they need. They personally identify with characters; they learn how others, especially hobbits, survive chaotic times and live to see better days. Although Tolkien may not have wanted his stories read only as allegories or interpreted as sociopolitical metaphors for conflicts during and beyond his lifetime, *LotR*, and to a lesser extent *The Hobbit*, typically offer more than entertainment to the fans who read the books many times, sometimes within a single year. The depth of characterisation and expansive plot invite interpretation, and readers throughout the years have enjoyed debating just what might be inferred from or inspired by Tolkien's stories.

Frodo, more than the other hobbits, takes on widely diverse or contradictory roles, as determined by individual fans or critics. Readers often 'adapt' or interpret Frodo's actions to fit their idea of what his character means not only in the story but in their lives; they choose to emphasise certain characteristics more than others or to focus on one section of *LotR* more than another. Also, because Frodo is a well-known character, his role in *LotR* has been taken out of context to fit a number of political situations, and politicians, academics, sociologists – anyone who analyses the text for historical, psychological, religious or sociological meanings – often interpret especially *LotR* as an allegory for their particular time or situation. Even the *concept* of hobbits has been interpreted by journalists and politicians to fit scenarios far outside anything Tolkien intended.

Fans making individualised, personal meaning from the lives of hobbits often share their 'findings' or perspectives in a variety of ways that reflect their individual interests or talents. Typical fan activities include writing or reading fanfiction or creating art, videos, poetry or costumes; initiating a gathering, ranging from cosplay (costumed role play) to scholarly conferences to social events; creating newsletters and magazines; attending film screenings and discussions; travelling to England to see where Tolkien lived and worked; or travelling to New Zealand filming locations. Even writing this book is a 'fan' activity born from love for hobbits. Tolkien fandom is participative, and we fans emphasise those details, characters or activities that have the greatest meaning to us.

The concept of *adaptation* especially applies to the fiction written purely for the enjoyment or enlightenment of other fans – not for profit or professional gain. These stories may incorporate dialogue, characters or events found in the original stories (or popular adaptations), but they are also supplemented by the writer's imagination. When Peter Jackson adapts Tolkien's *LotR*, he develops a script and shoots a movie. It might include new characters or scenes not found in the original. When a fanfiction writer adapts Tolkien's work, the result is often a serialised story involving alternate universes (AUs, a drastic departure from the direction Tolkien's stories take), new characters, or 'filler' stories that fit within gaps in Tolkien's tales (for example, what is happening back in the Shire while Bilbo is off with the dwarves). However, Jackson's adaptation is (the studio hopes) a for-profit endeavour, one made with the approval of those who hold the legal rights to the story. Fanfiction writers share their stories freely, with no expectation of remuneration, and develop their works without the permission of rights holders. The legality of fanfiction aside, the prevalence of fan-created works, including fanfiction, helps ensure that hobbits remain a viable part of popular culture. The constant updating of fanfiction websites and the number of new (and often well-written, memorable) stories uploaded daily ensure that hobbit fans always have something new to read. Fanfiction is likely the only form of adaptation that provides new material every day.

Two final ways in which Tolkien's hobbits have been integrated into the lives of individuals, as well as societies, are the political interpretations of Frodo or hobbits in general and the social phenomenon of fanfiction, a not-for-profit form of adaptation. These allegorical interpretations and prose adaptations, as much as the formal, for-profit, multimedia adaptations discussed in previous chapters, indicate the many ways that hobbits have become a permanent part of Western culture. Whether we are acknowledged fans of Tolkien's characters or not, we all are familiar with Frodo and his kin.

A Frodo for Every Decade and Conflict

No other type of interpretation has polarised readers (or audiences) more than political interpretations either of Tolkien's words or adaptations, especially Jackson's. In the 1960s and 2000s, in particular, politicised reviews and commentary illustrated the extremes of interpretation. Although every generation and era has its specific domestic and global problems and conflicts, the politically turbulent 1960s and the globally violent, economically chaotic 2000s provided plenty of backstory for new interpretations involving Frodo Baggins.

In the US during the 1960s, many young people often projected their dissatisfaction with political leaders or the Vietnam War onto one of their favourite book characters. They did not want to see Frodo represent the Establishment whose policies, to their mind, led to warfare abroad and sociopolitical upheaval at home. They wanted Frodo to be one of them. He became a powerful voice for mercy, which became interpreted as pacifism for his refusal to take up arms at home against the ruffians and his willingness to forgive Saruman/Sharkey and send him peacefully on his way.

A Tolkien fan blog, written during the time when Jackson's films were highly anticipated but not yet released, questions how audiences in the 2000s would interpret the cinematic adaptation, noting that *LotR* had been adopted by

> the hippie generation of the '60's who were reading all sorts of messages with the Vietnam War and the atomic bomb... [T]he young American reading the book today certainly isn't thinking about Vietnam, yet it still has a message... [Tolkien's] themes are universal and timeless, so you can obviously take from the book or the movie whatever you choose to take.[1]

Scholars have long analysed *LotR* and interpreted the work in many ways. A passage from C.N. Manlove's literary criticism well summarises the popular political usage of *LotR* as an allegory arising from responses to wars from World War II and the atomic age to Vietnam:

[*LotR*] came just when disillusion among the American young at the Vietnam war and the state of their own country was at a peak. Tolkien's fantasy offered an image of the kind of rural conservationist ideal or escape for which they were looking (it also could be seen as describing, through the overthrow of Sauron, the destruction of the U.S.). In this way *The Lord of the Rings* could be enlisted in support of passive resistance and idealism on the one hand and of draft-dodging and drugs on the other.[2]

For audiences who saw Jackson's films while serving in the military in Iraq or Afghanistan in the early 2000s, Frodo was often a representative of the army fighting on the side of Good against Evil. Frodo became a role model who did not realise all ramifications of the upcoming war and could not really prepare for all horrors he would experience. Nevertheless, he kept going forward with his mission, at great risk to himself, simply because Sauron had to be stopped. Frodo was perceived as fighting valiantly to protect his homeland from the invasion of evildoers.[3]

Another strong political interpretation arose after 11 September 2001, in the US. The hobbits were often politically less important during the 'War on Terror', but other characters, including Aragorn, became glorified as stronger, more decisive battle leaders fighting on the side of Good against Evil in a black-and-white interpretation of global events. There were also vastly different interpretations of Saruman and Sauron and who might 'play' them on the global stage.

Conservative audiences favoured the hobbits as protectors of their homeland, those who were afraid of change from outside or invaders who would destroy their way of life. They were perceived as fighting on behalf of their loved ones and as innocent victims who would have peacefully lived in the Shire had they not been suddenly and without provocation attacked by outside Evil forces.

One science-fiction website described the importance of *FotR* in a post-9/11 US: 'Christmas would have been strange without the needed distraction. America needed the uplifting story of heroism and good vs. evil. While America and her allies forged ahead with its war on evil, a timely epic played in the theatres in these same nations.' In this scenario, Frodo played one of two roles, either as the

US taking on an unwanted burden that was necessary to rid the world of Evil or as privileged US youth who inherits global ire as a result of the improper actions of previous generations. The comparison was made that Frodo

> was not unlike America today, burdened with a seemingly insurmountable task of defeating evil. Frodo, the child of wealth, was often scorned by his own kindred for his inheritance. Some may have even blamed his guardian Bilbo, for the burdens left to him. So too, you can find Americans who blame history, their own ancestors and the nation itself for the attacks upon it.[4]

Other political analogies involve hobbits, even without a wartime crisis to prompt comparisons. The US political association between Tolkien's characters and Tea Party hobbits, as mentioned in the Introduction, is one of the latest in a long line of political uses of Tolkien's literary characters.

Politically, *LotR* has been a literary powder keg. Sometimes the hobbits play a direct role in a political interpretation; sometimes their role is lessened as popular culture emphasises the role of men, wizards, or even an Evil Eye as powerful leaders trying to decide the fate of all Middle-earth (that is, modern earth). In hindsight, flaws abound in these interpretations, which sometimes seem to be straining to make a point or may present Frodo in contradictory roles during the same time period (for example, Frodo as pacifist/Frodo as warrior). Nevertheless, the point here is that hobbits in particular attract this type of interpretation, and *LotR* has often been used to put present crises in perspective, to make meaning out of what, at the time, may seem an insurmountable problem. Although not a true adaptation, as defined in Chapter 1, such political analogies are significant interpretations because of the way they colour contemporary perspectives of hobbits.

Tell Me a Story, or Better Yet, Upload it to Fanfiction.net

Popular multi-fandom fiction site Fanfiction.net lists stories based on *LotR* under 'Books' (not 'Movies'). By late 2011, the archive included more than 45,000 *LotR*-themed stories, averaging more than a thousand new stories each year from 2008 to 2011.[5] This archive is only one of many fanfiction sites housing thousands of hobbit stories.

During summer 2007, my online *LotR* fan survey asked several questions about fandom, including fanfiction, both 'gen' (general stories involving characters from the book or Jackson's films) and 'slash' (stories with sexual overtones involving same-sex relationships). Of the 1272 people who submitted surveys, only 756 answered questions about fanfiction. Whether they had never heard of fanfiction, did not read it, or did not want to admit reading it (possibly because of its questionable legality) is unknown. Of the 756 who described their fanfiction interests, 257 said they read fanfiction regularly (a term left undefined in the survey), 329 said they read fanfiction occasionally (another undefined term), and 170 said they both read and write fanfiction. The 202 fans listed favourite characters Frodo, who received more than twice the number of 'votes' than runner up Pippin, followed by Sam and Merry. Several surveys simply listed 'hobbits'. Even Bilbo was included on a survey, as was Rosie Cotton. Only Aragorn and Legolas were more popular than hobbits in this survey, receiving only one or two more 'votes' than Frodo. Possibly fan interest in Viggo Mortensen and Orlando Bloom, as much as their respective characters, was a reason behind the votes. Both the actors and their characters are prominently featured in online RPG (real person – general [not role playing game in this case]) or RPS (real person – slash) as well as gen and slash character fiction.

In a separate section about slash fanfiction, 189 fans wrote that they read slash, but, perhaps more important, 573 people wrote that they *did not* read slash. Some provided comments about the reasons why they do not approve of or like slash stories, which were the most adamant responses in the whole survey. In contrast, those who enjoy slash stories elaborated on their reasons: they like the loving relationships that contrast with much of Tolkien's darker story; they think that sexual relationships are a natural result of the close relationships shown in the book or on film; they simply like slash stories. Slash is clearly a dividing point among fans, who either love the loving same-sex relationships portrayed in the stories or hate the concept of slash, either on moral grounds or as completely against Tolkien's portrayal of the characters.

When choosing their favourite character pairs in a slash relationship, 147 fans preferred hobbit pairings. Frodo/Sam was most often selected, with Merry/Pippin a close second. Only Aragorn/Legolas received a similar tally. Even a threesome (Frodo/Sam/Rosie) was a popular choice, although it received fewer 'votes' than the pairings.

Although the Internet provides fanfiction writers with a forum and a potentially wide readership that encourages the production of everything from long, serialised stories ('WIP', or works in progress) to shorter, often fluffier one-time stories ('PWP', meaning plot what plot), the web alone cannot account for a surge in the number of stories beginning around 2001. *LotR* fanfiction in more 'old-school' bound volumes still exists, but online access to fanfiction allows hobbit fans to enjoy fiction whenever and wherever they want. The global popularity of Jackson's *LotR* films and the fan-friendly group of actors who starred in them inspire fanfiction writers to speculate on what might have taken place before, between or after the scenes captured by the camera or written by Tolkien. Furthermore, the actors' openness with each other, and genuine friendships, encourage fans to speculate about their off-camera antics as well.

The Professor's enduring theme of the strength of loving families and friends during troubling times is well represented in *LotR*. Fanfiction writer 'Pearl Took' explained that Tolkien-themed fanfiction provides hobbit fans with

> more of the world they have come to love. Even though all stories aren't of a 'Tolkien' quality, they are based on his characters and places... The Professor is gone. He will never write any more stories, but through Tolkien-based fanfiction, we can still have stories about... his hobbits... The movies merely increased the number of people exposed to *LotR*, thereby increasing the number of people who now loved the story and adding to the numbers of those whose minds began to imagine more adventures for the characters.[6]

In these stories writers often analyse one key aspect of Tolkien's story through a twenty-first-century lens. Male friendships are often a focal point for fan stories, perhaps because of ongoing debates about the legality or societal acceptance of homosexual or bisexual relationships. The camaraderie of characters (hobbits, elves, dwarves, men) in combat, as Tolkien perceived them, and rituals of male bonding in British society, especially within the confines of academia with which Tolkien was familiar, are largely absent from his readers' world more than fifty years after *LotR*'s publication and nearly a century after the author began drafting his epic. Western readers or movie audiences who see male characters gently touching, much less kissing – even the brush of lips on brow – are more likely to interpret these expressions of brotherly love as homosexual.

What is surprising is that fanfiction writers often do not seem squeamish about incestuous pairings between first cousins (Merry and Pippin) or slightly more distant kinships (as among Frodo, Merry and Pippin); 'pure' same-sex love is acceptable in AUs, and neither large age differences nor family ties prove to be major obstacles in these tales of abiding male love. Because many modern readers matured in a less class-obvious society, Sam's devotion to Frodo seems natural and not inappropriate, and Frodo, although he is Sam's older employer, is not portrayed as taking advantage of younger, less worldly Sam. Love is the only concern for readers, and the 'true love' between male characters overcomes any societal challenges.

In part, the fictionalised 'real-person' stories involving the actors who played hobbits are a variation on the 'pure love' theme in fanfiction. Again interpreting the world through a cultural lens in which close male friendships are often not the norm, or only 'manly buddy' anecdotes are perceived as acceptable evidence of such friendships, fans have used the bond among actors to rationalise slash stories.

When asked about hobbits during a 2004 *TV Guide* interview, Dominic Monaghan (Merry) concluded that they are 'very openhearted…very genuine…very pure with their emotions. If they feel love, they show it. If they're sad, they cry. [Director] Pete [Jackson] cast four hobbits who were very open with their emotions.'[7] The 'hobbits' in particular seemed a close-knit group off set. Stories of humorous or suggestive comments made during promotional junkets and interviews, as well as candid commentaries packaged with the *LotR* DVDs, initially prompted fans to speculate about the actors' and their characters' friendships and sexual orientation.

Later in the *TV Guide* interview, shortly after a comment about liking female company, Monaghan teased the interviewer in response to questions about hobbit sexuality, which, in turn, referenced his friendship with Boyd. Asked about Boyd's girlfriend, Monaghan confirmed that his friend had been seriously involved for several years, adding, 'which is terribly heartbreaking to me. No more long winter nights together like we used to,' before concluding smartly, 'No, that's not true.' With a little more prompting, Monaghan noted that

> There's been scandalous gay rumours...flying around me and Elijah [Wood], and me and Billy. I remember reading in the press that I had stayed at Elijah's house – and [that] we had made up some rumour that I was seeing Elijah's sister, so that Elijah and I could continue our lurid affair with each other. It cracks us both up... And then there's stuff about me and Billy being lovers because we're such good friends. It's an interesting thing, because you look at...actresses who are tight [friends]. There's never any stuff like 'Oooh, maybe they're gay.' But with guys, it's like the media and the fans can't come to terms with the fact that guys can be so connected in that way. We can be overjoyed to be in each other's company.[8]

Even in an article published online in early 2008 by Exclusive Movie News, Wood (most likely tongue firmly in cheek) commented that the hobbits were, indeed, gay, and that filmed scenes included more touching than absolutely necessary. According to the interviewer,

> Wood was reluctant to reveal anything at first, but that reluctance provoked me to ask even further. 'Okay, I'll tell you, but I know I am going to get killed for this,' Wood began. 'After reading the script I spoke with Sean, Dom and Billy and we all agreed there was a relative – let's say softness – to our characters and we started hamming it up and no one ever stopped us.'
>
> Wood began laughing, 'There are some scenes where you can actually see Sam trying to grope Frodo. You have to look close, but they are there. Nothing was meant by it, it just started out as a joke and some may say it went too far, but hell the films made billions of dollars so I don't think anyone is complaining.'[9]

By now, of course, the actors know that their fans know every little detail ever released about the films, and so they can play to the crowd with humorous, if outrageous, comments guaranteed to generate yet more fanfiction.

During promotional interviews prior to each film's premiere, the actors often came across as modern counterparts to their Middle-earth characters. Monaghan and Boyd were often jointly interviewed by the press and played well off each other, just as their on-screen characters do. They joked and often finished each other's sentences. Even years later, Monaghan and Boyd (often accompanied by 'Frodo') are frequently photographed together, including at personal events, such as Boyd's wedding.[10]

Sean Astin showed a genuine fondness and concern for Elijah Wood similar to the way that Sam related to Frodo. In his 2005 autobiography, Astin wrote that he often went out of his way during filming to make sure Wood had an easier time. In particular, he questioned the safety of Wood's harness during a scene in which the Watcher in the Water holds Frodo upside down. Whereas Wood was game for such a stunt, Astin worried about his co-star's safety and made sure that he would be protected. Even off set, when Wood forgot his house key and inadvertently locked himself out, Astin took it upon himself to track down a locksmith and get the key, while Wood enjoyed a night out.[11] The on- and off-set relationships endeared the actors to fans, who probably like to think that the close friendships Tolkien described, and Jackson filmed, could be transferred to real life.

Fanfiction often pays homage to such abiding friendships, whether between hobbits or the actors who played them in Jackson's films. The blurring between the films and Tolkien's story, or between hobbits and their actor counterparts, increases the amount of fanfiction adapted from either the books or Jackson's films. Interpreting hobbit relationships is an especially personal way to make meaning of Tolkien's characters, one that today is often combined with interest in celebrities. Fans of Monaghan or Boyd, separately or as a friendly duo, may see that real-life friendship as an embodiment of Merry and Pippin's bond. The resulting creative outlet for immortalising such friendships – fanfiction – may be a fan writer's way to celebrate the reality of same-sex love, whether platonic or sexual. In doing so, the resulting adaptation is far more likely to blur lines between fiction and reality, as well as several culturally conflicting time periods: the hobbits', Tolkien's and the writer's. Although fanfiction adaptations are an effective way to keep Tolkien's characters a daily part of fans' lives, these adaptations are also the most likely to stray from the original texts and to make hobbits memorable in unexpected ways.

Why Hobbits?

Why have hobbits remained so popular and been the focus of so many adaptations and interpretations? Certainly, as many adaptations have portrayed them, they often look cuddly and cute. Their nobility of spirit and dedication to friends and family are inspirational, and at least the 'lead hobbits' in *The Hobbit* and *LotR* display qualities that, much of the time, qualify them as role models. Even when hobbits make mistakes, they seem to learn from them and have only the best interests of others at heart. Because of their purity and perceived innocence, they are often idealised in fandom, as is the Shire as an idyllic place and culture removed from the corruption of the outside world.

Although this interpretation is popular, it glosses over rough spots in hobbit personalities and ignores hobbit society's isolationism and parochialism, especially prior to the War of the Ring. In an increasingly chaotic, technologically complex world, the idealised Shire may provide a respite from everyday problems, and hobbits serve as entry characters into this 'perfect' world. As the majority of these adaptations illustrate, the Shire is outside the realm of men (or humankind), and apparently many hobbit fans would also like to escape the world as it stands today.

The idea that hobbits are 'common', in the sense of being less worldly, is also appealing to many readers and audiences. Hobbits are accessible, non-threatening characters with whom to identify on the shared journey through Middle-earth. Bilbo, Frodo, Sam, Merry and Pippin, however, are not common in the sense of 'average'. Readers who identify with these characters may want to emulate them because they display what Tolkien considered the best qualities of hobbits. They have what Tolkien called a 'spark'; they are 'specially graced and gifted individuals'. Most hobbits stay at home, content with what they have and with no desire to extend themselves either above their station in life or outside their self-contained Shire. In contrast, Bilbo displays hobbit virtues of 'shrewd sense, generosity, patience and fortitude',[12] as well as this spark that marks him as different from most hobbits.

Gandalf chooses Bilbo to be the dwarves' hired burglar because he is a different type of hobbit. He displays that spark of adventure, and Gandalf helps fan the flames of Bilbo's inquisitive, intelligent nature. The Bilbo who returns to Bag End after his adventures in the wider world becomes an interesting role model for Frodo, Sam, Merry and Pippin. The hobbits of successive generations who take after him or benefit from his influence also share this spark – of curiosity, willingness to learn and open-mindedness.

Fans who look to hobbits as role models today are often looking for validation of what makes themselves special or different. The hobbits who return to the Shire can never become average. In fact, they might not ever have been 'average' hobbits, not just because of who they were in the community, as representatives of important families, but because of their unique characteristics. They are willing to step beyond what is familiar and comfortable, to do things that no other hobbits have done before, to take on unexpected responsibilities.

The hobbits of the Fellowship come back to the Shire changed; because of that difference, they are able to make their homeland better. They not only lead the fight to scour the Shire of ruffians, but because they expanded their horizons, they try to get other hobbits to do the same. They are no longer satisfied with the status quo, and, although they do not attempt to remake the Shire in the image of Rohan or Gondor, they encourage a multicultural appreciation of races heretofore unknown to hobbits.

That ability to transcend expectations is appealing to a new generation of fans who look to stories like *LotR* for inspiration as well as entertainment. Although Tolkien did not create a guidebook for successful living, the hobbits often take on that role, particularly for adolescents who first read the book during their formative years or who see Jackson's trilogy and find something to admire or emulate in hobbits. These characters inspire fans to self-improvement.

Whether formed in online communities, among attendees at special events, or continued in formal gatherings sponsored by the Tolkien Societies and their many small smials around the world, a devoted fellowship of fans honours Tolkien and his characters. Perhaps it is not surprising to read that many who adapt Tolkien's works – including Peter Jackson and other prominent artists, musicians and actors mentioned in this book – are also fans who celebrate Tolkien's works through professional adaptations and interpretations of characters. Whether purely personal or professional and commercial, adaptations are both a blessing and a curse to Tolkien's texts. What is certain is that, like a relentless river, adaptations carve their own path through Tolkien's Middle-earth, eroding some once-defining features and branching out in new directions. The river – or road – may go on, but its direction will be determined by the fans who carry this beloved story into the future.

NOTES

Introduction

1 Broadway, Cliff. TORN panel. San Diego Comic-Con. San Diego, CA. 21 July 2011.
2 Wood, Elijah. *Wilfred* panel. San Diego Comic-Con. San Diego, CA. 21 July 2011.
3 Ressner, Jeffrey. 'A New Spin.' *American Way*. 1 August 2011, p.38.
4 'For Big Talent, Multi-Platform is the New Multiplex.' San Diego Comic-Con. San Diego, CA. 21 July 2011.
5 Monaghan, Dominic. 'A Conversation with Dominic Monaghan.' Nerd HQ. San Diego, CA. 22 July 2011.
6 Jackson, Peter. 'Paramount: *The Adventures of Tin-Tin*.' San Diego Comic-Con. San Diego, CA. 22 July 2011.
7 Media coverage resulting from the 'hobbit' comment was widespread in the US in late July 2011. A few pertinent examples are these: 'The GOP's Reality Test.' *The Wall Street Journal*, 27 July 2011; Port, Rob, *The Wall Street Journal:* '"Tea Party Hobbits" Should Drop Opposition to Raising Debt Ceiling.' SayAnthingBlog.com. 27 July 2011; Erickson, Erick, 'The Closing Argument: We Are Filthy Hobbitses.' RedState. com. 27 July 2011.
8 '"Lord of the Rings" Script Seized at Guantanamo.' *USA Today*. 10 April 2008. http://www.usatoday.com/news/world/2008-04-10-guantanamo_N.htm
9 Jackson, Peter. 'LOTR Infographic.' TheHobbitBlog.com. 14 May 2011.
10 Daly, Steve. 'Action Jackson.' *Entertainment Weekly*. 22 September 2006. http://www.ew.com/ew/article/0,,1538494,00.html
11 *LotR* references can be found in these *Family Guy* episodes: Sulkin, Alec and Borstein, Alex. 'Sibling Rivalry.' Fox. 26 March 2006. Callaghan, Steve and McFarland, Seth. 'I Take Thee Quagmire.' Fox. 12 March 2006.

12 Selman, Matt. 'That '90s Show.' *The Simpsons*. Fox. 27 January 2008.

13 Sherman, Amy. 'The Hobbit, the Sofa, and Digger Stiles.' *Gilmore Girls*. CW. 7 October 2003.

14 Koh, Ryan. 'Business Ethics.' *The Office*. NBC. 9 October 2008.

15 Schwartz, Josh and Fedak, Chris. 'Chuck Versus the Break-up.' *Chuck*. NBC. 13 October 2008.

16 Molaro, Steven, Prady, Bill and Rosenstock, Richard. 'The Precious Fragmentation.' *The Big Bang Theory*. CBS. 8 March 2010.

17 Straughan, Peter. *The Men Who Stare at Goats*. BBC Films, Smoke House, Westgate Film Services and Winchester Capital Partners. 2009.

18 Black, Michael Ian and Pegg, Simon. *Run, Fatboy, Run*. Entertainment Films and Material Entertainment. 2007.

19 'A Long-Expected Party.' Shaker Village, KY. 25–28 September 2008. http://www.alongexpectedparty.org

20 'A Long-Expected Party 2.' Shaker Village, KY. 28 September–2 October 2011. http://alep2.us/About.htm

Chapter 1

1 Sibley, Brian. *Peter Jackson: A Film-maker's Journey*. London: HarperCollins, 2006.

2 Lacon, Ruth. *The Art of Ruth Lacon: Illustrations Inspired by the Works of J.R.R. Tolkien*. Moreton-in-Marsh: ADC Publications, 2005, p.10.

3 Reynolds, Pat. '*The Lord of the Rings:* The Text of a Tale'. The Tolkien Society. 2003. http://www.tolkiensociety.org/tolkien/tale.html

4 Beard, Henry N. and Kinney, Douglas C. *Harvard Lampoon. Bored of the Rings*. New York: ROC/Penguin, 1993.

5 *Fellowship!* CD original cast recording. 'Home's never too far away.' Lyrics by Kelly Holden, Joel McCrary, Allen Simpson, Ryan Smith, Cory Rouse and Peter Allen Vogt. Music by Kelly Holden, Joel McCrary, Cory Rouse and Peter Allen Vogt. Venice, CA, 2004.

6 *Fellowship!* CD original cast recording. 'The song of destiny.' Lyrics by Kelly Holden, Joel McCrary, Allen Simpson, Ryan Smith, Cory Rouse and Peter Allen Vogt. Music by Cory Rouse and Allen Simpson. Venice, CA, 2004.

7 *Fellowship!* CD original cast recording. 'The Balrog blues.' Lyrics by Kelly Holden, Joel McCrary, Allen Simpson and Peter Allen Vogt. Music by Kelly Holden, Joel McCrary and Allen Simpson. Venice, CA, 2004.

8 Kleinau, Marian. Play Cycle. Reading of *LotR*. 9–11 and 16–18 November 1967. Southern Illinois University. Script read from Series 8, Box 1, Folder 5. Marquette University, manuscripts, Milwaukee, WI.

9 Bakshi, Ralph. 'The Tackling of a Classic.' *Appendix*. September 1978, p.5. (*Appendix* was the official monthly bulletin of the American Tolkien Society, edited by Philip W. and Marc Helms in Union Lake, MI.)

10 Tolkien, J.R.R. *The Hobbit*. rev. ed. New York: Ballantine, 1982, p.300.

11 Tolkien, J.R.R. *The Lord of the Rings*. New York: Houghton Mifflin, 1994, p.35.

12 Peter Jackson (dir.). *The Lord of the Rings: The Fellowship of the Ring*. New Line Cinema, 2001.

13 *The Lord of the Rings*. CD original London Production. 'The road goes on.' Music by A.R. Rahman, Värthinä and Christopher Nightengale. Lyrics by Shaun McKenna and Matthew Warchus. London: Kevin Wallace Ltd, 2007.

14 Burry, Dean. Personal email. 7 June 2008.

15 Child, Ben. 'Will Peter Jackson's Tolkien Tinkering Make or Break The Hobbit?' *Guardian*. 2 June 2011. http://www.guardian.co.uk/film/2011/jun/02/peter-jackson-tolkien-the-hobbit

16 Reputable sites visited by Tolkien fans, such as the following National Geographic site, reinforce the idea that Tolkien wrote a mythology for England. National Geographic Society. 'Creating a Mythological Identity for England.' *National Geographic*. 1996. http://www.nationalgeographic.com/ngbeyond/rings/myth.html

17 Tolkien, J.R.R. *The Hobbit*. rev. ed. New York: Ballantine, 1982, p.1.

Chapter 2

1 The changes to the riddle game may be noted by comparing early and later editions of *The Hobbit* and *LotR*. Several fan sites and encyclopedias, however, also comment on this revision. A few examples of such fan commentary may be found at 'Riddles in the Dark, the Long Version' (http://www.ringgame.net/riddles.html), Tolkien Gateway (http://tolkiengateway.net/wiki/The_Hobbit) and The Hobbit-Lord of the Rings Wiki (http://lotr.wikia.com/wiki/The_Hobbit).

2 Scoville, Chester N. 'The Hobbit.' In Michael C. Drout (ed.), *J.R.R. Tolkien Encyclopedia: Scholarship and Critical Assessment*. London: Routledge, 2006, p.279.

3 Peter Jackson (dir.). *The Lord of the Rings: The Fellowship of the Ring*. New Line Cinema, 2001.

4 Tolkien, J.R.R. *The Hobbit*. New York: Houghton Mifflin, 2002.

5 Tolkien, J.R.R. *The History of* The Hobbit. *Part One: Mr. Baggins*. John D. Rateliff (ed.). Boston: Houghton Mifflin, 2007, p.62, note 19.

6   Tolkien, J.R.R. *The History of* The Hobbit. *Part One: Mr. Baggins.* John D. Rateliff (ed.). Boston: Houghton Mifflin, 2007, p.62, note 20.

7   Tolkien, J.R.R. *The History of* The Hobbit. *Part One: Mr. Baggins.* John D. Rateliff (ed.). Boston: Houghton Mifflin, 2007, p.376.

8   Anderson, Douglas A. *The Annotated Hobbit.* Boston: Houghton Mifflin, 2002, p.15.

9   Tolkien, J.R.R. 'A Long-Expected Party.' *Holograph.* Series 3, Box 1, Folder 7. Marquette University, Milwaukee, WI.

10 Tolkien, J.R.R. *The Lord of the Rings.* New York: Houghton Mifflin, 1994, Appendix A.

11 Tolkien, J.R.R. *The History of Middle-earth.* Vol. XII: *The Peoples of Middle-earth.* Christopher Tolkien (ed.). Boston: Houghton Mifflin, 1996, p.50.

12 Several online wiki sites include similar musings about Tolkien's use of the name Meriadoc: http://www.indopedia.org/Meriadoc.html, http://en.wikipedia.org/wiki/Meriadoc and http://www.maryjones.us/jce/conan.html

13 Tolkien, J.R.R. *The History of Middle-earth.* Vol. XII: *The Peoples of Middle-earth.* Christopher Tolkien (ed.). Boston: Houghton Mifflin, 1996, p.51.

14 Tolkien, J.R.R. *The History of Middle-earth.* Vol. XII: *The Peoples of Middle-earth.* Christopher Tolkien (ed.). Boston: Houghton Mifflin, 1996, p.51.

15 Christopher Tolkien's edited *History*, especially volumes I and III, provide many more details about the four phases of revision and the numerous changes that occurred in the development of the early chapters. I also noted these changes to Tolkien's handwritten and typed manuscripts, especially Series 3, Box 1, Folders 13–15.

16 Tolkien, J.R.R. *The History of* The Lord of the Rings. *Part 2: The Treason of Isengard.* Christopher Tolkien (ed.). Boston: Houghton Mifflin, 1989, p.31.

17 Tolkien, J.R.R. 'Shadow of the Past.' *Holograph.* Series 3, Box 1, Folder 9. Marquette University, Milwaukee, WI.

18 Tolkien, J.R.R. 'Shadow of the Past.' *Holograph.* Series 3, Box 1, Folders 10–11. Marquette University, Milwaukee, WI.

19 Tolkien, J.R.R. *The History of* The Lord of the Rings. *Part 2: The Treason of Isengard.* Christopher Tolkien (ed.). Boston: Houghton Mifflin, 1989, p.8.

20 Tolkien, J.R.R. 'A Conspiracy Unmasked.' Series 3, Box 1, Folder 15. Marquette University manuscripts, Milwaukee, WI.

21 Tolkien, J.R.R. 'At the Sign of the Prancing Pony.' Series 3, Box 1, Folder 20. Marquette University manuscripts, Milwaukee, WI.

22 Tolkien, J.R.R. 'At the Sign of the Prancing Pony.' Series 3, Box 1, Folder 20. Marquette University manuscripts, Milwaukee, WI.

23 Tolkien, J.R.R. *The History of* The Lord of the Rings. *Part 3: The War of the Ring.* Christopher Tolkien (ed.). Boston: Houghton Mifflin, 1990, p.345.

24 Tolkien, J.R.R. *The History of* The Lord of the Rings. *Part 3: The War of the Ring.* Christopher Tolkien (ed.). Boston: Houghton Mifflin, 1990, pp.346–48.

25 Tolkien, J.R.R. *The History of* The Lord of the Rings. *Part 3: The War of the Ring.* Christopher Tolkien (ed.). Boston: Houghton Mifflin, 1990, p.348.

26 Tolkien, J.R.R. *The Lord of the Rings.* New York: Houghton Mifflin, 1994, p.787.

27 Bratman, David. 'The Artistry of Omissions and Revisions in *The Lord of the Ring*.' In Wayne G. Hammond and Christina Scull (eds), The Lord of the Rings, *1954–2004: Scholarship in Honor of Richard E. Blackwelder* (pp.113–38). Milwaukee, WI: Marquette UP, 2006, p.129.

28 Bratman, David. 'The Artistry of Omissions and Revisions in *The Lord of the Ring*.' In Wayne G. Hammond and Christina Scull (eds), The Lord of the Rings, *1954–2004: Scholarship in Honor of Richard E. Blackwelder* (pp.113–38). Milwaukee, WI: Marquette UP, 2006, p.129.

29 Acker, Robert. 'Introduction.' *Beyond Bree.* September 1996, pp.6–7.

30 Acker, Robert. 'Introduction.' *Beyond Bree.* September 1996, p.7.

31 Tolkien, J.R.R. *The History of* The Lord of the Rings. *Part 4: The End of the Third Age.* Christopher Tolkien (ed.). Boston: Houghton Mifflin, 1992, pp.81–101.

32 Hyde, Paul Noble. '"Gandalf Please Should Not Sputter."' *Mythlore* 13 (Spring 1987), p.22.

33 Hyde, Paul Noble. '"Gandalf Please Should Not Sputter."' *Mythlore* 13 (Spring 1987), p.23.

34 Hyde, Paul Noble. '"Gandalf Please Should Not Sputter."' *Mythlore* 13 (Spring 1987), p.26.

35 Reynolds, Pat. '*The Lord of the Rings:* The Text of a Tale.' The Tolkien Society. http://www.tolkiensociety.org/tolkien/tale.html

36 Reynolds, Pat. '*The Lord of the Rings:* The Text of a Tale.' The Tolkien Society. http://www.tolkiensociety.org/tolkien/tale.html

Chapter 3

1 Painter, Deborah. *Forry: The Life of Forrest J Ackerman.* Jefferson, NC: McFarland, 2010.

2 Tolkien, J.R.R. *The Letters of J.R.R. Tolkien.* Humphrey Carpenter (ed.). Boston: Houghton Mifflin, 1981, Letter 202, 11 September 1957, p.261.

3 Zimmerman, Morton Grady. Series 8 Screen Treatments, Box 1, Folder 1. Annotated treatment of *LotR.* 1957, p.2. Marquette University manuscripts, Milwaukee, WI.

4 Tolkien, J.R.R. *The Letters of J.R.R. Tolkien.* Humphrey Carpenter (ed.). Boston: Houghton Mifflin, 1981, Letter 210, June 1958, p.271.

5 Tolkien, J.R.R. Letter to Rayner Unwin and Geo Allen & Unwin Ltd. From Forrest J. Ackerman. 6 December 1957. Series 8, Box 1, Folder 3. Marquette University manuscripts, Milwaukee, WI.

6 Croft, Janet Brennan. 'Three Rings for Hollywood: Scripts for *The Lord of the Rings* by Zimmerman, Boorman, and Beagle.' Paper presented at the Southwest-Texas Popular Culture Association Annual Conference, 2004. http://faculty-staff.ou.edu/C/Janet.B.Croft-1/three_rings_for_hollywood.htm

7 McNamee, Gregory. 'John Boorman, *Deliverance*, and Films Never Made.' Encyclopaedia Britannica. http://www.britannica.com/blogs/2007/07/1049

8 Croft, Janet Brennan. 'Three Rings for Hollywood: Scripts for *The Lord of the Rings* by Zimmerman, Boorman, and Beagle.' Paper presented at the Southwest-Texas Popular Culture Association Annual Conference, 2004. http://faculty-staff.ou.edu/C/Janet.B.Croft-1/three_rings_for_hollywood.htm

9 Gorel. TORN forum post. 10 July 2001. http://forums.theonering.com/viewtopic.php?t=51271&postdays=0&postorder=asc&start=0

10 Lemons, Stephen. 'John Boorman.' *Salon.* 2 April 2001. http://www.salon.com/people/conv/2001/04/02/boorman/print.html

11 Lemons, Stephen. 'John Boorman.' *Salon.* 2 April 2001. http://www.salon.com/people/conv/2001/04/02/boorman/print.html

12 Zimmerman, Morton Grady. Unproduced screen treatment of *The Lord of the Rings*, annotated by J.R.R. Tolkien, 1957. Series 8, Box 1, Folder 1, p.5. Marquette University manuscripts, Milwaukee, WI.

13 Zimmerman, Morton Grady. Unproduced screen treatment of *The Lord of the Rings*, annotated by J.R.R. Tolkien, 1957. Series 8, Box 1, Folder 1, p.5. Marquette University manuscripts, Milwaukee, WI.

14 Zimmerman, Morton Grady. Unproduced screen treatment of *The Lord of the Rings*, annotated by J.R.R. Tolkien, 1957. Series 8, Box 1, Folder 1, p.6. Marquette University manuscripts, Milwaukee, WI.

15 Zimmerman, Morton Grady. Unproduced screen treatment of *The Lord of the Rings*, annotated by J.R.R. Tolkien, 1957. Series 8, Box 1, Folder 2, p.1. Marquette University manuscripts, Milwaukee, WI.

16 Zimmerman, Morton Grady. Unproduced screen treatment of *The Lord of the Rings*, annotated by J.R.R. Tolkien, 1957. Series 8, Box 1, Folder 2, pp.4–5. Marquette University manuscripts, Milwaukee, WI.

17 Boorman, John and Pallenberg, Rospo. *The Lord of the Rings*. Unproduced screenplay for United Artists, 1970. Series 8, Box 2, Folder 1, p.9. Marquette University manuscripts, Milwaukee, WI.

18 Boorman, John and Pallenberg, Rospo. *The Lord of the Rings*. Unproduced screenplay for United Artists, 1970. Series 8, Box 2, Folder 1, p.11. Marquette University manuscripts, Milwaukee, WI.

19 Conkling, Chris. *The Lord of the Rings Part One: The Fellowship*. Unproduced screenplay, 21 September 1976. Series 8, Box 2, Folder 2, pp.3–5. Marquette University manuscripts, Milwaukee, WI.

20 Conkling, Chris. *The Lord of the Rings Part One: The Fellowship*. Unproduced screenplay, 21 September 1976. Series 8, Box 2, Folder 2, pp.28–29. Marquette University manuscripts, Milwaukee, WI.

21 Conkling, Chris and Beagle, Peter S. *The Lord of the Rings Part 1*. Unproduced screenplay, 3 May 1977. Series 8, Box 2, Folder 3, p.29. Marquette University manuscripts, Milwaukee, WI.

22 Conkling, Chris and Beagle, Peter S. *The Lord of the Rings Part 1*. Unproduced screenplay, 3 May 1977. Series 8, Box 2, Folder 3, p.29. Marquette University manuscripts, Milwaukee, WI.

23 Conkling, Chris and Beagle, Peter S. *The Lord of the Rings Part 1*. Unproduced screenplay, 3 May 1977. Series 8, Box 2, Folder 3, p.29. Marquette University manuscripts, Milwaukee, WI.

24 Zimmerman, Morton Grady. Unproduced screen treatment of *The Lord of the Rings*, annotated by J.R.R. Tolkien, 1957. Series 8, Box 1, Folder 1, p.1. Marquette University manuscripts, Milwaukee, WI.

25 Zimmerman, Morton Grady. Unproduced screen treatment of *The Lord of the Rings*, annotated by J.R.R. Tolkien, 1957. Series 8, Box 1, Folder 1, p.1. Marquette University manuscripts, Milwaukee, WI.

26 Boorman, John and Pallenberg, Rospo. *The Lord of the Rings*. Unproduced screenplay for United Artists, 1970. Series 8, Box 2, Folder 1, p.134. Marquette University manuscripts, Milwaukee, WI.

27 Boorman, John and Pallenberg, Rospo. *The Lord of the Rings*. Unproduced screenplay for United Artists, 1970. Series 8, Box 2, Folder 1, p.139. Marquette University manuscripts, Milwaukee, WI.

28 Zimmerman, Morton Grady. Unproduced screen treatment of *The Lord of the Rings*, annotated by J.R.R. Tolkien, 1957. Series 8, Box 1, Folder 1, p.52. Marquette University manuscripts, Milwaukee, WI.

29 Morton Grady Zimmerman, unproduced screen treatment of *The Lord of the Rings*, annotated by J.R.R. Tolkien, 1957. Series 8, Box 1, Folder 1, p.53. Marquette University manuscripts, Milwaukee, WI.

Chapter 4

1 See also McIntire, Sarah. 'The Unlikely Hero Bandwagon.' Victorian Web, Brown University, 2003; Brondtkamffer, W., 'J.R.R. Tolkien.' 'Gods and Men: Reading Fantasy as Literature.' 20 May 2011; and a lengthy fan discussion at The Barrow-Downs, 'Fantasy: Pre and Post Tolkien.' 10–18 September 2007.

2 One list of fantasy authors who seem to emulate Tolkien is posted on RPG.net under the question 'Which fantasy novels are very similar to Tolkien's Middle-earth?' 12 February 2007 – 7 July 2008. Author Greg Hamerton also discusses Tolkien's influence as a possible pitfall for new fantasy writers in 'Are the best fantasy books like Tolkien's or not?' GregHamterton.com

3 Several polls report similar results. After the Bible, which US men and women chose as their favourite book, the second choice for men – and people living in the Eastern US – was *LotR*. Mollins, Julie. 'Bible is America's Favorite Book – Poll.' Reuters. 9 April 2008. Voters in the BBC's 'Big Read' poll chose *LotR* as the number 1 book. 'The Big Read. Top 21.' BBC. 13 December 2003.

4 The BBC produced its first *LotR* adaptation shortly after the book's publication, in 1955 and 1956, but reportedly no copies exist today. The quality of the dramatisation did not impress Tolkien, who sometimes reluctantly advised the production. (For further information, see 'Lord of the Rings Movie Forum.' http://www.sf-fandom.com.) US National Public Radio broadcast a production in 1979. See 'The Lord of the Rings Mind's Eye 1979.' SF-Fandom Tolkien and Inklings Forum, http://www.sf-worlds.com

5 Decades later, Sibley wrote a biography of Peter Jackson and books about Jackson's trilogy.

6 Duriez, Colin. 'Celebrating Tolkien and Popular Media: Interview with Brian Sibley.' *Festival in the Shire Journal.* 2009. http://www.festivalintheshire.com/journal4kde/4intbsibley.html

7 Kearney, James. 'The Lord of the Rings: The B.B.C. Radio 4 Serial.' *Mallorn* 25 (September 1988), p.5.

8 'The Ring in Your Ear.' *Radio Times*, London. March 7–13 1981, p.70.

9 Duriez, Colin. 'Celebrating Tolkien and Popular Media: Interview with Brian Sibley.' *Festival in the Shire Journal.* 2009. http://www.festivalintheshire.com/journal4kde/4intbsibley.html

10 Kearney, James. 'The Lord of the Rings: The B.B.C. Radio 4 Serial.' *Mallorn* 25 (September 1988), p.5.

11 Kearney, James. 'The Lord of the Rings: The B.B.C. Radio 4 Serial.' *Mallorn* 25 (September 1988), p.6.

12 Kearney, James. 'The Lord of the Rings: The B.B.C. Radio 4 Serial.' *Mallorn* 25 (September 1988), pp.6–7.

13 Kearney, James. 'The Lord of the Rings: The B.B.C. Radio 4 Serial.' *Mallorn* 25 (September 1988), p.7.

14 BBC. *Return of the King.* CD set. Disk 1. BBC Audiobooks Ltd, 2002.

15 BBC. *Return of the King.* CD set. Disk 1. BBC Audiobooks Ltd, 2002.

16 BBC. *Return of the King.* CD set. Disk 2. BBC Audiobooks Ltd, 2002.

17 BBC. *Return of the King.* CD set. Disk 2. BBC Audiobooks Ltd, 2002.

18 BBC. *Return of the King.* CD set. Disk 2. BBC Audiobooks Ltd, 2002.

19 Brundige, Ellen. '*The Lord of the Rings* by J.R.R. Tolkien: Prepared for BBC Radio in 13 Episodes by Brian Sibley and Michael Bakewell. A Masterpiece Worthy of the Masterpiece.' http://www.istad.org/tolkien/sibley.html

20 The series originally was broadcast as 26 half-hour episodes, later recombined into 13 hour-long episodes.

21 'Lord of the Rings Back on Radio 4.' BBC News. 29 November 2001.

22 'Dominic Monaghan: Interview.' *The Scene.* http://www.scene-magazine.com/archive/filmarchive.php?filmarcid=9 (link no longer working).

23 'Lord of the Rings Back on Radio 4.' BBC News. 29 November 2001.

24 'The Lord of the Rings – Pure Magic for Radio 4 Listeners.' 9 May 2002. Press release. BBC News. A post-filming connection is Sibley's books about the cinematic trilogy and his biography of Peter Jackson.

25 Culhane, John. 'Will the Video Version of Tolkien Be Hobbit Forming?' *New York Times.* 27 November 1977, p.D33.

26 Tolkien, J.R.R. *The Hobbit.* New York: Houghton Mifflin, 2002.

27 Culhane, John. 'Will the Video Version of Tolkien Be Hobbit Forming?' *New York Times.* 27 November 1977, p.D33.

28 Rankin, Arthur, Jr. and Bass, Jules (dirs). *The Hobbit.* 'The greatest adventure: the ballad of the hobbit.' Music by Maury Laws. Lyrics by Jules Bass. Warner Bros. Family Entertainment. DVD. 2001. (Originally broadcast in 1977.)

29 Most readers 'hear' a character's voice when they read a story. Older readers often admit that their Gandalf sounds like John Huston, who voiced the Rankin–Bass character, whereas younger readers prefer their Gandalf to sound like Ian McKellen of the more recent films.

30 Tolkien Geek. '"The Hobbit" Cartoon: What's Wrong with It?' Blog. 22 July 2005. http://tolkiengeek.blogspot.com/2005/07/hobbit-cartoon-whats-wrong-with-it.html

31 Gardella, Kay. 'TV Version of "The Hobbit" To Be Bankrolled by Xerox.' *Daily News*. 6 May 1976, p.148.

32 Scheib, Richard. Review of *The Hobbit*. http://www.moria.co.nz/fantasy/hobbit.htm

33 Rankin, Arthur, Jr. and Bass, Jules (dirs). *The Return of the King*. Warner Home Video. DVD. 2001. (Originally broadcast in 1980.)

34 Although the programme was first broadcast on 11 May 1980, the animation took place in the late 1970s, and that style is clearly shown in the choice of hairstyles and music.

35 Although depictions of smokers and smoking were certainly on the decline by 1980, tobacco (pipeweed) was an integral part of hobbit life, according to Tolkien. Jackson's trilogy specifically mentions pipeweed and shows Bilbo and Gandalf blowing smoke rings, and parodies, such as *Fellowship!*, question just what exactly hobbits smoke. Although smoking a pipe is not as socially acceptable today (or even in 1980) as it was in Tolkien's day, tobacco still did not have as many negative connotations in 1980 as it does now. Hobbits would not have been considered 'bad' because they smoke.

36 *Veggie Tales: Lord of the Beans*. Created by Phil Vischer and Mike Nawrocki. Big Idea. DVD. 2005.

37 Campbell, Joseph. *The Hero with a Thousand Faces*. Bollingen Series No 17. Princeton, NJ: Princeton UP, 1972.

38 Mitchell, S., 'A Down Under Perspective,' Amazon.com review. 16 January 2007.

39 Zampino, David, '21st Century Hobbit,' Amazon.com review. 8 February 2007.

40 Loree, L., 'Nothing But Great Entertainment!' Amazon.com review. 28 August 2006.

41 Beadnell, Maria. 'Who, Exactly, is the Audience?' Amazon.com review. 12 June 2006.

42 Reich, C. 'Probably the Stupidest Veggie Tales So Far.' Amazon.com review. 2 January 2008.

Chapter 5

1 Selman, Matt. 'That '90s Show.' *The Simpsons*. Fox. 27 January 2008. With the episode's title indicating that Marge attended university in the '90s, the joke is obviously in reference to Peter Jackson's filmed *LotR*

trilogy, but, intentionally or not, the lack of acknowledgement of the Bakshi 1978 film is a telling reference to this adaptation's general lack of acceptance by the *LotR* fan community.

2 'How the *Lord of the Rings* Movies Came to Be.' Xenite.Org News. http://www.xenite.org/faqs/lotr_movie/lotr_background.htm

3 The Saul Zaentz Company. http://www.zaentz.com/index.html

4 Demosthenes. 'Saul Zaentz on The Hobbit.' TORN. 23 November 2006. http://www.theonering.net/torwp/2006/11/23/24050-saul-zaentz-on-the-hobbit-2

5 Harmetz, Aljean. 'Bakshi Journeys to Middle Earth to Animate "Lord of the Rings."' *New York Times*. 8 November 1978, p.C17.

6 Harmetz, Aljean. 'Bakshi Journeys to Middle Earth to Animate "Lord of the Rings."' *New York Times*. 8 November 1978, p.C17.

7 Harmetz, Aljean. 'Bakshi Journeys to Middle Earth to Animate "Lord of the Rings."' *New York Times*. 8 November 1978, p.C17.

8 Canby, Vincent. 'Film: "Lord of the Rings" From Ralph Bakshi.' *New York Times*. 15 November 1978, p.C21.

9 Malcolm, Derek. 'One Way to Break Yourself of Some Bad Hobbits.' *Guardian*. 5 July 1979, p.8.

10 Meador, Sarah. 'The Lord of the Rings (Bakshi Version).' Greenman Review. http://www.greenmanreview.com/film/film_lotr.bakshi.psb.html

11 Sibley, Brian. *Peter Jackson: A Film-maker's Journey.* 'Chapter 2: Getting Serious.' London: HarperCollins, 2006, pp.47–48.

12 Buckley, Tom. 'At the Movies.' *New York Times*. 8 December 1978, p.C8.

13 Harmetz, Aljean. 'Bakshi Journeys to Middle Earth to Animate "Lord of the Rings."' *New York Times*. 8 November 1978, p.C17.

14 Sharp, O. 'Ralph Bakshi's *Lord of the Rings, Part One:* A Critique.' 26 October 2000. http://www.speakeasy.org/ohh/bakshi.htm

15 Boardman, John. 'Oooh, Those Awful United Artists!' *Dagon* 197 (15 December 1978), p.1.

16 Buckley, Tom. 'At the Movies.' *New York Times*. 8 December 1978, p.C8.

17 The following information summarises scenes from *The Lord of the Rings*, Ralph Bakshi (dir.), Warner Brothers, 1978.

18 *Man of La Mancha* debuted in the mid-1960s and, to date, has had four Broadway revivals, including the famed Richard Kiley version in 1972.

19 Data gathered in September 2008. 'All Time Box Office Gross.' Box Office Mojo. http://www.boxofficemojo.com/alltime/world

20 This comment is based upon my observations at Creation Entertainment's ORC and ELF conventions and Orlando, Florida's Megacon in the US in the mid-2000s, as well as representative UK events like the Tolkien 2005 celebration in Birmingham and Fellowship Festival in London.

21 Astin, Sean, and Layden, Joe. *There and Back Again: A Hobbit's Tale*. New York: St. Martin's, 2004, p.209. To Astin's dismay, Merry and Pippin are portrayed so broadly in this scene that he deems their antics 'clownish'.

22 Person, Martin. *The Unfinished Spelling Errors of Bolkien*. CD. The CD is based on his parody of *LotR*. Further descriptions of the live performance can be found at JAM-NWS Folk Federation's site, http://jam.org.au/moxie/venues/thedog/DOG-february-2006.shtml

23 In the online survey of Tolkien fans I conducted in June 2007, fans who selected Pippin as their favourite character often explained that their preference was based on two factors: Pippin is 'cute', and Boyd's Scottish accent is attractive. Young female fans in particular liked the way Pippin looks and sounds and often identified the likeable Boyd as similar to his character.

24 Jackson, Peter (dir.). *The Lord of the Rings: The Return of the King*. Extended DVD. New Line Cinema. 2004.

25 Comments made by fans on TORN forums (for example, http://forums.theonering.com/viewtopic.php?t=75574) as well as by Astin at the ELF fan convention attest to the actor's memorable, award-worthy performance.

26 Jackson, Peter (dir.). *The Lord of the Rings: The Fellowship of the Ring*. New Line Cinema. 2001.

27 In comparison, Aragorn received the most votes, 24.4 percent, followed by Gandalf with 14.4 percent, as 'favourite character'.

28 Jackson, Peter (dir.). *The Lord of the Rings: The Two Towers*. New Line Cinema. 2002.

29 Jackson, Peter (dir.). *The Lord of the Rings: The Return of the King*. New Line Cinema. 2003.

30 Astin, Sean and Layden, Joe. *There and Back Again: A Hobbit's Tale*. New York: St. Martin's, 2004, p.221.

31 Sibley, Brian. *Peter Jackson: A Film-maker's Journey*. 'Chapter 7: Quest for the Ring.' London: HarperCollins, 2006, p.342.

32 Sibley, Brian. *Peter Jackson: A Film-maker's Journey*. 'Chapter 7: Quest for the Ring.' London: HarperCollins, 2006, p.366.

33 Sibley, Brian. *Peter Jackson: A Film-maker's Journey*. 'Chapter 7: Quest for the Ring.' London: HarperCollins, 2006, p.345.

34 Sibley, Brian. *Peter Jackson: A Film-maker's Journey*. 'Chapter 7: Quest for the Ring.' London: HarperCollins, 2006, p.370.

35 Sibley, Brian. *Peter Jackson: A Film-maker's Journey*. 'Chapter 7: Quest for the Ring.' London: HarperCollins, 2006, p.351.

36 Sibley, Brian. *Peter Jackson: A Film-maker's Journey*. 'Chapter 9: Ring Master.' London: HarperCollins, 2006, p.510.

37 Lalumière, Francis K. 'Put Your Best Foot Forward.' *Lord of the Rings Fan Club Official Movie Magazine* 2 (April–May 2002), p.39.

38 Madsen, Dan. 'The Costumes of Middle-Earth.' *Lord of the Rings Fan Club Official Movie Magazine* 4 (August–September 2002), p.55.

39 Madsen, Dan. 'The Costumes of Middle-Earth.' *Lord of the Rings Fan Club Official Movie Magazine* 4 (August–September 2002), p.54.

40 Madsen, Dan. 'The Costumes of Middle-Earth.' *Lord of the Rings Fan Club Official Movie Magazine* 4 (August–September 2002), p.54.

41 Madsen, Dan. 'The Costumes of Middle-Earth.' *Lord of the Rings Fan Club Official Movie Magazine* 4 (August–September 2002), p.55.

42 Atkinson, Carla. 'Making Merry.' *Lord of the Rings Fan Club Official Movie Magazine* 9 (June–July 2003), p.30.

43 Jackson, Peter (dir.). *The Lord of the Rings: The Two Towers*. New Line Cinema. 2002.

44 Atkinson, Carla. 'Making Merry.' *Lord of the Rings Fan Club Official Movie Magazine* 9 (June–July 2003), p.31.

45 Atkinson, Carla. 'Making Merry.' *Lord of the Rings Fan Club Official Movie Magazine* 9 (June–July 2003), p.31.

46 Atkinson, Carla. 'The Artful Dodger.' *Lord of the Rings Fan Club Official Magazine* 8 (April–May 2003), p.40.

47 Perhaps it is appropriate that Pippin's scarf becomes iconically identified with the character and resembles a child's security blanket; one of Boyd's early theatrical roles was Linus, the blanket-carrying sage of *You're a Good Man, Charlie Brown*.

48 Madsen, Dan. 'The Costumes of Middle-Earth.' *Lord of the Rings Fan Club Official Movie Magazine* 4 (August–September 2002), p.55.

49 Tolkien, J.R.R. *The History of Middle-earth: Sauron Defeated*. Vol. IX. Christopher Tolkien (ed.). Boston: Houghton Mifflin, 1992, p.115.

50 Tolkien, J.R.R. *The Lord of the Rings*. Boston: Houghton Mifflin, 1994, p.163.

51 Snyder, Jon B. 'Update with Peter Jackson.' *Lord of the Rings Official Movie Magazine* 1 (February–March 2002), p.19.

52 Astin, Sean, and Layden, Joe. *There and Back Again: An Actor's Tale*. New York: St. Martin's, 2004.

53 Snyder, Jon B. 'Update with Peter Jackson.' *Lord of the Rings Official Movie Magazine* 1 (February–March 2002), pp.19–20.

54 Chernoff, Scott. 'Into the Wood.' *Lord of the Rings Official Movie Magazine* 1 (February–March 2002), p.32.

55 Chernoff, Scott. 'Sam I Am.' *Lord of the Rings Official Movie Magazine* 1 (February–March 2002), p.38.

56 Chernoff, Scott. 'Sam I Am.' *Lord of the Rings Official Movie Magazine* 1 (February–March 2002), p.38.

57 McNary, Dave. 'Guillermo Del Toro to Direct "Hobbit".' *Variety.* 24 April 2008. http://www.variety.com/article/VR1117984595.html?categoryid= 13&cs=1

58 Xoanon. 'Guillermo Del Toro Departs "The Hobbit".' TORN. 30 May 2010. http://www.theonering.net/torwp/2010/05/30/36920-guillermo-del-toro-departs-the-hobbit

59 Taylor, Matthew. 'McKellen Back as Gandalf in "Hobbit" Films.' *Guardian.* 1 May 2008. http://www.guardian.co.uk/film/2008/may/01/ lordoftherings.jrrtolkien

60 Adler, Shawn. 'Viggo Mortensen Still Waiting for Del Toro's "Hobbit" Call.' MTV Movies Blog. 17 September 2008. http://moviesblog.mtv. com/2008/09/17/viggo-mortensen-still-waiting-for-guillermo-del-toros-hobbit-call

61 Altaira. 'James McAvoy Continues to Deny "Hobbit" Rumors; Plans "Me-Time".' TORN. 21 June 2008. http://www.theonering.net/ torwp/2008/06/21/29065-james-mcavoy-continues-to-deny-hobbit-rumors-plans-%E2%80%9Cme-time%E2%80%9D

62 TORN panel. San Diego Comic-Con. San Diego, CA. 21 July 2011.

63 Adetunji, Jo. 'Martin Freeman Cast as The Hobbit's Bilbo Baggins.' *Guardian.* 22 October 2010. http://www.guardian.co.uk/culture/2010/ oct/22/martin-freeman-hobbit-bilbo-baggins

64 Rottenberg, Josh. '"Hobbit" First Look: 3 Pics!' *Entertainment Weekly.* 24 June 2011. http://www.ew.com/ew/gallery/0,,20504849,00.html. The post linking readers to the *EW* photos was made at TheHobbitBlog. com on the same day.

65 Tehanu. 'Thirteen Singing Dwarves and a Very Funny Hobbit.' TORN. 10 February 2011. http://www.theonering.net/torwp/2011/02/10/42176-thirteen-singing-dwarves-and-a-very-funny-hobbit/#more-42176

66 Child, Ben. 'Hobbit Slip Reveals Holmes and Watson Reunion on Rings Prequel.' *Guardian.* 24 May 2011. http://www.guardian.co.uk/ film/2011/may/24/hobbit-reveals-holmes-watson-reunion

67 Tyler, Josh. 'Peter Jackson Confirms The Hobbit Will Send White Council In To Battle.' CinemaBlend.com. 30 May 2011. http://www. cinemablend.com/new/Peter-Jackson-Confirms-The-Hobbit-Will-Send-The-White-Council-In-To-Battle-24959.html. The original message was posted on Jackson's Facebook page (Peter Jackson NZ) on 29 May 2011. https://www.facebook.com/notes/peter-jackson/question-1/10150267552216558

Chapter 6

1   Critics even questioned whether *LotR* fits the definition of a true 'musical'. It has show-stopping singing and dancing numbers, but the majority of the story is not told through song. In response, later promotional materials used terms like 'musical play', 'play with music', or 'theatrical event' rather than classify *LotR* as a musical. Nevertheless, during awards season, *LotR* was considered alongside more traditional musicals.

2   Ken Wallace, quoted by Xoanon. 'LOTR Musical Ends London Run.' TORN. 14 March 2008, http://www.theonering.net/torwp/2008/03/14/28512-lotr-musical-ends-london-run/#more-28512. This article also mentions discussions about bringing the musical to Germany and Australia by 2009, but these talks apparently fell through. The official website (http://www.lotr.com/home/) later revised the projected touring date to 2011, but no announcements of future bookings were forthcoming by late in the year.

3   Begum, Jenny. Facebook post. 24 July 2011. The Lord of the Rings Musical. https://www.facebook.com/pages/The-lord-of-the-Rings-Musical/46888235569?sk=wall

4   Early preview performances from February through May sometimes stopped when a moving stage became stuck or lifts failed to work as expected. In a high-tech theatrical extravaganza like this, the risks of using so much technology most often paid off with a wowed audience who had never before seen such stagecraft. Occasionally, though, the risk did not pan out, and everything came to a standstill until a glitch could be fixed. Audience comments, such as those posted by Xoanon on TORN, attested to problems not always reported in the press. Xoanon, 'Problems with the (Musical) Helms Deep?' TORN. 29 March 2006. http://www.theonering.net/torwp/2006/03/29/24143-problems-with-the-musical-helms-deep

5   I talked with approximately twenty-five audience members during intermissions and after performances to gauge their awareness of Tolkien's story and their overall appraisal of the show.

6   *The Lord of the Rings*. CD original London Production. 'The road goes on.' Music by A.R. Rahman, Värthinä and Christopher Nightengale. Lyrics by Shaun McKenna and Matthew Warchus. London: Kevin Wallace Ltd, 2007.

7   Jackson, Peter (dir.). *The Lord of the Rings: The Fellowship of the Ring*. New Line Cinema, 2001. Also found in Tolkien, J.R.R., *The Lord of the Rings: The Fellowship of the Ring*. New York: Houghton-Mifflin, 1994, p.35.

8   *The Lord of the Rings*. CD original London Production. 'The cat and the moon.' Music by A.R. Rahman, Värthinä and Christopher Nightengale. Lyrics by Shaun McKenna and Matthew Warchus. London: Kevin Wallace Ltd, 2007.

9   Tolkien, J.R.R. *The History of Middle-earth: Sauron Defeated*. Vol. IX. Christopher Tolkien (ed.). Boston: Houghton Mifflin, 1992, p.115.

10 *The Lord of the Rings*. CD original London Production. 'Tell me a story.' Music by A.R. Rahman, Värthinä and Christopher Nightengale. Lyrics by Shaun McKenna and Matthew Warchus. London: Kevin Wallace Ltd, 2007.

11 Tilley, Steve. '"LOTR" Musical to Close Early.' *Toronto Sun*. 29 June 2006. http://jam.canoe.ca/Theatre/Lord_Of_The_Rings/2006/06/29/1659321.html

12 Tilley, Steve. '"LOTR" Musical to Close Early.' *Toronto Sun*. 29 June 2006. http://jam.canoe.ca/Theatre/Lord_Of_The_Rings/2006/06/29/1659321.html

13 'Rings Musical Halted by Accident.' BBC News. 31 May 2007. http://news.bbc.co.uk/2/hi/entertainment/6707791.stm

14 'Rings Musical Halted by Accident.' BBC News. 31 May 2007. http://news.bbc.co.uk/2/hi/entertainment/6707791.stm

15 Russell, Gary. *The Lord of the Rings: The Official Stage Companion*. London: HarperCollins, 2007, pp.154–55.

16 Battle, Laurie. 'The Lord of the Rings Synopsis.' *The Lord of the Rings Programme*, June–August 2006. Toronto: Mirvish, p.15.

17 Battle, Laurie. 'The Lord of the Rings Synopsis.' *The Lord of the Rings Programme*, June–August 2006. Toronto: Mirvish, p.16.

18 Battle, Laurie. 'The Lord of the Rings Synopsis.' *The Lord of the Rings Programme*, June–August 2006. Toronto: Mirvish, p.18.

19 Battle, Laurie. Act/scene list. *The Lord of the Rings Programme*, November–December 2007. London: Kevin Wallace, n.p.

20 Russell, Gary. *The Lord of the Rings: The Official Stage Companion*. London: HarperCollins, 2007, p.61.

21 Russell, Gary. *The Lord of the Rings: The Official Stage Companion*. London: HarperCollins, 2007, p.61.

22 Russell, Gary. *The Lord of the Rings: The Official Stage Companion*. London: HarperCollins, 2007, p.13.

23 'Mixed Reviews for "Lord of the Rings" Musical.' CBC Arts. 25 March 2006. http://www.cbc.ca/story/arts/national/2006/03/24/lordoftherings-reviews.html

24 Corliss, Richard. 'Gandalf in Greasepaint.' *Time*. 19 March 2006. http://www.time.com/time/printout/0,8816,1174695,00.html

25 Pastorek, Whitney. '"Rings" Master.' *Entertainment Weekly.* 11 January 2006. http://www.ew.com/ew/article/0,,1148025,00.html

26 Toronto Alliance for the Performing Arts (TAPA). 'Dora Awards. Past Winners 2007.' http://www.tapa.ca/doras/past_winners

27 'The Lord of the Rings Nominated for 7 Whatsonstage Theatregoer's Choice Awards.' http://www.lotr.com/pr_theatregoers_awards.php

28 Theatregoer's Choice Awards. 2008 Award Winners. 22 February 2007. http://awards.whatsonstage.com/index.php?pg=493

29 In April 2006 *Fellowship!* won as Best Comedy Ensemble and Musical of the Year at the 27th annual LA Weekly Theater Awards. Morris, Stephen Leigh. 'Welcome to Our Party.' *LA Weekly.* 12 April 2006. http://www.laweekly.com/index.php?option=com_lawcontent&task=view&id=13103&Itemid=47

30 Valdez, Mike. *Comedy LA.* 'Fly, You Fools, to Fellowship!' http://www.fellowshipthemusical.com/reviews/comedyla.html (link no longer working).

31 Bradley, Brian D. Interview. 17 April 2008.

32 Bradley, Brian D. Interview. 17 April 2008.

33 Bradley, Brian D. Interview. 17 April 2008.

34 McCrary, Joel. Interview. 20 April 2008.

35 Holden-Bashar, Kelly. Interview. 22 April 2008.

36 Morgan, Terry. 'Fellowship!' Backstage.com. http://www.fellowshipthemusical.com/reviews/bswreview.html (link no longer working).

37 Holden-Bashar, Kelly. Interview. 22 April 2008.

38 *Fellowship!* CD original cast recording. 'Home's never too far away.' Lyrics by Kelly Holden, Joel McCrary, Allen Simpson, Ryan Smith, Cory Rouse and Peter Allen Vogt. Music by Kelly Holden, Joel McCrary, Cory Rouse and Allen Simpson. Venice, CA, 2004.

39 *Fellowship!* CD original cast recording. 'The song of destiny.' Lyrics by Kelly Holden, Joel McCrary, Cory Rouse, Allen Simpson, Ryan Smith and Peter Allen Vogt. Music by Cory Rouse and Allen Simpson. Venice, CA, 2004.

40 Holden-Bashar, Kelly. Interview. 22 April 2008.

41 Holden-Bashar, Kelly. Interview. 22 April 2008.

42 Simpson, Allen. Interview. 10 April 2008.

43 Simpson, Allen. Interview. 10 April 2008.

44 *Fellowship!* CD original cast recording. 'The lament of the ring.' Lyrics and music by Joel McCrary, Steve Purnick, Cory Rouse and Allen Simpson. Venice, CA, 2004.

45 Jackson, Peter (dir.). *The Lord of the Rings: The Fellowship of the Ring.* New Line Cinema. 2001.

46 Holden-Bashar, Kelly. Interview. 22 April 2008.

47 *Fellowship!* CD original cast recording. 'It's a hobbit thing.' Lyrics and music by Kelly Holden, Joel McCrary and Allen Simpson. Venice, CA, 2004.

48 *Fellowship!* CD original cast recording. 'Home's never too far away.' Lyrics by Kelly Holden, Joel McCrary, Allen Simpson, Ryan Smith, Cory Rouse and Peter Allen Vogt. Music by Kelly Holden, Joel McCrary, Cory Rouse and Allen Simpson. Venice, CA, 2004.

49 *Fellowship!* CD original cast recording. 'The song of destiny.' Lyrics by Kelly Holden, Joel McCrary, Cory Rouse, Allen Simpson, Ryan Smith and Peter Allen Vogt. Music by Cory Rouse and Allen Simpson. Venice, CA, 2004.

50 FellowshiptheMusical.com

51 'The Lord of the Rings.' Johan de Meij.com. http://www.johandemeij. com. CDs of this symphony include *The Lord of the Rings: Symphony No. 1*, Johan de Meij, the London Symphony Orchestra and David Warble, Madacy 2 Label Group, 2001, and *Lord of the Rings Symphonie No. 1*, Andre Jutras, Johan de Meij and Jan Van Der Roost, Atma Classique, Montreal, 1998 (which is the version I used in reviewing the symphony). The symphony is also included in other live CDs, such as *The Lord of the Rings & Firebird Suite*, Johan de Meij, Mark Masters, 2001, performed by the US Marine Band.

52 'The Lord of the Rings.' Johan de Meij.com. http://www.johandemeij.com.

53 Mason, Doug. 'Wind Symphony Performs "Lord of the Rings" Piece.' *Knoxville News Sentinel*. 2 March 2008. http://knoxnews.com/ news/2008/mar/02/wind-symphony-performs-lord-of-the-rings-piece

54 Forrester, Marshall. Personal email. 25 March 2008.

55 Xoanon. 'Sarasota Youth Opera to Present The Hobbit.' TORN. 7 February 2008. http://www.theonering.net/torwp/2008/02/07/28365-sarasota-youth-opera-to-present-the-hobbit

56 Wood, Raven von. 'Dean Burry, Composer of The Hobbit Visits Sarasota to Promote the Opera.' *Herald Tribune*. 2 April 2008. http:// www.heraldtribune.com/apps/pbcs.dll/article?AID+/20080402/ BLOG99/22596387

57 'Hobbits Set for Opera Stage.' CBC Arts. 19 March 2004. http://www. cbc.ca/arts/story/2004/03/19/thehobbit20040319.html

58 Burry, Dean. Personal email. 7 June 2008.

59 Burry, Dean. Personal email. 7 June 2008.

60 Burry, Dean. Interview. 14 July 2008.

61 Burry, Dean. Personal email. 7 June 2008.

62 Burry, Dean. Personal email. 7 June 2008.

63 Burry, Dean. Personal email. 7 June 2008.

64 Rankin, Arthur, Jr. and Bass, Jules (dirs). *The Hobbit*. 'The greatest adventure: the ballad of the hobbit.' Music by Maury Laws. Lyrics by Jules Bass. Warner Bros. Family Entertainment. DVD. 2001. (Originally broadcast in 1977.)

65 An unidentified writer promoting 'The greatest adventure' on a marketing website offered this testimonial to the song's empowerment: 'Many times, both as a child and as an adult I've drawn inspiration from this simple, yet powerful song. Often, as I've debated whether or not to take a risk or start something new, the line "the mold of your life is in your hands to break" has come to the fore in my mind. The lesson of this song and all those in *The Hobbit* have stayed with me from innumerable viewings as a child... there are pieces of your childhood that you never left behind, items that helped shape your thinking, and began to mold you into the person you would become. For me, *The Hobbit* (and especially this song) was one of the latter.' 'The greatest adventure: the ballad of the hobbit.' http://www.jjjwebdevelopment. com/306sites/hobbitsong/hobbitsong.shtml

66 Xoanon. 'Classic Hobbit Song Re-recorded for "Ringers"!' TORN. 2 September 2004. http://www.theonering.net/torwp/2004/09/02/6257-classic-hobbit-song-re-recorded-for-ringers

67 Rankin, Arthur, Jr. and Bass, Jules (dirs). *The Return of the King*. 'Frodo of the nine fingers.' Music by Maury Laws. Lyrics by Jules Bass. Warner Home Video. DVD. 2001. (Originally broadcast in 1980.)

68 Pirate Girl Productions. 'Frodo of the nine fingers.' Fan video. YouTube. Posted 5 May 2006. http://www.youtube.com/watch?v=jAvOI3uChsk. An interesting musical addition to the clip is Pippin's (Billy Boyd's) song from *RotK* over the video's closing credits. Although this version has been superseded by others in the years since my first research for this chapter, the YouTube link still provides several similar fan versions of the song over clips of Elijah Wood's portrayal of Frodo.

69 'Frodo of the nine fingers.' Rankin–Bass version. YouTube. Posted 29 October 2006. http://www.youtube.com/watch?v=yW_ocZLaRdI& feature=related

70 Flowers, Claude. 'Looking Back at the Animated "Hobbit" and "R.O.T.K."' LordoftheRingsGuide.com. 30 December 2003. http:// www.figures.com/databases/action.cgi?setup_file=lotrnews2.setup&cate gory=lotr&topic=5&show_article=108

71 Adams, Doug. 'The Music of *The Lord of the Rings* Films. Part I: *The Fellowship of the Rings*.' *The Lord of the Rings: The Fellowship of the Ring. The Complete Recordings* (CD booklet), 2005, p.1.

72 'Awards Won by LotR: RotK.' LotR Fan Club Scrapbook. http://lotrscrapbook.bookloaf.net/ref/awards_rotk.html. Several awards are also listed in the 'Howard Shore: Biography' section of his website, www.howardshore.net

73 'Awards Won by LotR: FotR.' LotR Fan Club Scrapbook. http://lotrscrapbook.bookloaf.net/ref/awards_fotr.html

74 'Awards Won by LotR: TT.' LotR Fan Club Scrapbook. http://lotrscrapbook.bookloaf.net/ref/awards_ttt.html

75 Adams, Doug. 'The Music of *The Lord of the Rings* Films. Part I: *The Fellowship of the Rings.*' *The Lord of the Rings: The Fellowship of the Ring. The Complete Recordings.* 2005, p.4.

76 Adams, Doug. 'The Music of *The Lord of the Rings* Films. Part I: *The Fellowship of the Rings.*' *The Lord of the Rings: The Fellowship of the Ring. The Complete Recordings.* 2005, p.10.

77 Adams, Doug. 'The Music of *The Lord of the Rings* Films. Part I: *The Fellowship of the Rings.*' *The Lord of the Rings: The Fellowship of the Ring. The Complete Recordings.* 2005, pp.10–12.

78 Jackson, Peter (dir.). *The Lord of the Rings: The Fellowship of the Ring.* New Line Cinema, 2001.

79 Jackson, Peter (dir.). *The Lord of the Rings: The Return of the King.* New Line Cinema, 2003.

80 Jackson, Peter (dir.). *The Lord of the Rings: The Return of the King.* New Line Cinema, 2003.

81 HowardShore.net. www.howardshore.net

82 Garfeimeo. 'Let the Music Begin – Thoughts on the Hobbit Score.' TORN. 6 April 2011. http://www.theonering.net/torwp/2011/04/06/43274-let-the-music-begin-thoughts-on-the-hobbit-score

83 'Howard Shore on Scoring The Hobbit.' King Under the Mountain. com. 4 March 2011. http://kingunderthemountain.com/2011/03/04/howard-shore-on-scoring-the-hobbit. This article summarises Shore's comments about *The Hobbit*, which were made in an article published by Canada's *National Post:* Atkinson, Nathalie. 'Q&A: Composer Howard Shore Wins Governor General's Award.' *National Post.* 3 March 2011. http://arts.nationalpost.com/2011/03/03/qa-composer-howard-shore-wins-governor-generals-award

84 Morris, Larry. Personal email. 8 March 2009.

85 Emerald Rose Press Kit. EmeraldRose.com. http://www.emeraldrose.com/pressbox.htm

86 Morris, Larry. Personal email. 8 March 2009.

87 Gilbert, Clyde. Personal email. 4 March 2009.

88 Gilbert, Clyde. Personal email. 4 March 2009.

89 Brobdingnagian Bards. http://thebards.net/cds.shtml
90 Gunn, Marc. Personal email. 23 October 2008.
91 McKee, Andrew. Personal email. 2 November 2008.
92 McKee, Andrew. Personal email. 2 November 2008.
93 Gunn, Marc. Personal email. 23 October 2008.
94 Gunn, Marc. Personal email. 23 October 2008.

Chapter 7

1 In this chapter I discuss two-dimensional art (for example, a painting, a calendar illustration, a backdrop for a film), but Tolkien art encompasses many more types of art. It includes architectural design, such as that developed in collaboration with artists John Howe and Alan Lee, for the buildings constructed for the Edoras set in Peter Jackson's *LotR* films, as well as reproductions, models and sculptures, such as those created by Weta Workshop. The adaptation of hobbits as 'art' has a limited definition for the purposes of this chapter.

2 Beahm, George. *The Essential J.R.R. Tolkien Sourcebook: A Fan's Guide to Middle-earth and Beyond.* Franklin Lakes, NJ: Career Press, 2004, p.187.

3 Beahm, George. *The Essential J.R.R. Tolkien Sourcebook: A Fan's Guide to Middle-earth and Beyond.* Franklin Lakes, NJ: Career Press, 2004, p.174.

4 Tolkien, J.R.R. *The Letters of J.R.R. Tolkien.* Carpenter, Humphrey (ed.). Boston: Houghton Mifflin, 1981, Letter 27 To the Houghton Miffliin Company, p.35.

5 Tolkien, J.R.R. *The Letters of J.R.R. Tolkien.* Carpenter, Humphrey (ed.). Boston: Houghton Mifflin, 1981, Letter 27 To the Houghton Miffliin Company, p.35.

6 Hammond, Wayne G. and Scull, Christina. *J.R.R. Tolkien: Artist and Illustrator.* London: HarperCollins, 1995, and *The Art of* The Hobbit *by J.R.R. Tolkien.* London: HarperCollins, 2011.

7 'Interview with Wayne Hammond and Christina Scull about *The Art of* The Hobbit.' Tolkien Library. 8 February 2011. http://www.tolkienlibrary.com/press/1002-Interview_Art_Hobbit.php

8 Hammond, Wayne G. and Scull, Christina. 'The Art of The Hobbit.' The weblog of Wayne G. Hammond and Christina Scull. 10 April 2011. http://wayneandchristina.wordpress.com/2011/04/10/the-art-of-the-hobbit

9 These illustrations may be seen on many Tolkien or Hobbit fan sites. One that includes both art and a brief history of each work is www.

hobbit.ca. *The Hill: Hobbiton Across the Water* is discussed at http://www. hobbit.ca/History.html

10 The Tolkien Gateway also discusses Tolkien's art and includes examples of his most famous illustrations, but a large-scale version of *Bilbo Comes to the Huts of the Raft Elves* can be seen at the Museum Syndicate website, http://www.museumsyndicate.com/item.php?item=34462

11 Murray, Jef. 'A Journey Through Middle-earth: Using Art to Explore Tolkien's World.' A Long-Expected Party. Presentation. Shaker Village, KY. 27 September 2008.

12 Murray, Jef. Personal email. 13 October 2008.

13 Jef Murray's art, including the works mentioned in this chapter, are listed at his website, http://www.adcbooks.co.uk, as well as ADC Art and Books' catalogue, where other Tolkien-themed art is also displayed at http://www.adcbooks.co.uk

14 Murray, Jef. Personal email. 14 October 2008.

15 Murray, Jef. Personal email. 14 October 2008.

16 Murray, Jef. Personal email. 14 October 2008.

17 Murray, Jef. Personal email. 14 October 2008.

18 Murray, Jef. 'A Journey Through Middle-earth: Using Art to Explore Tolkien's World.' A Long-Expected Party. Presentation. Shaker Village, KY. 27 September 2008.

19 Murray, Jef. 'A Journey Through Middle-earth: Using Art to Explore Tolkien's World.' A Long-Expected Party. Presentation. Shaker Village, KY. 27 September 2008.

20 Ted Nasmith's paintings described in this chapter can be seen at the artist's official website, http://www.tednasmith.com/tolkien.html

21 'Ted Nasmith.' Wikipedia. This tidbit is interesting, but because it comes from an uncredited Wikipedia source and is not verified on Nasmith's website or in other recent interviews it should be considered as undocumented.

22 Nasmith, Ted. 'About Me.' TedNasmith.com. http://www.tednasmith. com/about.html

23 Nasmith, Ted. 'Inspired by J.R.R. Tolkien.' TedNasmith.com. http:// www.tednasmith.com/tolkien.html

24 Murray, Jef. 'The Catholic Genius: Middle Earth as Muse.' *St. Austin Review*, July/August 2008, p.24.

25 Wendy. Interview with Ted Nasmith. Dreamish.com. 3 February 2004. http://www.dreamish.com/artist/tednasmith.shtml

26 Herring, Michael. *The Scouring of the Shire*. J.R.R. Tolkien Calendar 1979. London: George Allen & Unwin, 1978.

27 Sweet, Darrell K. *The West-Door of Moria*. J.R.R. Tolkien Calendar 1982. New York: Random House, 1981.

28 Kaluta, Michael. *Meriadoc the Magnificent and the Children of Samwise Hamfast.* J.R.R. Tolkien Calendar 1994. New York: Random House, 1993.

29 Sfiligoi, Andrea. *Due Hobbit nella tama di Shelob.* J.R.R. Tolkien Calendario 1996. Glasgow: HarperCollins, 1995.

30 Tim Kirk illustrated a fan calendar in 1969, for example. It was inserted into a Los Angeles science-fiction society's December 1968 publication. 'The Complete Gyde to Tolkien Calendars.' http://www.angelfire.com/tn3 /tolkiencalendars/1969_1977.html

31 'The Complete Gyde to Tolkien Calendars.' http://www.angelfire.com/tn3/tolkiencalendars

32 Summers, Ian. In *Greg and Tim Hildebrandt: The Tolkien Years.* Glenn Herdling (ed.). New York: Watson-Guptill Publications, 2001, n.p.

33 'Biography.' TheBrothersHildebrandt.com. http://www.brothershildebrandt.com/bio.htm

34 'Biography.' TheBrothersHildebrandt.com. http://www.brothershildebrandt.com/bio.htm

35 Hildebrandt, Gregory, Jr. In *Greg and Tim Hildebrandt: The Tolkien Years.* Glenn Herdling (ed.). New York: Watson-Guptill Publications, 2001, p.17.

36 The Hildebrandt brothers' Tolkien-themed art is part of online career-spanning galleries at their official website, http://www.brothershildebrandt.com/tolkien.htm

37 Herdling, Glenn (ed.). *Greg and Tim Hildebrandt: The Tolkien Years.* New York: Watson-Guptill Publications, 2001, pp.26–27.

38 Herdling, Glenn (ed.). *Greg and Tim Hildebrandt: The Tolkien Years.* New York: Watson-Guptill Publications, 2001, p.23.

39 Singh, Arune. 'Legendary Artist Tim Hildebrandt Has Passed Away.' CBR News. 12 June 2006. http://www.comicbookresources.com/?page=article&id=7280

40 'Rest in Peace Tim Hildebrandt.' Ain't It Cool News. 13 June 2006. http://www.aintitcool.com/node/23585

41 Beahm, George. *The Essential J.R.R. Tolkien Sourcebook: A Fan's Guide to Middle-earth and Beyond.* Franklin Lakes, NJ: Career Press, 2004, p.170.

42 Beahm, George. *The Essential J.R.R. Tolkien Sourcebook: A Fan's Guide to Middle-earth and Beyond.* Franklin Lakes, NJ: Career Press, 2004, p.178.

43 Maudlin, Lynn. 'History of the "NOT Tolkien Calendar".' http://www.angelfire.com/tn3/tolkiencalendars/maudlin.html

44 'The Complete Gyde to Tolkien Calendars'. http://www.angelfire.com/tn3/tolkiencalendars

45 See Chapter 5, 'Hobbits on the Big Screen' for a further description of film merchandise, including art, based on Jackson's films.

46 In 1998, Alan Lee was acclaimed Best Fantasy Artist during the World Fantasy Awards, an honour reflecting Lee's reputation among fans as one of the best artists ever to work in this genre. Lee may be best known to Tolkien fans for his illustrations of *The Hobbit, LotR* and *Children of Hurin*. What has been called Lee's 'crowning Tolkien achievement' is a collection of 50 paintings for the *LotR* centenary edition. Lalumière, Francis K. 'Conceptual Artist Alan Lee.' *The Lord of the Rings Fan Club Official Movie Magazine* 1 (February–March 2002), p.53.

47 Beahm, George. *The Essential J.R.R. Tolkien Sourcebook: A Fan's Guide to Middle-earth and Beyond.* Franklin Lakes, NJ: Career Press, 2004, p.173.

48 Lalumière, Francis K. 'Conceptual Artist Alan Lee.' *The Lord of the Rings Fan Club Official Movie Magazine* 1 (February–March 2002), p.54.

49 Lee, Alan. Tolkien 2005 presentation. 13 August 2005. Aston University. Birmingham, England.

50 Horowitz, Josh. 'Guillermo Del Toro Talks "Hobbit" Casting, Creatures.' MTV.com. 14 October 2008. http://www.mtv.com/movies/news/articles/1596909/story.jhtml

51 Goldberg, Matt. 'Peter Jackson Starts Answering Fan Questions for The Hobbit.' Collider.com. 30 May 2011. http://collider.com/hobbit-peter-jackson-white-council-dol-guldur/93613

52 Lee, Alan. *The Lord of the Rings Sketchbook.* New York: HarperCollins, 2005, p.14.

53 Lee, Alan. *The Lord of the Rings Sketchbook.* New York: HarperCollins, 2005, p.12.

54 Lalumière, Francis K. 'Master of High Drama: An Interview with *The Lord of the Rings* Conceptual Artist John Howe.' *The Lord of the Rings Fan Club Official Movie Magazine* 3 (June–July 2002), p.57.

55 Murray, Jeff. 'The Catholic Genius: Middle Earth as Muse.' *St. Austin Review,* July/August 2008, p.23.

56 Lalumière, Francis K. 'Master of High Drama: An Interview with *The Lord of the Rings* Conceptual Artist John Howe.' *The Lord of the Rings Fan Club Official Movie Magazine* 3 (June–July 2002), pp.50–51.

57 Lalumière, Francis K. 'Master of High Drama: An Interview with *The Lord of the Rings* Conceptual Artist John Howe.' *The Lord of the Rings Fan Club Official Movie Magazine* 3 (June–July 2002), p.53.

58 A Tolkien fan since childhood, Reeve achieved global cinematic fame for his work as a calligrapher and cartographer for Jackson's *LotR* and *King Kong*. His work for these and other films can be viewed at his website, www.danielreeve.co.nz.

59 Reeve, Daniel. Presentation. Wellington, New Zealand. 16 February 2007.

60 Reeve, Daniel. Personal interview. Wellington, New Zealand. 16 February 2007.

61 Reeve, Daniel. Official website: http://www.danielreeve.co.nz. Reeve's illustrations and examples of film- or character-specific fonts, for example, are showcased at this site. His work on Jackson's *LotR* and *Hobbit* films can be seen in the 'Calligraphy' and 'Cartography' sections of the website.

62 Vanderstelt, Jerry. Personal email. 7 December 2007.

63 Vanderstelt, Jerry. Official website: http://www.vandersteltstudio.com

64 Vanderstelt, Jerry. Personal email. 7 December 2007.

65 Vanderstelt, Jerry. Personal email. 7 December 2007.

66 Vanderstelt, Jerry. Personal email. 7 December 2007.

67 Vanderstelt, Jerry. Personal email. 7 December 2007.

68 Vanderstelt, Jerry. Personal email. 2 October 2008.

69 One of the earliest references took place on 27 February 2002, *The Dork Tower*, TORN. http://www.theonering.net/torwp/2002/02/27/14921-the-dork-tower/, but the TORN archives still provide articles and links to several comics from Dork Tower.

70 *Sheldon* comic strip. June 1, 2008. http://www.sheldoncomics.com/archive/080601.html

71 Meriadoc. 'Mad Magazine Goofs on RotK.' TORN. 3 May 2004.

72 Snyder, Jon B. 'Famous Fan Profile: Bill Amend.' *The Lord of the Rings Fan Club Official Movie Magazine* 1 (February–March 2002), p.15.

73 'Real Undead Ringwraiths.' *Fox Trot*. 2 February 2001. Reprinted in Snyder, Jon B. 'Famous Fan Profile: Bill Amend.' *The Lord of the Rings Fan Club Official Movie Magazine* 1 (February–March 2002), p.15.

74 Xoanon. 'More Fox Trot.' TORN. 18 April 2000. http://www.theonering.net/torwp/2000/04/18/21105-more-foxtrot

75 Many of Amend's *LotR*-themed cartoons ran in April 2000 and periodically throughout 2001 in anticipation of *FotR*'s December 2001 release date, but even in 2007, *Fox Trot* occasionally returned to the *LotR* theme. The cartoons were published online at http://www.ucomics.com/foxtrot

76 Xoanon. 'Fox Trot Still Going Geek.' TORN. 17 December 2007. http://www.theonering.net/torwp/2007/12/17/28149-fox-trot-still-going-geek

Chapter 8

1   Fischer, Paul. '"Hobbit Man" Talks Tolkien.' Iofilm.com. n.d. http://www.iofilm.co.uk/feats/interviews/p/peter_jackson.shtml

2   Manlove, C.N. *Modern Fantasy: Five Studies*. Cambridge: Cambridge University Press, 1975. Excerpts appear online, such as at http://www.bookrags.com/criticism/tolkien-john-ronald-reuel-18921973-crit3_20

3   During Creation Entertainment's ELF fan convention in July 2008, I talked with recently returned veterans who discussed the importance of *LotR* while they were deployed. They frequently watched the Jackson films and valued the hobbits' camaraderie and devotion to duty, which they related to their own combat experiences. A soldier even shared a similar story during a Q&A session with Sean Astin, during which the veteran thanked Astin for his portrayal of Sam.

4   Hay, Noelle. 'September 11 and Lord of the Rings.' Sffworld.com. n.d. http://www.sffworld.com/authors/h/hay_noelle/articles/september.html

5   Fanfiction.net. I kept tabs on the number of stories between November 2008 and September 2011. The count should increase significantly with the release of the *Hobbit* films.

6   Took, Pearl. Personal email. 8 November 2008.

7   Rudolph, Ileane and Coleridge, Daniel R. 'LOTR's Hobbits: Are They Gay?' *TV Guide*. 8 December 2004. http://www.tvguide.com/News-Views/Interviews-Features/Article/default.aspx?posting=%7B66559701-A9D7-4E05-8B0F-22A460BE8FFB%7D

8   Rudolph, Ileane, and Coleridge, Daniel R. 'LOTR's Hobbits Are They Gay?' *TVGuide*. 8December2004.http://www.tvguide.com/News-Views/Interviews-Features/Article/default.aspx?posting=%7B66559701-A9D7-4E05-8B0F-22A460BE8FFB%7D

9   Black, Walter. 'Confirmed: Merry, Pip, Samwise, and Even Frodo Are Gay!' Exclusive Movie News. 11 January 2008. http://www.exclusivemovienews.com/2008/01/11/confirmed-merry-pip-samwise-and-even-frodo-are-gay. In addition, several fan sites, such as Aristan's 'Hobbits Are Very Very Gay!' site (http://www.malbela.com/hobbitsareveryverygay), complete with photographic 'evidence', and the Masked Reviewer's *RotK* commentary at http://maskedreviewer.com/Reviews/LOTRROTK.htm, among others, suggest the same 'conclusion'.

10 Bull, Sarah. 'Hobbits Reunited: Lost Star Dominic Monaghan and Elijah Wood Celebrate Co-star Billy Boyd's Wedding.' *Mail Online*. 30 December 2010. http://www.dailymail.co.uk/tvshowbiz/article-1342524/Dominic-Monaghan-Elijah-Wood-Lord-Of-The-Rings-star-Billy-Boyds-wedding.html

11 Astin, Sean and Layden, Joe. *There and Back Again: A Hobbit's Tale.* New York: St. Martin's, 2004, pp.156–57.

12 Tolkien, J.R.R. *The Letters of J.R.R. Tolkien.* Humphrey Carpenter (ed.). Boston: Houghton Mifflin, 1981, Letter 281 To Rayner Unwin, 15 December 1965, p.261.

BIBLIOGRAPHY

Acker, Robert. 'Introduction.' *Beyond Bree*. September 1996.

Adams, Doug. 'The Music of *The Lord of the Rings* Films. Part I: *The Fellowship of the Rings.*' *The Lord of the Rings: The Fellowship of the Ring. The Complete Recordings.* CD. 2005.

Adetunji, Jo. 'Martin Freeman Cast as The Hobbit's Bilbo Baggins.' *Guardian.* 22 October 2011. http://www.guardian.co.uk/culture/2010/oct/22/martin-freeman-hobbit-bilbo-baggins

Adler, Shawn. 'Viggo Mortensen Still Waiting for Del Toro's "Hobbit" Call.' MTV Movies Blog. 17 September 2008. http://moviesblog.mtv.com/2008/09/17/viggo-mortensen-still-waiting-for-guillermo-del-toros-hobbit-call

'All Time Box Office Gross.' Box Office Mojo. http://www.boxofficemojo.com/alltime/world

Altaira. 'James McAvoy Continues to Deny "Hobbit" Rumors; Plans; "Me-Time".' TORN. 21 June 2008. http://www.theonering.net/torwp/ 2008/06/21/29065-james-mcavoy-continues-to-deny-hobbit-rumors-plans-%E2%80%9Cme-time%E2%80%9D

Anderson, Douglas A. *The Annotated Hobbit.* Boston: Houghton Mifflin, 2002.

Astin, Sean and Layden, Joe. *There and Back Again: A Hobbit's Tale.* New York: St. Martin's, 2004.

Atkinson, Carla. 'Making Merry.' *Lord of the Rings Fan Club Official Movie Magazine* 9 (June–July 2003).

Atkinson, Nathalie. 'Q&A: Composer Howard Shore Wins Governor General's Award.' *National Post.* 3 March 2011. http://arts.nationalpost.com/2011/03/03/qa-composer-howard-shore-wins-governor-generals-award

'Awards Won by LotR: FotR.' LotR Fan Club Scrapbook. http://lotrscrapbook.bookloaf.net/ref/awards_fotr.html

Bakshi, Ralph. 'The Tackling of a Classic.' *Appendix.* September 1978.

Bakshi, Ralph (dir.). *The Lord of the Rings.* Warner Bros. 1978. DVD.

The Barrow-Downs. 'Fantasy: Pre and Post Tolkien.' 10–18 September 2007. http://forum.barrowdowns.com/showthread.php?t=14202

Battle, Laurie. 'The Lord of the Rings Synopsis.' *The Lord of the Rings Programme*, Toronto: Mirvish.

BBC. *Return of the King*. BBC Audiobooks Ltd. CD. 2002.

Beahm, George. *The Essential J.R.R. Tolkien Sourcebook: A Fan's Guide to Middle-earth and Beyond*. Franklin Lakes, NJ: Career Press, 2004.

Beard, Henry N. and Kinney, Douglas C. *Harvard Lampoon. Bored of the Rings*. New York: ROC/Penguin, 1993.

Begum, Jenny. Facebook post. 24 July 2011. The Lord of the Rings Musical. https://www.facebook.com/pages/The-lord-of-the-Rings-Musical/46888235569?sk=wall

'Biography.' TheBrothersHildebrandt.com. http://www.brothershildebrandt.com/bio.htm

Black, Michael Ian and Pegg, Simon. *Run, Fatboy, Run*. Entertainment Films and Material Entertainment. 2007.

Black, Walter. 'Confirmed: Merry, Pip, Samwise, and Even Frodo Are Gay!' Exclusive Movie News. 11 January 2008. http://www.exclusivemovienews.com/2008/01/11/confirmed-merry-pip-samwise-and-even-frodo-are-gay

Boardman, John. 'Oooh, Those Awful United Artists!' *Dagon* 197 (15 December 1978).

Boorman, John, and Pallenberg, Rospo. *The Lord of the Rings*. Unproduced screenplay for United Artists, 1970. Series 8, Box 2, Folder 1, Marquette University manuscripts, Milwaukee, WI.

Bradley, Brian D. Interview. 17 April 2008.

Bratman, David. 'The Artistry of Omissions and Revisions in *The Lord of the Ring*.' In Wayne G. Hammond and Christina Scull (eds), The Lord of the Rings, *1954–2004: Scholarship in Honor of Richard E. Blackwelder*. Milwaukee, WI: Marquette UP, 2006.

Broadway, Cliff. TORN panel. San Diego Comic-Con. San Diego, CA. 21 July 2011.

Brobdingnagian Bards. http://thebards.net/cds.shtml

Brondtkamffer, W. 'J.R.R. Tolkien.' 'Gods and Men: Reading Fantasy as Literature.' 20 May 2011. Introduction to podcast. http://wbrondtkamffer.com/2011/05/20/j-r-r-tolkien

Brundige, Ellen. '*The Lord of the Rings* by J.R.R. Tolkien: Prepared for BBC Radio in 13 Episodes by Brian Sibley and Michael Bakewell. A Masterpiece Worthy of the Masterpiece.' http://www.istad.org/tolkien/sibley.html

Buckley, Tom. 'At the Movies.' *New York Times*. 8 December 1978, p.C8.

Bull, Sarah. 'Hobbits Reunited: Lost Star Dominic Monaghan and Elijah Wood Celebrate Co-star Billy Boyd's Wedding.' *Mail Online*. 30 December 2010. http://www.dailymail.co.uk/tvshowbiz/article-

1342524/Dominic-Monaghan-Elijah-Wood-Lord-Of-The-Rings-star-Billy-Boyds-wedding.html

Burry, Dean. Interview. 14 July 2008.

Callaghan, Steve, and McFarland, Seth. 'I Take Thee Quagmire.' *Family Guy.* Fox. 12 March 2006.

Campbell, Joseph. *The Hero with a Thousand Faces.* Bollingen Series No 17. Princeton, NJ: Princeton UP, 1972.

Canby, Vincent. 'Film: "Lord of the Rings" From Ralph Bakshi.' *New York Times.* 15 November 1978, p.C21.

'The cat and the moon.' *The Lord of the Rings.* CD original London Production. Music by A.R. Rahman, Värthinä and Christopher Nightengale. Lyrics by Shaun McKenna and Matthew Warchus. London: Kevin Wallace Ltd, 2007.

Carpenter, Humphrey (ed.). *The Letters of J.R.R. Tolkien.* Boston: Houghton Mifflin, 1981.

Chernoff, Scott. 'Into the Wood.' *Lord of the Rings Official Movie Magazine* 1 (February–March 2002).

—. 'Sam I Am.' *Lord of the Rings Official Movie Magazine* 1 (February–March 2002).

Child, Ben. 'Hobbit Slip Reveals Holmes and Watson Reunion on Rings Prequel.' *Guardian.* 24 May 2011. http://www.guardian.co.uk/film/2011/may/24/hobbit-reveals-holmes-watson-reunion

—. 'Will Peter Jackson's Tolkien Tinkering Make or Break The Hobbit?' *Guardian.* 2 June 2011. http://www.guardian.co.uk/film/2011/jun/02/peter-jackson-tolkien-the-hobbit

'The Complete Gyde to Tolkien Calendars.' http://www.angelfire.com/tn3/tolkiencalendars

Conkling, Chris. *The Lord of the Rings Part One: The Fellowship.* Unproduced screenplay, 21 September 1976. Series 8, Box 2, Folder 2. Marquette University manuscripts, Milwaukee, WI.

Corliss, Richard. 'Gandalf in Greasepaint.' *Time.* 19 March 2006. http://www.time.com/time/printout/0,8816,1174695,00.html

Croft, Janet Brennan. 'Three Rings for Hollywood: Scripts for *The Lord of the Rings* by Zimmerman, Boorman, and Beagle.' Paper presented at the Southwest-Texas Popular Culture Association Annual Conference, 2004. http://faculty-staff.ou.edu/C/Janet.B.Croft-1/three_rings_for_hollywood.htm

Culhane, John. 'Will the Video Version of Tolkien Be Hobbit Forming?' *New York Times.* 27 November 1977, p.D33.

Daly, Steve. 'Action Jackson.' *Entertainment Weekly.* 22 September 2006. http://www.ew.com/ew/article/0,,1538494,00.html

De Meij, Johan. 'The Lord of the Rings.' Johan de Meij.com. http://www.johandemeij.com

Demosthenes. 'Saul Zaentz on The Hobbit.' TORN. 23 November 2006. http://www.theonering.net/torwp/2006/11/23/24050-saul-zaentz-on-the-hobbit-2

'Dominic Monaghan: Interview.' *The Scene.* http://www.scene-magazine. com/archive/filmarchive.php?filmarcid=9 (link no longer working).

Duriez, Colin. 'Celebrating Tolkien and Popular Media: Interview with Brian Sibley.' *Festival in the Shire Journal.* 2009. http://www.festivalintheshire. com/journal4kde/4intbsibley.html

Emerald Rose Press Kit. EmeraldRose.com. http://www.emeraldrose.com/ pressbox.htm

Erickson, Erick, 'The Closing Argument: We Are Filthy Hobbitses.' RedState. com. 27 July 2011. http://www.redstate.com/erick/2011/07/27/the-closing-argument-were-filthy-hobbitses

Fellowship! CD original cast recording. Fellowshipthemusical.com. Venice, CA, 2004.

Fischer, Paul. '"Hobbit Man" Talks Tolkien.' Iofilm.com. n.d. http://www. iofilm.co.uk/feats interviews/p/peter_jackson.shtml

Flowers, Claude. 'Looking Back at the Animated "Hobbit" and "R.O.T.K."' LordoftheRingsGuide.com. 30 December 2003. http://www.figures. com/databases/action.cgi?setup_file=lotrnews2.setup&category=lotr&t opic=5&show_article=108

'For Big Talent, Multi-Platform is the New Multiplex.' San Diego Comic-Con. San Diego, CA. 21 July 2011.

Forrester, Marshall. Personal email. 25 March 2008.

'Frodo of the nine fingers.' Rankin, Arthur, Jr. and Bass, Jules (dirs). *The Return of the King.* Music by Maury Laws. Lyrics by Jules Bass. Warner Home Video. DVD. 2001.

'Frodo of the nine fingers.' Rankin–Bass version. YouTube. Posted 29 October 2006. http://www.youtube.com/watch?v=yW_ocZLaRdI& feature=related

Gardella, Kay. 'TV Version of "The Hobbit" To Be Bankrolled by Xerox.' *Daily News.* 6 May 1976, p.148.

Garfeimeo. 'Let the Music Begin – Thoughts on the Hobbit Score.' TORN. 6 April 2011. http://www.theonering.net/torwp/2011/04/06/43274-let-the-music-begin-thoughts-on-the-hobbit-score

Gilbert, Clyde. Personal email. 4 March 2009.

Goldberg, Matt. 'Peter Jackson Starts Answering Fan Questions for The Hobbit.' Collider.com. 30 May 2011. http://collider.com/hobbit-peter-jackson-white-council-dol-guldur/93613

'The GOP's Reality Test.' *Wall Street Journal.* 27 July 2011. http://online. wsj.com/article/ SB100014240531119035911045764700619868374 9.html?mod=WSJ_Opinion_LEADTop

Gorel. TORN forum post. 10 July 2001. http://forums.theonering.com/viewtopic.php?t=51271&postdays=0&postorder=asc&start=0

'The greatest adventure: the ballad of the hobbit.' Rankin, Arthur Jr. and Bass, Jules (dirs). *The Hobbit.* Music by Maury Laws. Lyrics by Jules Bass. Warner Bros. Family Entertainment. DVD. 2001. http://www.jjjwebdevelopment.com/306sites/hobbitsong/hobbitsong.shtml

Gunn, Marc. Personal email. 23 October 2008.

Hammond, Wayne G. and Scull, Christina. 'The Art of The Hobbit.' The Weblog of Wayne G. Hammond and Christina Scull. 10 April 2011. http://wayneandchristina.wordpress.com/2011/04/10/the-art-of-the-hobbit

—. *The Art of* The Hobbit *by J.R.R. Tolkien.* London: HarperCollins, 2011.

—. *J.R.R. Tolkien: Artist and Illustrator.* London: HarperCollins, 1995.

Harmetz, Aljean. 'Bakshi Journeys to Middle Earth to Animate "Lord of the Rings."' *New York Times.* 8 November 1978, p.C17.

Hay, Noelle. 'September 11 and Lord of the Rings.' Sffworld.com. N.d. http://www.sffworld.com/authors/h/hay_noelle/articles/september.html

Herdling, Glenn (ed.). *Greg and Tim Hildebrandt: The Tolkien Years.* New York: Watson-Guptill Publications, 2001.

Herring, Michael. *The Scouring of the Shire.* J.R.R. Tolkien Calendar 1979. London: George Allen & Unwin, 1978.

Hildebrandt, Gregory, Jr. In *Greg and Tim Hildebrandt: The Tolkien Years.* Glenn Herdling (ed.). New York: Watson-Guptill Publications, 2001.

'Hobbits Set for Opera Stage.' CBC Arts. 19 March 2004. http://www.cbc.ca/arts/story/2004/03/19/thehobbit20040319.html

Holden-Bashar, Kelly. Interview. 22 April 2008.

'Home's never too far away.' *Fellowship!* CD original cast recording. Lyrics by Kelly Holden, Joel McCrary, Allen Simpson, Ryan Smith, Cory Rouse and Peter Allen Vogt. Music by Kelly Holden, Joel McCrary, Cory Rouse and Peter Allen Vogt. Venice, CA. 2004.

Horowitz, Josh. 'Guillermo Del Toro Talks "Hobbit" Casting, Creatures.' MTV.com. 14 October 2008. http://www.mtv.com/movies/news/articles/1596909/story.jhtml

'How the *Lord of the Rings* Movies Came to Be.' Xenite.Org News. http://www.xenite.org/faqs/lotr_movie/lotr_background.htm

'Howard Shore on Scoring The Hobbit.' King Under the Mountain. 4 March 2011. http://kingunderthemountain.com/2011/03/04/howard-shore-on-scoring-the-hobbit

Hyde, Paul Noble. '"Gandalf Please Should Not Sputter."' *Mythlore 13.* Spring 1987.

'Interview with Wayne Hammond and Christina Scull about *The Art of* the Hobbit.' Tolkien Library. 8 February 2011. http://www.tolkienlibrary. com/press/1002-Interview_Art_Hobbit.php

'It's a hobbit thing.' *Fellowship!* CD original cast recording. Lyrics and Music by Kelly Holden, Joel McCrary and Allen Simpson. Venice, CA. 2004.

Jackson, Peter (dir.). *The Lord of the Rings: The Fellowship of the Ring.* New Line Cinema. 2001.

—. *The Lord of the Rings: The Return of the King.* New Line Cinema. Extended DVD. 2004.

—. *The Lord of the Rings: The Two Towers.* New Line Cinema. 2002.

—. Facebook. 29 May 2011. https://www.facebook.com/notes/peter-jackson/question-1/10150267552216558

—. 'LOTR Infographic.' TheHobbitBlog.com. 14 May 2011. http://www. thehobbitblog.com/?cat=7

—. 'Paramount: *The Adventures of Tin-Tin.*' San Diego Comic-Con. San Diego, CA. 22 July 2011.

Kaluta, Michael. *Meriadoc the Magnificent and the Children of Samwise Hamfast.* J.R.R. Tolkien Calendar 1994. New York: Random House, 1993.

Kearney, James. 'The Lord of the Rings: The B.B.C. Radio 4 Serial.' *Mallorn* 25 (September 1988).

Kleinau, Marian. Play Cycle. Reading of *LotR.* 9–11 and 16–18 November 1967. Southern Illinois University. Script read from Series 8, Box 1, Folder 5. Marquette University manuscripts, Milwaukee, WI.

Koh, Ryan. 'Business Ethics.' *The Office.* NBC. 9 October 2008.

Lacon, Ruth. *The Art of Ruth Lacon: Illustrations Inspired by the Works of J.R.R. Tolkien.* Moreton-in-Marsh: ADC Publications, 2005.

Lalumière, Francis K. 'Conceptual Artist Alan Lee.' *The Lord of the Rings Fan Club Official Movie Magazine* 1 (February–March 2002).

—. 'Master of High Drama: An Interview with *The Lord of the Rings* Conceptual Artist John Howe.' *The Lord of the Rings Fan Club Official Movie Magazine* 3 (June–July 2002).

—. 'Put Your Best Foot Forward.' *Lord of the Rings Fan Club Official Movie Magazine* 2 (April–May 2002).

'The lament of the ring.' *Fellowship!* CD original cast recording. Lyrics and Music by Joel McCrary, Steve Purnick, Cory Rouse and Allen Simpson. Venice, CA. 2004.

Lee, Alan. *The Lord of the Rings Sketchbook.* New York: HarperCollins, 2005.

—. Tolkien 2005 presentation. 13 August 2005. Aston University Birmingham, UK.

Lemons, Stephen. 'John Boorman.' *Salon.* 2 April 2001. http://www.salon. com/people/conv/2001/04/02/boorman/print.html

'A Long-Expected Party.' Shaker Village, KY. 25–28 September 2008. http://www.alongexpectedparty.org

'A Long-Expected Party 2.' Shaker Village, KY. 28 September–2 October 2011. http://alep2.us/About.htm

'Lord of the Rings Back on Radio 4.' BBC News. 29 November 2001. http://news.bbc.co.uk/2/hi/entertainment/1681480.stm

'The Lord of the Rings Nominated for 7 Whatsonstage Theatregoer's Choice Awards.' http://www.lotr.com/pr_theatregoers_awards.php

'The Lord of the Rings – Pure Magic for Radio 4 Listeners.' 9 May 2002. Press release. BBC News. http://www.bbc.co.uk/pressoffice/pressreleases/stories/2002/ 05_may/09/lordoftherings.shtml

"Lord of the Rings" Script Seized at Guantanamo.' USA Today. 10 April 2008. http://www.usatoday.com/news/world/2008-04-10-guantanamo_ N.htm

Loree, L. 'Nothing But Great Entertainment!' Amazon.com review. 28 August 2006. http://www.amazon.com/gp/product/customer-reviews/B0006IION6/sr=1-1/qid=1191761811/ref=cm_cr_dp_all_top/103-7909369-6429428?ie=UTF8&n=130&s=dvd&qid=1191761811&sr=1-1#customerReviews

Madsen, Dan. 'The Costumes of Middle-Earth.' Lord of the Rings Fan Club Official Movie Magazine 4 (August–September 2002).

Malcolm, Derek. 'One Way to Break Yourself of Some Bad Hobbits.' Guardian. 5 July 1979, p.8.

Manlove, C.N. Modern Fantasy: Five Studies. Cambridge: Cambridge University Press, 1975.

Mason, Doug. 'Wind Symphony Performs "Lord of the Rings" Piece.' Knoxville News Sentinel. 2 March 2008. http://knoxnews.com/news/2008/mar/02/wind-symphony-performs-lord-of-the-rings-piece

Maudlin, Lynn. 'History of the "NOT Tolkien Calendar".' http://www.angelfire.com/tn3/tolkiencalendars/maudlin.html

McCrary, Joel. Interview. 20 April 2008.

McIntire, Sarah. 'The Unlikely Hero Bandwagon.' Essay written for English 65 Fantasy Literature in the Victorian Web, Brown University, 2003. http://www.victorianweb.org/courses/fiction/65/tolkien/mcintire14.html

McKee, Andrew. Personal email. 2 November 2008.

McNamee, Gregory. 'John Boorman, Deliverance, and Films Never Made.' Encyclopaedia Britannica. http://www.britannica.com/blogs/2007/07/1049

McNary, Dave. 'Guillermo Del Toro to Direct "Hobbit".' Variety. 24 April 2008. http://www.variety.com/article/VR1117984595.html?categoryid=13&cs=1

Meador, Sarah. 'The Lord of the Rings (Bakshi Version).' Greenman Review. http://www.greenmanreview.com/film/film_lotr.bakshi.psb.html

Meriadoc. 'Mad Magazine Goofs on RotK.' TORN. 3 May 2004.

Mitchell, S., 'A Down Under Perspective.' Amazon.com review. 16 January 2007. http://www.amazon.com/gp/product/customer-reviews/ B0006IION6/sr=1-1/qid=1191761811/ref=cm_cr_dp_all_top/103-7909369-6429428?ie=UTF8&n=130&s=dvd&qid=1191761811&sr= 1-1#customerReviews

'Mixed Reviews for "Lord of the Rings" Musical.' CBC Arts. 25 March 2006. http://www.cbc.ca/story/arts/national/2006/03/24/lordoftherings-reviews.html

Molaro, Steven, Prady, Bill and Rosenstock, Richard. 'The Precious Fragmentation.' *The Big Bang Theory.* CBS. 8 March 2010.

Monaghan, Dominic. 'A Conversation with Dominic Monaghan.' Nerd HQ. San Diego, CA. 22 July 2011.

Morgan, Terry. 'Fellowship!' Backstage.com. http://www.fellowshipthemusical. com/reviews/bswreview.html (link no longer working).

Morris, Larry. Personal email. 8 March 2009.

Morris, Stephen Leigh. 'Welcome to Our Party.' *LA Weekly.* 12 April 2006. http://www.laweekly.com/index.php?option=com_lawcontent&task=vi ew&id=13103&itemid=47

Murray, Jef. 'The Catholic Genius: Middle Earth as Muse.' *St. Austin Review,* July/August 2008.

—. 'A Journey Through Middle-earth: Using Art to Explore Tolkien's World.' A Long-Expected Party. Presentation. Shaker Village, KY. 27 September 2008.

—. Personal email. 13–14 October 2008.

Nasmith, Ted. 'About Me.' TedNasmith.com. http://www.tednasmith.com/ about.html

—. 'Inspired by J.R.R. Tolkien.' TedNasmith.com. http://www.tednasmith. com/tolkien.html

—. TedNasmith.com. http://www.tednasmith.com/tolkien.html

National Geographic Society. 'Creating a Mythological Identity for England.' *National Geographic.* 1996. http://www.nationalgeographic. com/ngbeyond/rings/myth.html

Painter, Deborah. *Forry: The Life of Forrest J Ackerman.* Jefferson, NC: McFarland, 2010.

Pastorek, Whitney. '"Rings" Master.' *Entertainment Weekly.* 11 January 2006. http://www.ew.com/ew/article/0,,1148025,00.html

Person, Martin. *The Unfinished Spelling Errors of Bolkien.* JAM-NWS Folk Federation. CD. http://jam.org.au/moxie/venues/thedog/DOG-february-2006.shtml

Pirate Girl Productions. 'Frodo of the nine fingers.' Fan video. YouTube. Posted 5 May 2006. http://www.youtube.com/watch?v=jAvOI3uChsk

Port, Rob. 'The Wall Street Journal: "Tea Party Hobbits" Should Drop Opposition to Raising Debt Ceiling.' SayAnthingBlog.com. 27 July 2011. http://sayanythingblog.com/entry/wall-street-journal-tea-party-hobbits-should-drop-opposition-to-raising-debt-ceiling

Rankin, Arthur Jr. and Bass, Jules (dirs). The Return of the King. Warner Home Video. DVD. 2001.

'Real Undead Ringwraiths.' Fox Trot. 2 February 2001. Reprinted in Snyder, Jon B. 'Famous Fan Profile: Bill Amend.' The Lord of the Rings Fan Club Official Movie Magazine 1 (February–March 2002).

Reeve, Daniel. DanielReeve.co.nz. http://www.danielreeve.co.nz

—. Personal interview. Wellington, New Zealand. 16 February 2007.

—. Presentation. Wellington, New Zealand. 16 February 2007.

Ressner, Jeffrey. 'A New Spin.' American Way, 1 August 2011, 34–39.

'Rest in Peace Tim Hildebrandt.' Ain't It Cool News. 13 June 2006. http://www.aintitcool.com/node/23585

Reynolds, Pat. 'The Lord of the Rings: The Text of a Tale.' The Tolkien Society. 2003. http://www.tolkiensociety.org/tolkien/tale.html

'Riddles in the Dark, the Long Version.' RingGame.net. http://www.ringgame.net/riddles.html

'The Ring in Your Ear.' Radio Times, London. 7–13 March 1981, p.70.

'Rings Musical Halted by Accident.' BBC News. 31 May 2007. http://news.bbc.co.uk/2/hi/ entertainment/6707791.stm

'The road goes on.' The Lord of the Rings. CD original cast recording. Music by A.R. Rahman, Värthinä and Christopher Nightengale. Lyrics by Shaun McKenna and Matthew Warchus. London: Kevin Wallace Ltd, 2007.

Rottenberg, Josh. '"Hobbit" First Look: 3 Pics!' Entertainment Weekly. 24 June 2011. http://www.ew.com/ew/gallery/0,,20504849,00.html

Rudolph, Ileane and Coleridge, Daniel R. 'LOTR's Hobbits: Are They Gay?' TV Guide. 8 December 2004. http://www.tvguide.com/News-Views/Interviews-Features/Article/default.aspx?posting=%7B66559701-A9D7-4E05-8B0F-22A460BE8FFB%7D

Russell, Gary. The Lord of the Rings: The Official Stage Companion. London: HarperCollins, 2007.

The Saul Zaentz Company. http://www.zaentz.com/index.html

Scheib, Richard. Review of The Hobbit. http://www.moria.co.nz/fantasy/hobbit.htm

Schwartz, Josh and Fedak, Chris. 'Chuck Versus the Break-up.' Chuck. NBC. 13 October 2008.

Scoville, Chester N. 'The Hobbit.' In Michael C. Drout (ed.), J.R.R. Tolkien Encyclopedia: Scholarship and Critical Assessment. London: Routledge, 2006.

Selman, Matt. 'That '90s Show.' The Simpsons. Fox. 27 January 2008.

Sfiligoi, Andrea. *Due Hobbit nella tama di Shelob.* J.R.R. Tolkien Calendario 1996. Glasgow: HarperCollins, 1995.

Sharp, O. 'Ralph Bakshi's *Lord of the Rings, Part One:* A Critique.' 26 October 2000. http://www.speakeasy.org/ohh/bakshi.htm

Sherman, Amy. 'The Hobbit, the Sofa, and Digger Stiles.' *Gilmore Girls.* CW. 7 October 2003.

Shore, Howard. HowardShore.net. www.howardshore.net

Sibley, Brian. *Peter Jackson: A Film-maker's Journey.* 'Chapter 2: Getting Serious.' London: HarperCollins, 2006.

Simpson, Allen. Interview. 10 April 2008.

Singh, Arune. 'Legendary Artist Tim Hildebrandt Has Passed Away.' CBR News. 12 June 2006. http://www.comicbookresources.com/?page=article&id=7280

Snyder, Jon B. 'Famous Fan Profile: Bill Amend.' *The Lord of the Rings Fan Club Official Movie Magazine* 1 (February–March 2002).

—. 'Update with Peter Jackson.' *Lord of the Rings Official Movie Magazine* 1 (February–March 2002).

'The song of destiny.' *The Lord of the Rings.* CD original cast recording. Lyrics by Kelly Holden, Joel McCrary, Cory Rouse, Allen Simpson, Ryan Smith and Peter Allen Vogt. Music by Cory Rouse and Allen Simpson. Venice, CA. CD. 2004.

Straughan, Peter. *The Men Who Stare at Goats.* BBC Films, Smoke House, Westgate Film Services and Winchester Capital Partners. 2009.

Sulkin, Alec and Borstein, Alex. 'Sibling Rivalry.' *Family Guy.* Fox. 26 March 2006.

Summers, Ian. In *Greg and Tim Hildebrandt: The Tolkien Years.* Glenn Herdling (ed.). New York: Watson-Guptill Publications, 2001.

Sweet, Darrell K. *The West-Door of Moria.* The J.R.R. Tolkien Calendar 1982. New York: Random House, 1981.

Taylor, Matthew. 'McKellen Back as Gandalf in "Hobbit" Films.' *Guardian.* 1 May 2008. http://www.guardian.co.uk/film/2008/may/01/lordoftherings.jrrtolkien

Tehanu. 'Thirteen Singing Dwarves and a Very Funny Hobbit.' TORN. 10 February 2011. http://www.theonering.net/torwp/2011/02/10/42176-thirteen-singing-dwarves-and-a-very-funny-hobbit/#more-42176

'Tell me a story.' *The Lord of the Rings* CD original cast recording. Music by A.R. Rahman, Värthinä and Christopher Nightengale. Lyrics by Shaun McKenna and Matthew Warchus. London: Kevin Wallace Ltd, 2007.

Theatregoer's Choice Awards. 2008 Award Winners. 22 February 2007. http://awards.whatsonstage.com/index.php?pg=493

Tilley, Steve. '"LOTR" Musical to Close Early.' *Toronto Sun.* 29 June 2006. http://jam.canoe.ca/Theatre/Lord_Of_The_Rings/2006/06/29/1659321.html

Tolkien Geek. '"The Hobbit" Cartoon: What's Wrong with It?' Blog. 22 July 2005. http://tolkiengeek.blogspot.com/2005/07/hobbit-cartoon-whats-wrong-with-it.html

Tolkien, J.R.R. 'At the Sign of the Prancing Pony.' Series 3, Box 1, Folder 20. Marquette University manuscripts, Milwaukee, WI.

—. 'A Conspiracy Unmasked.' Series 3, Box 1, Folder 15. Marquette University manuscripts, Milwaukee, WI.

—. *The History of Middle-earth.* Vol. XII: *The Peoples of Middle-earth.* Christopher Tolkien (ed.). Boston: Houghton Mifflin, 1996.

—. *The History of Middle-earth: Sauron Defeated.* Vol. IX. Tolkien, Christopher (ed.). Boston, Houghton Mifflin, 1992.

—. *The History of* The Hobbit. *Part One: Mr. Baggins.* John D. Rateliff (ed.). Boston: Houghton Mifflin, 2007.

—. *The History of* The Lord of the Rings. *Part 2: The Treason of Isengard.* Christopher Tolkien (ed.). Boston: Houghton Mifflin, 1989.

—. *The History of* The Lord of the Rings. *Part 3: The War of the Ring.* Christopher Tolkien (ed.). Boston: Houghton Mifflin, 1990.

—. *The History of* The Lord of the Rings. *Part 4: The End of the Third Age.* Christopher Tolkien (ed.). Boston: Houghton Mifflin, 1992.

—. *The Hobbit.* New York: Houghton Mifflin, 2002.

—. Letter to Rayner Unwin and Geo Allen & Unwin Ltd. From Forrest J. Ackerman. 6 December 1957. Series 8, Box 1, Folder 3. Marquette University manuscripts, Milwaukee, WI.

—. *The Letters of J.R.R. Tolkien.* Humphrey Carpenter (ed.). Boston: Houghton Mifflin, 1981, Letter 27 To the Houghton Mifflin Company, p.35.

—. 'A Long-Expected Party.' *Holograph.* Series 3, Box 1, Folder 7. Marquette University, Milwaukee, WI.

—. *The Lord of the Rings.* Boston: Houghton Mifflin, 1994.

—. 'Shadow of the Past.' *Holograph.* Series 3, Box 1, Folder 9. Marquette University, Milwaukee, WI.

Took, Pearl. Personal email. 8 November 2008.

TORN panel. San Diego Comic-Con. San Diego, CA. 21 July 2011.

Toronto Alliance for the Performing Arts (TAPA). 'Dora Awards. Past Winners 2007.' http://www.tapa.ca/doras/past_winners

Tyler, Josh. 'Peter Jackson Confirms The Hobbit Will Send White Council In To Battle.' CinemaBlend.com. 30 May 2011. http://www.cinemablend.com/new/Peter-Jackson-Confirms-The-Hobbit-Will-Send-The-White-Council-In-To-Battle-24959.html

Valdez, Mike. *Comedy LA.* 'Fly, You Fools, to Fellowship!' http://www.fellowshipthemusical.com/reviews/comedyla.html (link no longer working).

Vanderstelt, Jerry. Personal email. 7 December 2007.

—. Personal email. 2 October 2008.

—. VandersteltStudio.com. http://www.vandersteltstudio.com

Veggie Tales: Lord of the Beans. Created by Phil Vischer and Mike Nawrocki. Big Idea. DVD. 2005.

Wood, Elijah. *Wilfred* panel. San Diego Comic-Con. San Diego, CA. 21 July 2011.

Wood, Raven von. 'Dean Burry, Composer of The Hobbit Visits Sarasota to Promote the Opera.' *Herald Tribune.* 2 April 2008. http://www.heraldtribune.com/apps/pbcs.dll/article?AID+/20080402/BLOG99/22596387

Wendy. Interview with Ted Nasmith. Dreamish.com. 3 February 2004. http://www.dreamish.com/artist/tednasmith.shtml

Xoanon. 'Classic Hobbit Song Re-recorded for "Ringers"!' TORN. 2 September 2004. http://www.theonering.net/torwp/2004/09/02/6257-classic-hobbit-song-re-recorded-for-ringers

—. 'Fox Trot Still Going Geek.' TORN. 17 December 2007. http://www.theonering.net/torwp/2007/12/17/28149-fox-trot-still-going-geek

—. 'Guillermo Del Toro Departs "The Hobbit".' TORN. 30 May 2010. http://www.theonering.net/torwp/2010/05/30/36920-guillermo-del-toro-departs-the-hobbit

—. 'LOTR Musical Ends London Run.' TORN. 14 March 2008, http://www.theonering.net/torwp/2008/03/14/28512-lotr-musical-ends-london-run/#more-28512

—. 'More Fox Trot.' TORN. 18 April 2000. http://www.theonering.net/torwp/2000/04/18/21105-more-foxtrot

—. 'Problems with the (Musical) Helms Deep?' TORN. 29 March 2006. http://www.theonering.net/torwp/2006/03/29/24143-problems-withthe-musical-helms-deep

—. 'Sarasota Youth Opera to Present The Hobbit.' TORN. 7 February 2008. http://www.theonering.net/torwp/2008/02/07/28365-sarasota-youth-opera-to-present-the-hobbit

Zampino, David, '21st Century Hobbit,' Amazon.com review. 8 February 2007. http://www.amazon.com/gp/product/customer-reviews/B0006IION6/sr=1-1/qid=1191761811/ref=cm_cr_dp_all_top/103-7909369-6429428?ie=UTF8&n=130&s=dvd&qid=1191761811&sr=1-1#customerReviews

Zimmerman, Morton Grady. Series 8 Screen Treatments, Box 1, Folder 1. Annotated treatment of *LotR.* 1957, p.2. Marquette University manuscripts, Milwaukee, WI.

—. Unproduced screen treatment of *The Lord of the Rings*, annotated by J.R.R. Tolkien, 1957. Series 8, Box 1, Folder 1. Marquette University manuscripts, Milwaukee, WI.

INDEX